No Exit: North Korea, Nuclear Weapons and International Security

Jonathan D. Pollack

No Exit: North Korea, Nuclear Weapons and International Security

Jonathan D. Pollack

IISS The International Institute for Strategic Studies

The International Institute for Strategic Studies

Arundel House | 13–15 Arundel Street | Temple Place | London | WC2R 3DX | UK

First published May 2011 by **Routledge**
4 Park Square, Milton Park, Abingdon, Oxon, OX14 4RN

for **The International Institute for Strategic Studies**
Arundel House, 13–15 Arundel Street, Temple Place, London, WC2R 3DX, UK
www.iiss.org

Simultaneously published in the USA and Canada by **Routledge**
270 Madison Ave., New York, NY 10016

Routledge is an imprint of Taylor & Francis, an Informa Business

© 2011 The International Institute for Strategic Studies

DIRECTOR-GENERAL AND CHIEF EXECUTIVE John Chipman
EDITOR Nicholas Redman
ASSISTANT EDITOR Janis Lee
EDITORIAL Jeffrey Mazo, Sarah Johnstone, Ayse Abdullah
COVER/PRODUCTION John Buck

The International Institute for Strategic Studies is an independent centre for research, information and debate on the problems of conflict, however caused, that have, or potentially have, an important military content. The Council and Staff of the Institute are international and its membership is drawn from almost 100 countries. The Institute is independent and it alone decides what activities to conduct. It owes no allegiance to any government, any group of governments or any political or other organisation. The IISS stresses rigorous research with a forward-looking policy orientation and places particular emphasis on bringing new perspectives to the strategic debate.

The Institute's publications are designed to meet the needs of a wider audience than its own membership and are available on subscription, by mail order and in good bookshops. Further details at www.iiss.org.

Printed and bound in the United States of America by Edwards Brothers, Inc.

British Library Cataloguing in Publication Data
A catalogue record for this book is available from the British Library

Library of Congress Cataloging in Publication Data

ADELPHI series
ISSN 1944-5571

ADELPHI 418-19
ISBN 978-0-415-67083-8

Contents

'It's mere chance that has brought us together. Mere chance? Then it's by chance this room is furnished as we see it. It's an accident that the sofa on the right is a livid green, and that one on the left's wine-red. Mere chance? Well, just try to shift the sofa and you'll see the difference quick enough …

I tell you they've thought it all out. Down to the last detail. Nothing was left for chance. This room was all set for us … we're chasing after each other, round and round in a vicious circle, like horses on a roundabout.'

Jean-Paul Sartre, *Huis Clos* [No Exit], 1944.

'The smaller a nation, the stronger a nation must be to keep its pride.'

Kim Jong-il, interview with South Korean media
representatives, *Chosun Ilbo*, 13 August 2000

'Where else was such a country, such a revolution?'

Rodong Sinmun, 8 January 2010

ACKNOWLEDGEMENTS

For Barbara

This book explores Korea's political-military development since the end of the Pacific War, how nuclear technology shaped these possibilities, and the effects of both issues on the Korean peninsula and beyond. I focus primarily on North Korea (the Democratic People's Republic of Korea, or DPRK); its leaders and institutions; and on how its actions have influenced the policies of the Republic of Korea (ROK), China, Japan, Russia and the United States. For Washington, there is an understandable focus on nuclear diplomacy and on US policy options. My primary focus, however, is on the Korean peninsula, which often gets lost amidst detailed accounts of the US policy debate.

Practitioners and analysts hew to highly divergent and intensely held views of the DPRK. Those analysing the North must do so from a distance. It remains largely sealed from the outside world, with observers at best having episodic and highly constrained access. Despite the system's inherent insularity, the DPRK's history and strategic calculations are neither unknown nor impossible to fathom, though any claims to definitive knowledge should be viewed sceptically. But this underscores the need for a continued close attention to North Korea and of how this isolated, highly idiosyncratic system has shaped and continues to shape international security in one of the world's pivotal strategic locations.

My understanding of the DPRK has been influenced by individuals with deep knowledge and long personal experience in Korea. In particular, I want to acknowledge Stephen Bradner, Andrei Lankov and Hans Maretzki. I do not expect any of them to agree fully with my arguments, but they have enriched my understanding and compelled me to carefully assess my assumptions and interpretations. I have also benefited from numerous exchanges with Stephen Linton, Alexandre Mansourov, Narushige Michishita, Chris Nelson, James Person, Joshua Pollack, Mitchell Reiss, Evans Revere and David Straub. I am indebted to Mitchell Reiss for a careful reading of the manuscript. In addition, I have learned much from an outpouring of studies on North Korean history, politics, economics, weapons development and nuclear diplomacy published in recent years, many of which I cite in the volume.

My analysis draws extensively on the DPRK's official media. Without access to decision-making in Pyongyang, careful scrutiny of these materials is crucial to understanding the language, logic and rhythms of North Korean policy. The primary sources compiled and disseminated by the Open Source Center were indispensable to this effort.[1] I am much indebted to the extraordinary work of the dedicated government researchers who grapple with these materials every day. Though I cannot acknowledge them by name, I have benefited greatly from their insights and their keen understanding of the North Korean media process.

I have also drawn extensively on the holdings of the Cold War International History Project of the Woodrow Wilson International Center for Scholars. The Center's dissemination of previously unavailable primary sources has enabled scholars to reconstruct pivotal events in far greater detail. As the volume neared completion, James Person alerted me to newly available materials on North Korea from the 1960s and 1970s, when leaders in Pyongyang approached decisions on nuclear-weapons development. His forthcoming PhD dissertation will delve much more deeply into North Korean domestic politics during the 1950s and 1960s.

The research and writing for this volume was supported by a generous grant from the Program on Global Security and Sustainability of the John D. and Catherine T. MacArthur Foundation. I owe special thanks to Amy Gordon, the Foundation's Director for International Peace and Security, for her support and encouragement. The grant enabled extensive international travel and repeated interactions with scholars, diplomats, technical specialists and government personnel on visits to China, Japan, the Republic of Korea and Russia, as well as to various EU states. Many of these individuals have first-hand experience with the DPRK, either through study or government service. Some provided important insights into policy debate within their own countries. These individuals must remain largely anonymous, but I have benefited greatly from their candor and their insights.

Over the course of this research, I twice visited the DPRK, where I participated in Track-Two dialogues with senior North Korean diplomatic personnel and other officials. Though these visits were relatively brief, they provided insight into North Korea that cannot be garnered from a distance. In addition, I benefited from discussions and interactions with past and present US officials. But this book is not an 'inside the Beltway' account. I am convinced that the how and why of the Korean nuclear impasse must begin with the DPRK system and its history.

I also want to acknowledge the ongoing support of the Naval War College, my professional home between October 2000 and November 2010. My research on the Korean nuclear issue began with a long article I published in the Naval War College Review in 2003 analysing the breakdown of the Agreed Framework, and my interest has persisted ever since.[2] The college's endorsement of this project and its administrative support freed me from many of my regular responsibilities. I owe particular thanks to Rear-Admiral James P. Wisecup, President of the Naval War College; Peter Dombrowski, Chairman of the Strategic Research Department; and Rear-Admiral Roger Nolan (Retd), Executive Director of the Naval War College Foundation. The views expressed in this book, however, are entirely my own.

I completed an earlier draft of this study before joining the Brookings Institution in December 2010. New information on the North's advances in enrichment technology became available at virtually the same time, necessitating revisions in the manuscript and a delay in final publication. Though I discuss some of the implications of the enrichment programme in several chapters, this issue warrants more extensive consideration than I was able to provide. I owe appreciation to Tim Huxley and Adam Ward of the IISS, who encouraged me to undertake this volume and who have patiently awaited its completion. Thanks are also owed to Nick Redman, Ayse Abdullah and Janis Lee, who did everything possible to expedite final publication.

Though this book culminates years of effort, it is by no means the end of this story. My title, expropriated from the translation of Jean-Paul Sartre's play, *Huis Clos*, is both metaphor and explanation. As a Korean colleague has explained to me, the Korean language has distinct words for entry (*eep-gu*) and exit (*chool-gu*). But a hybrid word (*chool-eep-gu*) is generally employed in describing a doorway – which is explained by the absence of rear doors from most Korean homes. In North Korean usage, the sequence is reversed (*eep-chool-gu*), thus placing entry before exit, which seems particularly apt.[3] Unlike Sartre's literary work, however, this saga is not a one-act play. There has been no exit from the nuclear issue for Koreans in the north or south, for other states in Northeast Asia, or for the United States. The intractability of this issue should sober analysts and policymakers alike.

Finally and by no means least, I express my deep gratitude to my wife, Barbara. She has repeatedly accommodated my deep preoccupation with this project and the extensive travel and endless hours it has required. American officials urge strategic patience in achieving Korean denuclearisation; she has had to exhibit the same with me. For both of us, completion of this volume represents an exit of a kind. I doubt that she ever imagined that a book with nuclear weapons in the title would be dedicated to her, and she probably wondered at times if I would ever finish it, but at long last here it is.

JDP
Washington, DC
January 2011

GLOSSARY

CCP	Chinese Communist Party
CPSU	Communist Party of the Soviet Union
CPV	Chinese People's Volunteers
DMZ	Demilitarised Zone
DPRK	Democratic People's Republic of Korea
GDR	German Democratic Republic
IAEA	International Atomic Energy Agency
KEDO	Korean Peninsula Energy Development Organisation
KWP	Korean Workers' Party
KPA	Korean People's Army
LWR	Light-Water Reactor
NDC	National Defence Commission
NPT	Nuclear Non-proliferation Treaty
PRC	People's Republic of China
ROK	Republic of Korea
SPA	Supreme People's Assembly
WFP	World Food Programme
WMD	Weapons of Mass Destruction

North Korea's nuclear infrastructure: known and suspected locations

INTRODUCTION

Despite episodic, partial diplomatic successes and repeated calls for the denuclearisation of the Korean peninsula, the behaviour of North Korea across the decades suggests the precise opposite. For a quarter of a century, the Democratic People's Republic of Korea (DPRK) has defied, stymied, deferred or circumvented repeated efforts by allies, adversaries and the International Atomic Energy Agency (IAEA) to inhibit its pursuit of nuclear weapons and ensure Pyongyang's compliance with its declared non-proliferation obligations. Any residual ambiguity in North Korea's nuclear intentions dissipated over the past decade, though the ultimate scope and purposes of the nuclear programme (beyond protecting the DPRK from supposed existential threats from the United States and its insistence on treatment on 'an equal footing with other nuclear weapons states') remain obscure.[1]

The DPRK signalled its final breach of the nuclear divide with its pull-out from the Nuclear Non-Proliferation Treaty (NPT) in January 2003; there followed an official statement in February 2005 that it had manufactured nuclear weapons and the conducting of nuclear tests in October 2006 and May 2009.

The North has also asserted that its entire inventory of pluto-nium has been weaponised; it has claimed advances in enriched uranium as an alternative source of fissile material and made efforts to develop long-range missiles as a presumed means to deliver a nuclear weapon. It has also provoked sharp responses from the international community by transferring materi-als and technology with nuclear-weapons potential to other nuclear aspirants. The DPRK persists in making explicit claims to standing as a nuclear power outside the NPT, and insists that any future negotiations acknowledge its status as a nuclear-armed state. Despite continued technological, economic and industrial impediments to a fully realised nuclear capability and periodic intimations that it would be prepared to forgo its nuclear-weapons programme, the leadership of the DPRK long ago concluded that its power, identity and interests were more effectively ensured and protected with nuclear weapons than without them.

Why and how has the nuclearisation of the Korean penin-sula reached this point, and what are the consequences? Is it more attributable to a failure of political will and diplomatic imagination on the part of those seeking to prevent the DPRK's nuclear-weapons development, or is it better explained by factors internal to the North Korean system and to the regime's perception of its place in the world? Perhaps more important is whether the pattern of the past decade will be sustained in future years, with no possibility of resolution or reversal.

These issues have long triggered intense debate among policy analysts. On one side of the debate are those who believe that North Korea's pursuit of nuclear weapons reflects anxieties triggered by the end of the Cold War and the DPRK's loss of explicit security guarantees from Russia and China.[2] But Pyongyang's quest for strategic autonomy has far deeper roots. The first meeting between senior US and DPRK officials occurred in January 1992, when Undersecretary of State for Political Affairs Arnold Kanter met in New York with the Korean Workers Party (KWP) Secretary for International Affairs, Kim Yong-sun.[3] These exchanges provided senior American policy-makers with initial exposure to the world as viewed by leaders in Pyongyang. However, America was a late entrant into the Korean nuclear saga, though it has been enmeshed in high-stakes diplomacy with North Korea ever since.

From the DPRK's earliest existence, North Korea's ruling elite has tried to define and build a state apart from the international system. Even during its period of maximal dependence on the Soviet Union and China, the DPRK insisted that its citizens envied no one, and that exclusionary strategies were necessary to protect it from the depredations of a malign outside world. Survivalism has long dominated the thinking of leaders in the North, who characterise the DPRK as a small, vulnerable system surrounded by far more powerful states unprepared to accord it requisite autonomy and international standing. Given the continuous deployment of US forces on the peninsula since the Korean War, the United States has loomed very large in Pyongyang's calculations. In the name of national defence, Pyongyang maintains in relative terms a level of military preparedness unmatched by any other state in the world. North Korea also denies outside powers information about its decision-making, on issues from the banal to the most conse-quential. Moreover, the information withheld from the outside world pales by comparison to what the North denies its own citizens.

Despite North Korea's extreme introversion, the docu-mentary record on the DPRK is more substantial than many observers realise.[4] Even before the collapse of the Soviet Union, the DPRK's official version of the Korean War had begun to unravel, and this trickle became a torrent during the tenure of

Russian President Boris Yeltsin. Invaluable information (mainly from Soviet and East European archives and to a lesser extent from Chinese sources, but also encompassing interviews with participants in early Cold War history) produced an outpouring of new scholarship.[5] Archival information also included important disclosures about North Korea's early interest in nuclear technology, which came to fruition in weapons development decades later. Individuals who worked in the North or who have dealt with North Korean officials, diplomats and engineers have furnished additional insight into the evolution of the system.[6] Despite the obfuscation and obscurity, the DPRK's negotiating strategies and propaganda can be highly revealing. North Korean diplomats exhibit discipline, diligence and utter mastery of their negotiating brief. Even Google Earth provides valuable information about the system's economic underpinnings, military deployments and leadership locations.[7]

The DPRK is America's longest-standing adversary in the international system. Since the establishment of the North Korean state in September 1948, Washington and Pyongyang have never experienced normal relations, and the Korean War cemented lasting animosity on both sides. America has dealt with the North primarily in four contexts: as an enemy in the Korean conflict; as a primary focus of US defence planning in Northeast Asia for more than 60 years; as a US intelligence priority (in particular American efforts to monitor the DPRK's nuclear-weapons and missile activities); and in negotiations seeking to end the nuclear impasse. Despite intermittent political and diplomatic contact over the past two decades, especially negotiations during the Clinton administration, animosities and mutual suspicions have deepened ever since. The North's nuclear tests and its accumulation of fissile material are the latest and most lethal manifestations of this deeply troubling legacy.

The relationship of the two Koreas is equally disconcerting, and (given the geographic contiguity of the two states) arguably more dangerous. More than 60 years since the founding of rival states on opposite sides of the 38th parallel and the outbreak of armed conflict on the peninsula, and nearly 20 years since the end of the Soviet–American confrontation, the cold war in Korea remains largely undiminished. Notwithstanding ethnic homogeneity, a common language and partial breakthroughs in economic, political and humanitarian ties over the past decade, the two Koreas continue to inhabit separate worlds.

Pyongyang and Seoul have engaged in periodic negotiations for nearly four decades, and these interactions have provided some revelatory moments. But neither has been prepared to confer genuine equality and legitimacy to the other. The developmental paths of the two systems most fully reveal this divergence. The Republic of Korea (ROK) has been a singular international success story. It has advanced rapidly to the front ranks of the world's industrial powers, with a parallel political transformation from repressive authoritarian rule to a contentious, highly personalistic but vibrant democratic system. By comparison, North Korea seems an artifact of a bygone era. It persists amidst acute economic dysfunction and with a political mythology all its own. But it remains politically and institutionally intact and militarily powerful in the face of seemingly insuperable odds.

Quite apart from Pyongyang's pursuit of nuclear weapons, the dangers of instability on the peninsula persist, and have if anything increased. There have been repeated oscillations in inter-Korean relations, sometimes including clashes between the two militaries, of which North Korea's March 2010 sinking of the ROK Navy corvette *Cheonan* was the most lethal of these episodes.[8] Pyongyang's November 2010 shelling of Yeongpyong Do (a ROK-controlled coastal island) constituted the first use of

North Korean artillery against South Korean territory since the Korean War. It resulted in the loss of civilian lives as well as those of military personnel, escalating tensions even further.[9] Pyongyang and Seoul have sustained a level of military confrontation unmatched in global politics. But the longer-term power asymmetries between the two Koreas perhaps bear even greater consideration. The economic imbalance between North and South is far larger than that between any two contiguous states on the globe. These economic disparities, the North's protracted international isolation, and its continued pursuit of nuclear weapons lend inherent instability to the peninsula and have had strategic reverberations well beyond Korea, deeply engaging the security interests of the United States and other major powers.

Pyongyang has sustained its quest for nuclear capabilities amidst grievous economic hardship and societal privation that many external observers have long believed would presage the state's extinction. Starting with the demise of the Soviet Union, there have been repeated cycles of 'collapsist' thinking propounded by analysts.[10] Political and security specialists have anticipated systemic disintegration during at least four periods over the past two decades: in the immediate aftermath of the end of communist rule in Eastern Europe and the Soviet Union; following the death of North Korean leader Kim Il-sung and the de-industrialisation and famine of the mid- to late-1990s; during the acute tensions prompted by the second nuclear crisis in 2003; and in the aftermath of Kim Jong-il's stroke in the late summer of 2008 and subsequent reports of heightened economic disequilibrium and societal alienation. But these predictions represent external characterisations and expectations, and none have materialised. Despite its political pathology and economic dysfunction, the DPRK has not gone out of business; the regime persists with an internal authenticity and institutional resilience that external observers (including foreign governments) often seem unable to grasp.

How has an acutely isolated, self-referential regime deflected or resisted various international pressures and inducements, outlasting partners and adversaries alike, and survived to the present day, simultaneously accumulating the requisite scientific, technical and industrial capabilities to undertake and sustain a nuclear programme? A closer analysis of the country's history offers important clues about the DPRK's ability to retain its nuclear capacities and the possibility of negotiated restraints on its nuclear activities as well as the risks that may arise should North Korea prove able to retain and enhance its nuclear holdings. There are also lessons to draw from the North's nuclear history for other states intent on pursuing a nuclear capability or on retaining a nuclear-weapons option.

Well before North Korea's nuclear breakout of the past decade, the United States strongly opposed nuclear proliferation on the Korean peninsula. When American officials first learned of ROK President Park Chung-hee's covert pursuit of nuclear weapons in the early 1970s, they moved quickly and decisively to shut down the programme. But the United States had influence, political reach and an understanding of the South Korean system that it wholly lacked with North Korea. US knowledge of decision-making in the North was (and remains) almost entirely from the outside looking in. Intelligence data on the North's earliest years of nuclear development was patchy and inconclusive, and more definitive evidence emerged only as the North pursued development of a complete nuclear fuel cycle, and when IAEA personnel were briefly able to undertake limited inspections at Yongbyon, the centre of the North's plutonium-based programme.[11]

Even as US attention to the DPRK's nuclear-weapons development increased in the early 1990s, few American officials sought a deeper understanding of the North Korean system. For many in the US Government, non-proliferation trumped every other policy concern, begging the question of whether the DPRK mattered to the United States beyond inherent worries about the acquisition of nuclear weapons technology by a long-standing adversary, and parallel fears that North Korea might opt to transfer such technology, know-how and materials to others. Officials in Pyongyang have posed this question as well: apart from the DPRK's pursuit of nuclear weapons, was there a larger US interest in relations with North Korea? If there was no larger American interest, what were the risks (as distinct from any presumed benefits) if the DPRK were to forgo its weapons potential in irreversible fashion? Asserting that the US has not provided satisfactory answers to these questions, the DPRK (even at moments of prospective negotiating break-throughs) has opted to preserve and then enhance its nuclear assets.

While the United States and other countries have influenced (or sought to influence) the DPRK's behaviour and intentions, they have met with determined resistance from a regime that attaches enormous importance to nuclear weapons. Policymakers must therefore look at what lies behind this strong desire to pursue nuclear weapons if they are to find a way out of the current impasse. It will also be crucial to consider how the major powers have responded to North Korea's actions. Does the North's pursuit of nuclear weapons reflect fixed leadership goals that are essentially independent of attempts by outside powers to inhibit their realisation? In particular, are the North's assertions of acute threat from the United States principally a contrivance and rationalisation to obscure plans that Pyongyang intended to pursue regardless of US strategy?

Previous accounts of negotiations with the DPRK (mainly focused on the history of US–North Korea nuclear diplomacy) have addressed some of these questions.[12] In addition, there have been repeated denuclearisation proposals, primarily focused on US policy choices or on the modalities that might ultimately govern a negotiated agreement.[13] But Pyongyang has rarely attended for long to the initiatives of the United States or other powers. Despite some periodic and partial successes in restraining its nuclear-weapons development, no approach has forestalled or prevented the DPRK's strategic breakout, even at a time when North Korea's industrial economy experienced acute degradation.[14]

US denuclearisation strategies have focused principally on two highly divergent approaches. The first approach has been incentive-oriented, on the presumed demand-side of the nuclear equation. It postulates that inducement, assurance and validation, combined with opportunities for economic betterment and the end of the DPRK's international isolation, will diminish the value that the North attaches to nuclear weapons, leading to a decision to restrain and ultimately to forgo these capabilities. Policy measures have encompassed bilateral and multilateral security assurances; technical assistance in securing nuclear materials and disabling nuclear facilities; seeking (for a time) to build replacement nuclear reactors deemed more 'proliferation resistant'; and other forms of economic compensation and political affirmation, including moves towards diplomatic normalisation and (more prospectively) negotiation of a peace accord that would supplant the Korean War armistice of 1953.

The second approach has emphasised constraints and prevention, focusing on the supply side of the nuclear equation. It has sought to deny the North the ability to pursue a nuclear programme and to mitigate the capabilities or weapons potential it already possesses. These measures have encompassed deterrence and defence; sanctions and interdiction of illicit technology acquisitions and weapons transfers; efforts to impede transfer of nuclear technology, materials and know-how to other parties; measures to isolate and pressure the DPRK; and consideration of preventive measures to eliminate the North's weapons programme, though the use of force has not been undertaken. Neither strategy has achieved its postulated goals. For added measure, Pyongyang exploited President George W. Bush's avowed hostility towards the DPRK (especially during his first term in office) to openly advance weapons development and to claim standing as a nuclear-weapons state. Denuclearisation seems ever more elusive, given the North's two nuclear tests, its accumulation of fissile material, and the DPRK's stated belief that nuclear weapons are essential to the regime's protection, preservation and international status.

Advocates of these rival approaches contend that their preferred strategies were never fully pursued. Proponents of engagement and reassurance argue that the US never demonstrated a sufficient or consistent commitment to reassurance and compensation, devoting excessive attention to punishment, containment or verification of North Korea's prior nuclear activities, thereby confounding the possibility of diplomatic success. Contrarily, advocates of constraint and prevention assert that diplomatic concessions and compromises repeatedly stymied realisation of policy goals, enabling North Korea to retain its nuclear holdings, conduct nuclear tests and lay claim to nuclear status. Both schools of thought subscribe to 'if only' interpretations of policy failure. But these competing explanations are for the most part speculative and counterfactual. At the same time, the rival policy approaches have often neglected the DPRK's determination to deflect US initiatives, defy American pressure and pursue its own strategic objectives.

Both approaches, moreover, offer at best a partial, imperfect window into North Korean decision-making. US nuclear negotiations with Pyongyang over the past two decades have been restricted largely to a small cadre of Foreign Ministry officials with career responsibilities for nuclear diplomacy. The total number of authoritative North Korean interlocutors involved in negotiations with the United States over the past two decades numbers approximately a dozen individuals, in particular a smaller core group of no more than five. American officials had additional dealings with diplomats and technical personnel during the negotiations over Pyongyang's missile development, the cancelled light-water reactor (LWR) project, and the now-suspended disablement of the DPRK's nuclear complex at Yongbyon.[15]

A fuller understanding of the North Korean system requires more in-depth inquiry, but such research is not easy to undertake. According to one estimate, the total number of foreign nationals residing in Pyongyang has seldom exceeded 120.[16] Moreover, some of those involved in humanitarian assistance are restricted to two-week visas; the requests of some organisations for a presence on the ground in the DPRK have been repeatedly denied.[17] But there is a cumulative record of the DPRK's external relations and its pursuit of nuclear technology over the past three decades as well as various antecedents in prior history. Without a fuller appreciation of the leadership's enduring belief in a nuclear identity, it is not possible to comprehend present circumstances, or what could lie ahead.

What factors best explain a state's decision to pursue or to forgo nuclear weapons? In a provocative study on the history and psychology of nuclear proliferation, international relations scholar Jacques Hymans argues that nuclear-weapons development derives from deeply held emotional beliefs of leaders about power, identity and risk. He characterises the belief system associated with pursuit of nuclear weapons as 'oppositional nationalism'. Kim Il-sung and Kim Jong-il (despite their differences in temperament and experience) both fit the profile.[18]

However, pursuit of nuclear weapons is not a momentary or impulsive action, even though it may be an aspiration initially well beyond a state's reach. As international security scholar Richard Betts has observed, no state has ever developed nuclear weapons by accident or inadvertence. It reflects purposive long-term commitment and the large-scale mobilisation of scientific, technological and material resources. It also requires open defiance of agreed international norms and the deflection of external pressure arrayed against states pursuing such capabilities.[19] The DPRK's nuclear development is thus inseparable from the history of the North Korean state.

To explore these issues, this volume will examine Kim Il-sung, who dominated North Korean politics for a half century; his formative experiences as a Korean nationalist; the history of the DPRK from its inception in 1948; and the mix of dependence, defiance and alienation that characterised his relations with the outside world, first with the Soviet Union and China and subsequently with the United States. It will then turn attention to the challenges faced first by Kim Il-sung and later by Kim Jong-il (his eldest son and successor) in achieving and sustaining strategic autonomy, and how nuclear weapons continue to shape this process.

CHAPTER ONE

A system like no other

North Korea's nuclear-weapons programme constitutes a major factor in regional security, inter-Korean relations and non-proliferation policy. Over the past 20 years, this issue has repeatedly appeared to verge on major crisis, interspersed by protracted, fitful negotiations or deliberations over protracted, fitful negotiations. Given the centrality of the Korean nuclear issue to regional geopolitics and nuclear proliferation, this attention is not surprising. However, without a clearer grasp of the underpinnings of power and leadership in North Korea, our understanding of the nuclear issue will be unsatisfactory and incomplete.

North Korea's political evolution, strategic identity and institutional goals must be analysed largely from the outside looking in. These include the protracted struggle between rival conceptions of Korean nationalism during the early twentieth century; the peninsula's division following Japan's surrender at the end of the Second World War; the outbreak and outcome of the Korean War; the persistence of a divided Korea; and the adversarial strategic identity that has shaped North Korea ever since.[1] The Korean Workers' Party (KWP) and various military and security organisations have long staked their claim to absolute power and internal legitimacy on their characterisations of this remembered history. The regime asserts that its conception of Korean nationalism is authentic and unsullied.

The forces that battled for power amidst war and revolution in the early years of the new regime and the lessons that the North Korean leadership drew from these experiences played a formative part in establishing the system that still defines the country today. At the centre of these rival forces was Kim Il-sung, who achieved victory amid the partisan struggles of the mid- and late 1940s and dominated the Democratic People's Republic of Korea from its establishment in 1948 until his death in 1994. There is a timeless quality to North Korea: Kim Jong-il, Kim Il-sung's eldest son and successor, has never wavered from the strategic identity established by his father more than a half century ago, or from the co-dependent relationship the elder Kim built with the coercive institutions that dominate the North Korean state. As Kim Jong-il endeavours to bequeath power to his youngest son and designated heir, Kim Chong-un, he continues to draw on the system his father built and that he has tried to sustain. The regime still refers to events from the distant past to justify its extraordinary reliance on military power (including its claim to status as a nuclear-armed state) and its effort to withstand external pressure and avoid dependence on any outside power.

The rise of Kim Il-sung

Kim Il-sung is the singular figure in the history of Korean communism. Born in 1912, his name at birth was Kim Song-ju. In the early 1930s he changed his given name from 'one star' to 'becoming the sun', a *nom de guerre* expropriated from a deceased guerrilla fighter. At this time Kim was involved in organising and helping to lead anti-Japanese activities in Manchuria in collaboration with Chinese forces.[2] Through guile, emotional manipulation, charisma, audacity and sheer ruthlessness, Kim overcame his youth, inexperience and absence from Korea during most of his formative years, enabling him to achieve outright domination in the struggle for power in the northern half of the peninsula. (The two individuals who triumphed in the political struggles in North and South – Kim Il-sung in the DPRK and Syngman Rhee in the ROK – were both absent from Korea for decades.) Kim and most of his family fled from northern Korea to Manchuria in 1919, when Kim was seven years old. Beyond two years of schooling in Pyongyang in the 1920s, his limited formal education took place almost exclusively in Chinese schools. Kim did not return to the peninsula until September 1945, on the heels of the Red Army's rapid consolidation of power in the northern half of Korea. An ardent Korean nationalist, Kim was portrayed in state propaganda as following in the footsteps of his father and grandfather, both of whom are routinely depicted as leaders in the struggle against hostile foreign powers – the United States in the late nineteenth century and Japan in the twentieth century.

Kim had two singular achievements: his rapid ascent to power in the northern half of the peninsula while still in his mid-thirties and the establishment of a system in which power passed from father to son, an accomplishment unprecedented in Marxist–Leninist history. He outwitted and outmanoeuvered various rivals within the Korean communist movement, and managed to cultivate and obligate far more powerful patrons to his cause, most notably the Soviet leader Josef Stalin and the Chinese leader Mao Zedong. As characterised by one observer and participant in the Korean revolutionary struggle, 'the choice of Kim Il-sung as the future Party and state leader had been somewhat accidental'.[3] His allegiances to the Chinese Communist Party (CCP), which he joined in the early 1930s, and to the Soviet Red Army following his escape to the Soviet Far East in late 1940, both proved essential to his personal survival and to his subsequent rise to top leadership.[4] His dependence on Chinese and Soviet support, however, bred resentment and frustration from which he sought to break free for the rest of his life. As American journalist Bradley Martin has observed, 'it is possible to see much of [Kim's] subsequent career as a conscious, decades-long effort to redeem the nationalist credentials he had soiled by [initially] taking orders from Moscow'.[5] This also involved Kim's experiences in China in the 1930s, including his arrest in 1932 by CCP personnel who suspected that he was aligned with a pro-Japanese Korean group; Kim narrowly avoided execution before his release.[6]

Kim had a much more lasting affinity with China than with the Soviet Union. He spoke fluent Chinese, whereas his Russian language skills were more rudimentary. In private conversations later in life, Kim spoke defiantly about his years in the Soviet Union, insisting that he had never been in service to the Soviet state, even though he had been trained and prepared for a central role in post-war Korea by Red Army officers.[7] His sojourn in the Soviet Far East between late 1940 and 1945 is almost completely whitewashed in official histories (characterised by one author as 'a shroud of silence'), which are replete with various dubious or false claims.[8] These include the supposed birthplace of Kim Jong-il: Mount Paektu (known in Chinese as Changbaishan), a sacred mountain on the Sino-Korean border steeped in mythological history. In contrast, Soviet records attest to the younger Kim's birth in a village near a Soviet army camp in Khabarovsk, where he was known as Yuri.[9] In addition, the younger Kim's birth date was altered from 1941 to 1942, since a 30-year gap between father and son was deemed more appropriate for the purposes of establishing lineal descent.[10] Even the date of founding of the Korean

People's Army (KPA) was changed in the late 1970s from 8 February 1948 to 25 April 1932, to buttress Kim's claim that he founded it while engaged in struggles against the Japanese.[11]

Upon his return to Korea in September 1945, Kim Il-sung moved quickly to supplant various rivals within the Korean communist movement, several of whom had stronger claims to top leadership. Exploiting differences among Koreans with longstanding relationships to the Communist Party of the Soviet Union (CPSU) and the CCP and those with more indigenous roots, Kim and his followers soon achieved a dominant power position. Even before the end of the Korean War, he initiated widespread purges and show trials of various political opponents (especially of South Korean communists), exhibiting the ruthlessness that repeatedly characterised his rule.[12] Kim's core supporters consisted principally of several hundred men whom he had recruited and led in Manchuria and who subsequently escaped with him to the Soviet Far East. To some subordinates, many of whom were reputedly orphans, Kim (despite his youth) became a father figure. This group, known as the Kapsan faction, and their progeny have maintained the Kim dynasty's supreme power in the North ever since.[13] Indeed, the practices that Kim enshrined and sustained bear immediate comparison to the pervasive cultural influence of the Chosun dynasty that dominated the peninsula for half a millennium until 1910.[14]

Despite his deeply nationalist convictions, Kim's allegiance to Moscow during the Soviet occupation period (1945–48) was essential to his consolidation of political power.[15] The imposition of a Soviet-style system enabled the establishment of structures and practices integral to Kim's larger strategy, and clearly served his immediate and long-term interests. At the same time, even during the period of Soviet occupation, Kim sought to adapt Stalinist rule to the North's internal circumstances and to his own political needs. Kim also borrowed extensively from other historical precedents that he deemed useful, including practices from Korea's past and from Japanese emperor worship.[16] As a highly knowledgeable observer of the North has noted, Kim sought to understand why Koreans seemed to overachieve as individuals but underachieve collectively, whereas Japanese behaviour suggested the reverse. Kim concluded that the DPRK needed both a kingly system and a cult, with an iconography that borrowed symbols and images directly from Japan.[17]

Kim eyes a hostile world

From the first, Kim viewed himself as a survivor in a hostile world. He directed his initial enmity at Japan and at anti-Communist forces mobilising in the southern half of the peninsula, but his underlying goal was to build a system that could withstand any external or internal challenge. He demanded unquestioned obedience from his subordinates and (while deferring to his Red Army minders during the years of Soviet occupation) he viewed all outside powers with ample suspicion, including his Soviet and Chinese allies. He trusted no foreign power, nor any Korean compatriots whom he suspected of residual loyalty to foreign forces. Although highly extroverted, Kim's durable trust extended only to his immediate family and his closest subordinates. He developed a power structure more dynastic and hereditary than Leninist, and this system persists to the present day.

Kim Il-sung built and sustained what one long-time student of North Korean politics describes as the Kim family regime.[18] Through a combination of inertia, confidence in the proven methods of asserting absolute power, and filial loyalty, Kim Jong-il has never wavered from this leadership system since succeeding his father. Australian scholar Adrian Buzo's characterisation of the movement and system led by Kim Il-sung is particularly apt: '[T]he net effect ... [of history] was a brand of resentful nationalism which characteristically evinced a profound sense of injustice, impotence and inequality and which had little faith that the world could be anything but a threatening place.' As Buzo also observes, Kim's consolidation of power enabled the creation of 'a post-Korean War ideological and policy framework ... that strongly reflected the tastes, prejudices and experiences of the Manchurian guerrilla mindset – militarist, Spartan, ruthless, conspiratorial, anti-intellectual, anti-bureaucratic, and insular'.[19] The essence of the system was a Korea-centred (and Kim-centred) vision, with only temporary accommodation of the preferences and needs of foreigners, dictated exclusively by exigencies of the moment or outright political expediency.

Kim's experiences during the Korean War (1950–53) profoundly reinforced these beliefs.[20] The origins and conduct of the war had lasting consequences for the DPRK. The conflict's indeterminate outcome helps to explain the persistence of war communism in North Korean policy and propaganda; to Pyongyang, the war never ended. Soviet and Chinese archival materials unambiguously establish that Kim was the principal advocate of the southward advance of North Korean forces. He overcame the reluctance and initial opposition of Stalin and Mao, both of whom worried that the war could divert the cause of international communism from more important objectives, or feared that Soviet and Chinese interests could suffer if Kim's expectations proved too optimistic. Through relentless lobbying and repeated expressions of confidence in rapid victory, Kim was able to sell the war to Stalin, and in turn garner Mao's acquiescence, transforming episodic guerrilla conflict into full-scale conventional hostilities.[21] But Kim's surprise attack across the 38th parallel on 25 June 1950 would not have been possible without major Soviet military assistance or China's transfer of ethnic Korean military units that had fought in Manchuria during the final stages of the Chinese civil war to DPRK control.

Kim understood the ironic inversion of the peninsula's strategic geography: the principal locations of peasant-based insurrectionist activity were well south of the 38th parallel.[22] With Korea internally divided and ill prepared for war, and with the US still in search of a coherent policy on Korea, Kim sensed an opportunity for early unification.[23] In late August 1950, with demoralised South Korean forces retreating to a perimeter established by the US and the ROK in the southeast corner of peninsula near the port of Pusan, Kim received direct encouragement from Stalin. The Soviet leader told him that 'Korea is not alone now … it has allies who are helping it and will continue to help it.'[24] Even with the benefit of hindsight, Kim's gamble does not seem all that outlandish, underscoring his lifelong frustration at his near miss in achieving unification.

However, the introduction of major US combat units during July 1950 shifted the tide of battle. The steady augmentation of US forces and the overextension of North Korea's supply lines slowed the advance of Pyongyang's army. The Inchon landing of 15 September 1950 under US General Douglas MacArthur was pivotal, severing the North's supply lines and leading to the abrupt collapse of DPRK forces. Rather than nearing final victory, Kim Il-sung's forces were soon in headlong retreat. The turn of events was a personal humiliation for Kim Il-sung.[25] With US forces soon threatening the regime's existence, Kim sent an urgent message to Stalin requesting a direct military intervention by Soviet forces. Stalin turned down Kim's request, and instead urged China to intervene. Lacking alternatives, Kim appealed directly to Mao Zedong in a letter beseeching the Chinese for support.[26] The CCP Politburo decided to enter the war in early October. Residual uncertainties about Soviet pledges of military support led Mao to equivocate momentarily, however, delaying the Chinese intervention by several weeks. With North Korean forces in full retreat, Stalin urged Kim to flee Korea and establish a government in exile in China.[27] To clarify the extent of Stalin's support for a Chinese intervention, Mao sent China's Premier and Minister of Foreign Affairs Zhou Enlai on a visit to the Soviet Union. Stalin pledged to Zhou that the Soviet Union would furnish large-scale aid to China. Reassured of Soviet commitments, Mao reaffirmed the CCP's decision to intervene. Chinese forces crossed the Yalu in strength in late October 1950.

From this point in the conflict, North Korea's survival and Kim's personal safety depended on Chinese support.[28] In November, on Stalin's direct orders, Kim was compelled to yield operational control of KPA forces to Marshal Peng Dehuai, the commander of the Chinese People's Volunteers (CPV). He also subsequently had to relinquish control of North Korea's roads, railways and ports to Chinese officers. Peng and Kim engaged in intense confrontations over war strategy, but Kim ultimately had to accommodate Chinese campaign plans. The Chinese intervention transformed the hostilities into a Sino-American conflict (albeit one fought entirely on Korean soil), and relegated Kim to a subordinate role during much of the war. As a North Korean general observed in a conversation with an Eastern European ambassador many years later, 'China put Kim Il-sung in the bunker and told him to keep quiet'.[29]

Desperation necessitated Kim's reliance on outside forces: it was his only means of survival. But these wartime experiences instilled in him 'never again' convictions that defined his subsequent outlook and goals. To obscure his subordinate position during much of the conflict, North Korean accounts of the war embellish Kim's wartime contributions and largely ignore China's crucial role, even though Beijing's cumulative deployments to Korea during the war numbered nearly 3 million soldiers as well as more than 600,000 civilian personnel.[30] The mythology evident in North Korean accounts of the conflict was necessary to enshrine and protect Kim's claims to omniscience and omnipotence. But Kim confronted an open-ended strategic challenge as hostilities drew to a close. How could he address the economic and security needs of a small state surrounded by much larger powers without mortgaging his fate to an external power? The tumultuous events of subsequent decades would turn on this defining issue, and it remains equally or more relevant today.

Building the system

At the end of the war, the DPRK's economy and infrastructure were largely in ruins. Up to a quarter of the North's pre-war population had reportedly been killed.[31] Just as Kim Il-sung had relied on China and the Soviet Union to prosecute the war, he now had to turn to both countries (but especially the latter) and to East European states to rebuild his country. Only two months after the signing of the armistice, Kim travelled to Moscow to secure a major aid package, enabling a three-year recovery plan for 1954–56. Moscow also agreed to cancel more than half of North Korea's wartime debt.[32] Two months later, during a visit to Beijing in pursuit of additional assistance, Kim persuaded China to cancel all of North Korea's debt and provide substantial direct aid, including extensive contributions by Chinese troops in rehabilitating facilities that had been badly damaged during the war.[33] (It was on this latter trip that Kim first came into contact with Deng Xiaoping, then serving as China's minister of finance.[34]) According to one estimate, between 1954 and 1956 the Soviet Union and its allies provided 75% of North Korea's capital investments and financed more than three quarters of its imports and nearly a quarter of the state budget through aid and credits.[35] Kim had no compunctions about accepting (nor indeed, demanding) large-scale assistance, even though he offered no assurances of lasting allegiance in return. Following the USSR's collapse, this pattern was repeated, but with North Korea urging its long-term adversaries to assume the role previously performed by the Soviet Union and other communist states.

The results of the large-scale assistance from the socialist camp, described by historian Charles Armstrong as 'the most ambitious multilateral development project ever undertaken by the socialist countries during the Cold War', were impressive.[36] By the end of the 1950s, the DPRK had rebuilt and expanded its pre-Korean War industrial infrastructure, and Pyongyang continued to enjoy rapid economic growth during much of the 1960s.[37] This was the most prosperous and successful period that the DPRK ever experienced, with the state able to fulfil basic provisions in housing, public health, food and clothing for most of its citizens. The gross output of the mining, manufacturing and energy sectors reportedly tripled in the five years between 1954 and 1959.[38] It also convinced Kim to initiate (beginning in late 1959) the repatriation of nearly 100,000 ethnic Koreans from Japan to the DPRK, including many with educational and professional skills as well as financial resources.[39] According to comparative economist Eui-Gak Hwang, as late as 1965 North Korea's per capita GNP was still more than twice that of the South (US$248 for the DPRK, versus $105 for the ROK); the per capita GNP of the South did not exceed that of the North until 1976.[40]

Kim Il-sung also wasted little time in putting forth doctrines and practices to justify a Korea-first strategy. The concept of *juche* (described by most analysts as self-reliance, but better characterised as self-determination) first emerged in the mid-1950s as North Korea's defining ideological rationale. As Kim observed in a speech in 1955 articulating these beliefs, 'we are not engaged in any other country's revolution, but solely in the Korean revolution … When we study the history of the

Communist Party of the Soviet Union, the history of the Chinese revolution, or the universal truth of Marxism–Leninism, it is entirely for the purpose of correctly carrying out our own revolution.'[41] Kim sought to depict his regime as distinctly and authentically Korean, and in its first decade the DPRK seemed to be on a path to successful modernisation, while the South continued to flounder economically and politically.

At the same time, Kim proved willing to expropriate symbols and concepts closely identified with mortal enemies if they served his political purposes. Charles Armstrong's observations warrant extended quotation:

> 'American Imperialism' became North Korea's main enemy primarily as a result of the Korean War. Ironically, North Korea's war against the US has created a mobilising, militaristic regime with some striking resemblances to Japan in World War II. The cult of the semi-divine leader, the indivisible organic nation-race, and later even the portrayal of 'suicide squads' (*kyolsadae*) to defend the motherland against the Americans ... all suggest a kind of (perhaps unconscious) continuity with Japanese wartime mobilisation ... Like much else in the North Korean system, war mobilisation ... maintained the form of Japanese colonial militarism while obviously jettisoning its specifically Japanese and colonial content. Even some of North Korea's most prominent economic and foreign policy slogans, such as *charyok gaengsaeng* (self-reliance) and *juchesong* (autonomy or subjectivity) are identical to Japanese wartime slogans.[42]

Like Mao, Kim was intent on building a system that bore his direct imprint and was autonomous from the Soviet Union. He sought to differentiate *juche* from the policies of both of his external patrons. But appreciable dissonance was already surfacing between Kim and his primary benefactors, especially the Soviet Union. Kim was increasingly intent on a nationalist strategy to ensure his unquestioned dominance of North Korean politics, and deny outside powers major influence or outright control.

These issues culminated in a major intra-party struggle during 1955 and 1956, the most serious challenge to Kim's power in the history of the KWP.[43] Emboldened by Soviet leader Nikita Khrushchev's secret speech of February 1956, delivered to a closed session of the 20th CPSU party congress, and further prompted by a severe food crisis and reports of widespread starvation in the North, Kim's critics openely voiced their grievances with Soviet and East European diplomats.[44] Kim Il-sung saw de-Stalinisation as a direct threat to his power. As Russian historian Andrei Lankov observes, Kim's counterattack against internal opponents 'marked the end of the early North Korean power structure and the birth of Pyongyang's version of "national Stalinism" ... [and] the only known open challenge to Kim's supremacy from within the North Korean political system in the almost half-century reign of the "Great Leader".'[45]

Kim initially launched a campaign against those whose loyalty he deemed suspect, proceeding to direct appeals to Korean nationalism at the third KWP Congress in April 1956, the first party congress since the formal establishment of the DPRK. Disputes persist among historians on whether the differences between Kim and other senior leaders warranted the charge of factionalism, though Kim repeatedly attached this label to his critics. Khrushchev's secret speech slowed but did not halt Kim's plans to move against his opponents. The North Korean leader was undeterred by the dramatic denunciation of Stalinist policy. However, in June and July 1956, while on an extended trip to the Soviet Union and Eastern Europe in search of additional economic aid, internal opposition festered among Koreans with ties to the Soviet Union and China.[46] This discontent and outright opposition extended to contacts and conversations between the internal opposition and the Soviet Embassy in Pyongyang, and possibly with the Chinese Embassy as well. Sensing a direct challenge to his rule, upon his return, Kim effected a major purge to deal with the plotters, ousting senior leaders, many with long-standing ties to Moscow and Beijing. Some of his opponents were imprisoned; others escaped to the Soviet Union and China.

Alarmed by Kim's sweeping actions, Moscow and Beijing sent an unprecedented joint mission to Pyongyang in September 1956 led by Anastas Mikoyan, the long-time Politburo member and diplomatic trouble shooter, and Peng Dehuai, Kim Il-sung's superior officer during the Korean War who was then serving as China's Minister of National Defence.[47] The trip constituted the high-water mark in Sino-Soviet political collaboration. Under pressure from Mikoyan and Peng (and with intimations that the two sought to identify a leader to replace him, though the latter hypothesis seems largely speculative), Kim relented on his reprisals and consented to measures emphasising intra-party democracy and criticism and self-criticism. In a conversation years later, Kim told the Romanian ambassador to Pyongyang that the Mikoyan–Peng visit had 'introduced unwanted layers' into relations with Moscow and Beijing, and that the visit had 'insulted' the KWP leadership, presumably meaning Kim.[48]

Kim's concessions did not last. As Cold War historian Balazs Szalontai observes, 'Kim outsmarted both his foreign and domestic critics … he could rely on … the miscalculations of his opponents, the passivity of the North Korean population, and the shock the Hungarian revolution gave to the "Communist camp".'[49] Less than a year later, there were widespread attacks on factionalism within the party, followed by thousands of leadership dismissals, the internal relocation of various 'unde-sirable elements', and fresh show trials, with various alleged conspirators either imprisoned or executed.[50] Kim also turned increasingly to on-the-spot guidance tours first undertaken in the late 1940s, conveying the image of a benign fatherly figure and thereby seeking to ingratiate himself with North Korean citizens at the local level.[51] Deflecting potential challenges to his authority required a larger-than-life image, including an emotional bond between the leader and population. If Moscow and Beijing had hoped to curb or caution Kim from actions that undermined Soviet or Chinese interests, they failed.

Between Moscow and Beijing

In the aftermath of the Sino-Soviet intervention of 1956 that followed the overt signs of opposition to Kim Il-sung, the North Korean leader turned the tables on Moscow and Beijing. The outcome of the DPRK leadership struggles of the late 1950s marked the definitive triumph of Kim's Manchurian partisans (the Kapsan faction). As Andrei Lankov observes, 'the guerilla movement in Manchuria … [was now] presented as the only proper form of Korean Communism … [that] was depicted as both Communist and nationalist'.[52] Though he led a small and needy state, Kim had defied his major patrons, neither of whom was inclined to confront the North Korean leader. He even elic-ited apologies from Moscow and Beijing for the Mikoyan–Peng mission of September 1956, with Mao delivering a direct expres-sion of regret for his intervention in North Korean internal affairs when he and Kim were both in Moscow in November 1957.[53]

To minimise any additional damage to Chinese interests, Mao informed Kim that China would quickly withdraw the remaining CPV military units from North Korea.[54] Though appreciable numbers of Chinese military personnel departed from the DPRK during 1954 and 1955, 440,000 troops still remained as late as April 1956. But a large, continuing foreign troop presence generated undoubted suspicions in Pyongyang about Chinese internal influence and undermined North Korea's claims to full sovereignty. Beijing continued unsuccessfully to call for the withdrawal of US troops from the peninsula, although this was largely for political effect. In three separate phases between April and October 1958, the Chinese withdrew more than 250,000 troops, and transferred their weaponry, equipment, and facilities gratis to the DPRK. Beijing also undertook major new economic commitments and additional weapons transfers to Pyongyang in subsequent years.[55]

By the late 1950s, Kim was firmly entrenched in power; neither the Soviets nor the Chinese were able to control events inside North Korea, leading to a major recalibration in power relations among the three capitals. As Khrushchev remarked to Mao Zedong in October 1959, 'Both you and we have Koreans who fled from Kim Il-sung. But this does not give us ground to spoil relations with Kim Il-sung, and we remain good friends.'[56] It seems clear that Khrushchev was trying to make the best of a bad situation, as far larger disputes were already emerging between Moscow and Beijing. These culminated with the 1959 cancellation of Soviet nuclear assistance to China (including a 1957 agreement to furnish Beijing with a sample nuclear weapon) and the abrupt withdrawal of all remaining Soviet advisers from China in 1960. But rancorous arguments between Khrushchev and senior Chinese leaders about what Beijing saw as a US 'two Chinas' plot and parallel actions by Moscow and Washington that implied Germany's permanent division had obvious implications for Korea as well.[57] There is no evidence that the Chinese discussed mounting Sino-Soviet differences with North Korean leaders, but Sino-Soviet frictions were becoming increasingly obvious at various party gatherings and even in some public settings. Fearful that Mao's strident attacks on the United States presaged potential Chinese risk-taking, the Soviet leader openly cautioned Mao that 'it is unwise to use military means to test the stability of the capitalist system'. But Khrushchev's message applied equally to Pyongyang, which (like Beijing) rankled at the possibility of Soviet control over its external behaviour.

Since by this time he was already dealing with an intransigent Mao, the Soviet leader was even less prepared to conciliate an equally independent-minded leader in North Korea. Khrushchev dismissed the DPRK's initial draft of a first five-year plan as wholly unrealistic and cancelled plans for a 1959 visit to Pyongyang, opting instead to meet first with US President Dwight D. Eisenhower at Camp David and then with Mao in Beijing.[58] This apparent slight (and the Soviet leader's pursuit of improved relations with Washington) reinforced Kim's determination to pursue an independent course. But he faced an ongoing challenge from US forces deployed in South Korea. The withdrawal of Chinese forces coincided with the introduction of US tactical nuclear weapons on the peninsula, to be discussed in the next chapter. Kim may have felt more secure in his domestic power position, but he was not able to confront American military power on his own.

Materials from Soviet and East European archives released by the Cold War International History Project indicate that Kim repeatedly sought a formal security guarantee from Moscow towards the end of the 1950s. Khrushchev initially turned aside these requests, arguing that improved Soviet–American relations invalidated the need for such a commitment. Khrushchev also postponed plans for a visit to North Korea time and again, and never visited the DPRK. Nor did any of his successors as CPSU first secretary.[59] (Vladimir Putin's 2000 state visit to Pyongyang remains the only instance of the top Soviet or Russian leader travelling to the DPRK.) Khrushchev nevertheless signed a treaty of friendship, cooperation and mutual assistance with North Korea in July 1961, with the terms taken nearly verbatim from the Sino-Soviet treaty of February 1950.

Khrushchev only consented to the treaty after Kim Il-sung stopped first in Beijing en route to the Soviet capital, when Kim informed him that Mao was prepared to sign a treaty regardless of Moscow's intentions. With the Soviet leader locked into increasingly rancorous contention with Beijing, he agreed to the treaty, though with little conviction.[60] Meeting with a visiting Albanian official three months later, Kim Il-sung characterised his co-dependence with Khrushchev in unusually frank terms:

> Whether we love Khrushchev or not, he is the one in power at the moment ... It is not in our hands to topple him. He is what we have to deal with and there is no one else to talk to. Whether we want to or not, we have to tip our hat to him ... [but] he [also] cannot remove me from power. I hold the power here and whoever rises up against me, I will cut his head off and take measures against him.[61]

The Moscow–Beijing–Pyongyang triangle was in the throes of major policy shifts in the early 1960s, and the increasing animosities between China and the Soviet Union were becoming pivotal. Kim grasped the opportunity to exploit these circumstances to North Korea's benefit, with his predominant sympathies resting with Beijing, especially as the Soviet Union and the United States sought to curtail the spread of nuclear weapons. (China was the principal source of American and Soviet worries about proliferation.[62]) But in the early 1960s North Korea was also beginning to reveal a nuclear agenda of its own that would later lead Pyongyang to embark on a strategic course independent of both Moscow and Beijing.

CHAPTER TWO

Nuclear memories and nuclear visions

Kim Il-sung was aware of the nuclear revolution well before the establishment of the DPRK. The Soviet Union's eleventh-hour entry into the conflict against Japan in the waning weeks of the Second World War and the abrupt collapse of Japanese military forces in Korea in the aftermath of the nuclear attacks on Hiroshima and Nagasaki in August 1945 denied Kim the role for which he had long prepared, direct participation in the liberation of his homeland from Japanese colonial rule, which would have brought him the legitimacy he craved. On 10 August 1945, just hours after the second nuclear attack on Nagasaki, Soviet forces crossed the Tumen River and undertook amphibious landings along Korea's east coast, encountering minimal resistance from outnumbered Japanese forces. Sweeping across the northern half of the peninsula, Soviet units faced only token opposition in most major cities, occupying Hamhung, Wonsan and Pyongyang in less than two weeks.[1]

Kim's plan was to enter Korea on the heels of Moscow's military intervention as commander of the Red Army's 88th Brigade, which was comprised primarily of his Manchurian guerrilla compatriots. But the destruction of a bridge across the

Yalu River denied him immediate entry into northern Korea, forcing him to arrive on a Soviet ship entering Wonsan on 19 September, more than two weeks after Japan's unconditional surrender. By the date that Kim (wearing a Red Army uniform) arrived on his native soil, the battle for the northern half of the peninsula was over, and victory had been secured by Soviet troops without participation by Kim's forces. As historian Sydney Seiler observes, Kim and his close followers 'were at once surprised and dismayed by the rapid surrender of the Japanese', which reduced his unit to a conspicuously subordinate role, without any involvement in combat.[2]

Kim's views in the immediate aftermath of the nuclear bombardment of Japan remain unknown, in contrast to Mao Zedong, who openly disparaged the belief that atomic bombs were all-powerful or decisive instruments of war in a speech to cadres in Yanan ten days after the attack on Hiroshima.[3] The Korean leader would certainly have followed the reports that circulated in communist media within days of the Hiroshima bombing. He undoubtedly recognised the overwhelming power of the bomb, given that it had so abruptly compelled Japan to sue for peace, bringing to an end a decade and a half of large-scale warfare on the Asian mainland.

There were also more immediate connections between Korea and the events at Hiroshima and Nagasaki. Significant numbers of Korean labourers in forced employment at Japanese factories were killed in the nuclear attacks. In addition, major chemical and industrial facilities linked to Tokyo's clandestine nuclear-weapons programme were located in northern Korea, and Japan was also exploring for uranium and various rare earth metals in the northern half of the peninsula.[4] According to top secret memos from Soviet archives, Moscow undertook uranium mining in northern Korea as early as 1946, presumably relying on Korean labour.[5] Such efforts must have prompted intense curiosity on Kim's part: if these resources were of such great value to Japan and to the Soviet Union, could they not serve Korean interests as well? Kim Il-sung was never a man to think small.

The Korean War and US military planning in the 1950s

The possible use of nuclear weapons in the Korean War was highly sobering to Kim Il-sung. The North Korean leader had been deeply affected by the overwhelming destruction wrought by US conventional bombardment during the war. In February 1952, Kim informed Mao that the toll of the bombing was leading to 'great losses', declaring that he had 'no desire to continue the war'.[6] But he also faced the chilling prospect of nuclear attack against the North. From the early months of the conflict until just before the armistice was signed, his fears were compounded by periodic statements from senior US civilian and military leaders about the use of nuclear weapons, training exercises undertaken with nuclear-capable aircraft in or near the peninsula, and open calls by members of Congress for the use of nuclear weapons to compel an end to the Korean conflict.[7]

China and North Korea both claimed that the threat of Soviet retaliation would inhibit the United States from using nuclear weapons, but it is doubtful that either one expressed these views with much confidence. Indeed, interviews during the war with Chinese and North Korean POWs suggested deep anxieties about nuclear use among soldiers on the front lines.[8] As the war ended, Kim may have begun to ponder the potential value of such weapons, but the war's horrific destruction, the imperatives of post-war reconstruction, and the North's modest scientific base made the prospect of a nuclear capability at best a distant aspiration.

The American decision to introduce nuclear weapons on the peninsula in the late 1950s heightened Kim's awareness of the nuclear revolution. Though developed principally for the European theatre, US tactical nuclear systems were deployed in significant numbers to South Korea.[9] By early 1958, the United States had begun to station various tactical nuclear systems in Korea, including nuclear-armed artillery and short-range nuclear-armed missiles, with additional deployments of longer-range missiles in 1959 intended for targets in China and the Soviet Union. Subsequent nuclear deployments included additional missile batteries and atomic demolition mines designed to blunt any renewed attack by North Korean forces across the 38th parallel. In addition, there were ample nuclear capabilities on US surface ships and attack submarines. Nuclear gravity bombs were also stored at US air bases in the ROK for potential use on US fighter-bombers.

According to declassified US government data, the total number of nuclear weapons deployed on the peninsula peaked at 763 in 1972.[10] The numbers were quietly reduced in subsequent years, with approximately 100 warheads still deployed on the peninsula in 1991, when President George H.W. Bush unilaterally decided to withdraw all remaining tactical nuclear weapons from Korea and to remove all nuclear weapons from the US Navy's surface fleet. For three decades, however, substantial nuclear assets were deployed in and near Korea and were fully integrated into US war planning.

North Korea undoubtedly viewed US strategy through a nuclear lens, but from the outside looking in, it is impossible to determine precisely how the US deployment of nuclear weapons affected Pyongyang's risk-taking calculus. The continued large-scale presence of US forces during the mid- and late-1950s presumably inhibited serious consideration of major military actions by Pyongyang. However, according to former Soviet diplomat and historian Alexandre Mansourov, when Kim Il-sung learned the details of President Harry S Truman's contemplated use of nuclear weapons during the Korean War, he expressed 'shock, anguish, and undisguised fear that one day his country could become held prey' to US nuclear attack.[11] As strategic specialist Peter Hayes has observed, North Korea's experience with nuclear weapons was 'unique among small states. No other state … faced four decades of continuous nuclear threat … without a countervailing nuclear retaliatory capability of its own or allied nuclear deployments in its own territory.'[12]

For much of the 1950s, however, there were few North Korean references to nuclear threats. This may have reflected Pyongyang's primary focus on economic recovery and the fact that US nuclear weapons were not deployed on the peninsula until the latter part of the decade. But US nuclear deployments increased steadily throughout the early 1960s. North Korea was increasingly attentive to US nuclear capabilities and to its own potential vulnerabilities. North Korea's first discussions of nuclear weapons, including reported preparations for defence against nuclear attack, date from this period.

Pyongyang and the peaceful atom

North Korea's earliest known interest in nuclear technology focused on the peaceful atom. Though the DPRK might have imagined a future weapons capability, any nuclear aspirations were held in check by the country's acute limitations in trained manpower, infrastructure and technology. The men who went on to form the DPRK's first generation of nuclear scientists, To Sang-rok, Lee Sung-ki and Han In-sok, were educated in Japanese universities in nuclear physics and related disciplines during the 1930s and only returned to Korea in the mid- and late 1940s. Kim Il-sung purportedly met with To Sang-rok upon the latter's arrival in Pyongyang in 1946, and explicitly encouraged the returning scientist to develop a cadre of specialists in mathematics, physics and other basic sciences.[13]

There are claims from South Korean sources that Kim Il-sung sought to initiate nuclear weapons research as early as 1950, but there is no documentary evidence to substantiate this assertion.[14] There were, however, initial investments in nuclear science during the war.[15] The DPRK National Academy of Sciences was established in 1952, with uranium exploration, basic research in nuclear physics and the training of nuclear scientists identified as early priorities. In March 1955, an Atomic and Nuclear Physics Research Institute was established under the Institute of Physics and Mathematics of the Academy of Sciences. Nuclear physics departments were also opened at Kim Il-sung University and at Kim Ch'aek Industrial College, later renamed a technical university. A ten-year plan for science and technology, promulgated in 1957, called for a comprehensive survey of North Korea's natural resources including uranium, and advocated an active programme of research in atomic energy, the training of scientific personnel, and pursuit of nuclear applications to the DPRK's economic development.[16]

After returning from additional advanced study in Moscow in the late 1950s, Han In-sok delivered lectures to high-ranking KWP cadres on the significance of nuclear energy and the need for the DPRK to pursue nuclear development.[17] Lee Sung-ki, a chemist best known for the invention of vinalon, a synthetic compound extolled in the North as 'juche fibre', was named the first director of the Atomic Energy Research Institute, where some of the DPRK's earliest nuclear-weapons research took place.[18] The ties of these scientists to Japan provided North Korea with early access to nuclear expertise and technology vital to building a nuclear infrastructure in subsequent decades. The returned scientists oversaw training of a second generation of nuclear specialists, many of whom benefited from advanced training in the Soviet Union. Subsequent generations of nuclear specialists were trained mainly in North Korea, though they also gained requisite knowledge from international contacts, including from ethnic Korean scientists in Japan loyal to the DPRK.

The DPRK had to build its initial nuclear competence from scratch, and Soviet assistance was indispensable to these efforts. China's nuclear scientific development was then in its infancy, and it seems doubtful that Chinese scientists played a meaningful role in assisting the North in the early and mid-1950s, though some sources claim Chinese involvement. The entire socialist camp depended on the Soviet Union's nuclear expertise and its willingness to share knowledge and train personnel. North Korea's circumstances differed from those of other states seeking Soviet nuclear assistance. Following the withdrawal of Soviet military forces in 1948 the DPRK was no longer subject to Moscow's direct control. North Korea was not an important actor in intra-bloc politics or a formal ally of the Soviet Union, so there may have been less reason for Moscow to encourage nuclear scientific and technological development in the DPRK. Pyongyang had also proven a problematic partner during the Korean War, and following the war it had refused to join the Council for Mutual Economic Assistance (COMECON), the principal mechanism for economic coordination between the Soviet Union and its East European allies.

Khrushchev nevertheless saw the training of nuclear scientific personnel as a means to develop bloc solidarity. The mining of uranium in the North for the Soviet nuclear programme during the late 1940s may have also created obligations to Pyongyang. Soviet leaders probably believed that such assistance would also cement Soviet–North Korean relations. Khrushchev was intent on matching President Eisenhower's 'atoms for peace' initiative with a parallel programme for communist states. This opened the door to the training of scientific personnel in the Soviet Union, and Pyongyang was eager to walk though it.

Following the signing of cooperative agreements with Moscow in the mid and late 1950s, the DPRK's opportunities for nuclear advancement increased significantly. In February 1956, the Joint Institute for Nuclear Research was established at Dubna, near Moscow, and North Korea was among its founding members.[19] Russian estimates place the number of North Korean scientists trained at the institute in the range of 250 to 300 or more.[20] Many North Korean personnel trained there were later associated with the nuclear-weapons programme, most notably Seo Sang-kuk, born in 1938. A Chinese account of the North Korean programme dates the DPRK's covert weapons development from 1969, shortly after Seo completed a PhD in the Soviet Union. According to this article, Seo's wide-ranging personal relationships from his years of study in the Soviet Union enabled illicit acquisitions of nuclear-weapons technology. He was also responsible in later years for a major expansion of North Korean uranium exploration.[21] Seo then served as the chairman of the Physics Department of Kim Il-sung University, and is deemed by some the true father of the North's nuclear-weapons programme.[22]

In March and September 1956, the Soviet Union and the DPRK signed agreements on the peaceful uses of atomic energy and on research collaboration in nuclear science. Soviet documents also allude to a 1956 inquiry from Pyongyang on provision of power reactors.[23] The DPRK and the Soviet Union signed an even more important protocol enabling joint nuclear undertakings in September 1959. This included planning for nuclear activities near Yongbyon, approximately 90km northeast of Pyongyang, where North Korea subsequently built the plutonium production reactor and related facilities for nuclear-weapons development. Yongbyon was purportedly one of the locations that Japan utilised for its covert nuclear activities during the 1940s. A Russian expert has noted that the Soviet code name for the facility was 'Object 9559' and that North Korean experts labelled it the 'Furniture Factory', suggesting that the activities carried out there were sensitive and highly restricted.[24] Yongbyon's designation as a Special District of the State Administrative Council (including specialised entry and exit requirements issued by the Ministry of Public Security) even more tightly controlled access to the area.[25]

The scope of activities at Yongbyon suggested ambitious goals. It included establishment of the Atomic Energy Research Center in November 1962; transfer of an IRT-2000 2 MWt research reactor and additional equipment from the Soviet Union to North Korea (construction began in March 1963 and the reactor achieved criticality in August 1965);[26] and building of additional facilities, including a radiochemical laboratory for isotope separation and waste storage sites, all constructed according to Soviet-supplied blueprints, with total costs in 1962 prices estimated at US$500 million.[27] Through subsequent indigenous efforts, the capacity of the reactor was later increased to 8 MWt. In 1974, North Korea joined the International Atomic Energy Agency (IAEA), and three years later Pyongyang agreed to an extension of the safeguards, detailed in information circular INFCIRC/66, that enabled the agency to monitor activities and the provision of fuel at the research reactor.[28] It was nearly a full decade before North Korea ratified the Nuclear Non-proliferation Treaty (NPT), and another seven years before a full safeguards agreement was signed with the IAEA, enabling agency personnel to uncover significant discrepancies in Pyongyang's declaration of the very limited amounts of plutonium that it had claimed to have separated from damaged fuel rods.[29]

Soviet commitments to North Korea were limited to civilian applications of nuclear science, but Moscow's deep involvement in planning and construction at Yongbyon seems puzzling. The DPRK and the Soviet Union signed the 1959 protocol only three months after Khrushchev's unilateral decision to cancel nuclear-weapons assistance to China.[30] Why was the Soviet Union prepared to initiate nuclear-technology transfer to yet another East Asian communist state, including the risk that Pyongyang might pursue nuclear collaboration with Beijing? Did leaders in the Kremlin calculate that North Korea's nuclear competencies (then in their infancy) would not prove a major worry? How did they propose to control the risks of any technology transfer? Alternatively, did the Russians fear that North Korea would turn to China if Moscow failed to provide meaningful assistance to Pyongyang? There are no certain answers to these questions.[31] Khrushchev probably hoped to pull Kim more firmly into the Soviet camp. US deliberations over nuclear-sharing arrangements within NATO represented another important factor. Khrushchev may have perceived the need for parallel possibilities in the socialist world, even with states as difficult to manage as Pyongyang.

The DPRK's repeated demands for major support from Moscow and its East European allies persisted until the waning years of the Soviet Union. Despite these expectations or perhaps because of them, Pyongyang also repeatedly criticised Soviet non-proliferation goals and challenged the steadfastness of Moscow's security commitments, even though Soviet scientists were deeply involved in Yongbyon's development. Moreover, as China prepared to carry out its first nuclear test, officials in Pyongyang intimated that the DPRK was contemplating nuclear-weapons ambitions of its own.

Nuclear technology and alliance politics

As construction of nuclear facilities at Yongbyon progressed in the early 1960s, Pyongyang put forward ambitious goals in nuclear-power development that vastly exceeded the requirements for a single research reactor and some ancillary facilities. The peaceful uses of nuclear energy, research on radioactive isotopes, and various measuring devices were all identified as priorities for the Seven Year Plan announced at the 4th KWP National Congress in September 1961.[32] Extensive mining efforts, chemical-processing facilities, and building of research and development centres were also under way at the time.[33] By the latter half of the decade (in meetings with Soviet and East European counterparts), North Korean officials asserted regularly that development of a nuclear-power industry was imperative to address unmet energy requirements.

North Korea also hinted at possible interest in nuclear weapons. There is no definitive evidence of a North Korean programme in archival materials from the early 1960s, but various documents reveal persistent inquiries about nuclear weaponry. In conversations with East European diplomats during the winter and spring of 1963, North Korean officials spoke of heightened war mobilisation in the North, purportedly as defensive measures against potential nuclear attack. In August, the GDR ambassador to North Korea reported to his Soviet counterpart that Pyongyang was seeking technical information about nuclear weapons and nuclear power from East German sources.

In September 1963, North Korean technical personnel informed Soviet specialists visiting the DPRK that they were planning extensive uranium exploration. But these visitors deemed North Korean plans grossly disproportionate to the requirements for a single research reactor, to which Moscow was already obligated to supply enriched uranium as fuel when it agreed to construct the reactor. In October 1963, when queried by a North Korean engineer about the DPRK's ability to fashion a nuclear weapon, Soviet nuclear personnel expressed scepticism. The engineer retorted that labour costs were far lower in the North, and that if workers were instructed to undertake such a project, they would work without compensation. Soviet diplomats saw a Chinese hidden hand in many of these inquiries and comments, but this may have reflected Moscow's deepening animosities with Beijing, rather than direct evidence of collaboration between China and the DPRK.[34] Over the next quarter century, Pyongyang repeatedly pressed the Soviet Union and other prospective nuclear suppliers to build nuclear reactors and facilitate extensive technology transfer, with at least one appeal coming directly from Kim Il-sung to the Soviet leadership, as well as from other senior North Korean officials and technical personnel.[35]

Kim Il-sung viewed nuclear power as a talisman that would affirm the country's standing as an advanced scientific and industrial power. Since the North relied heavily on Soviet assistance to advance its ambitions, it would also represent Moscow's readiness to treat the North as a worthy partner. But other socialist states had a more credible claim to Soviet aid. Eastern European states possessed greater indigenous industrial capabilities and scientific talent and enjoyed much closer relations with Moscow, thereby ensuring higher priority in Soviet nuclear assistance. The ROK's early pursuit of nuclear power was probably an even more important factor in Pyongyang's thinking. From its initial forays into nuclear power, North Korea lagged behind its southern rival, lending urgency to its repeated calls for heightened technology transfer. The ROK joined the IAEA in its first year of existence (1957), and Seoul established an Office of Atomic Energy in 1959. The South's first research reactor went critical in 1962, and construction of its first power reactor began in 1970.[36]

Pyongyang was also beginning to signal heightened interest in nuclear weapons. North Korea almost certainly perceived connections between civilian and military nuclear development; any large-scale technology transfer or major reactor project would serve both objectives. But many of the facilities that North Korea developed for the weapons programme were in remote locations, where Soviet advisers apparently had little access. In 1962, fears over China's nuclear-weapons development prompted Nikita Khrushchev to accelerate non-proliferation cooperation with the United States. Though China may have been Khrushchev's primary concern, the measures tabled by Moscow would have also impeded Pyongyang's pursuit of a weapons option.

On 23 August 1962 Soviet Foreign Minister Andrei Gromyko proposed to Secretary of State Dean Rusk an accord that would prohibit any transfer of nuclear weapons or know-how to non-nuclear states, including states allied to a nuclear-armed power.[37] A day later the Soviet ambassador to the DPRK, Vasily Moskovsky, briefed the DPRK Foreign Minister Pak Song-chol on the proposal. The foreign minister's response was unequivocal:

> Who can impose such a treaty on countries that do not have nuclear weapons, but are perhaps successfully working in that direction? Recently … I read a small report…that the Chinese comrades … are successfully working in this direction … [W]hy, indeed, wouldn't the Chinese comrades work on this?
>
> The Americans hold on to Taiwan, to South Korea, and South Vietnam, blackmail the people with their nuclear weapons and, with their help, rule on these continents and do not intend to leave. *Their possession of nuclear weapons, and the lack thereof in our hands, objectively helps them … They have a large stockpile, and we are forbidden even to think about the manufacture of nuclear*

weapons? I think that in such case the advantage will
be on the Americans' side.[38]

The Soviet Union was well aware of the Chinese nuclear
programme, but officials in Moscow may not have given
serious thought to parallel efforts in North Korea. They knew
Pyongyang did not yet possess the requisite technical, industrial
or financial resources for a dedicated weapons programme,
but Pak (perhaps reflecting internal deliberations within the
regime) was giving voice to the North's aspirations for nuclear
autonomy. Moreover, Soviet diplomats posted to Pyongyang
warned repeatedly that any nuclear assistance to North Korea
ran the risk of falling into Chinese hands.

Despite Soviet worst-case fears, there was minimal evidence
of nuclear collaboration between Beijing and Pyongyang.
Over the years, Chinese scientists have repeatedly denied any
involvement in the DPRK's nuclear pursuits, even though for
a time these scientists expressed skepticism about the North's
nuclear-weapons potential, which would seem to imply some
knowledge of and access to Pyongyang's nuclear facilities.[39]
Some analysts have made claims of Chinese nuclear assistance
to the DPRK, but it is more plausible that North Korea sought
such collaboration than that the Chinese provided it. A senior
Japanese military expert, Katsuichi Tsukamoto, asserts that in
1961 Beijing rejected a proposal from Pyongyang that North
Korean scientists be included in the Chinese programme.
He also claims that a month after China's first nuclear test in
October 1964, Kim wrote a letter to Mao Zedong requesting
data and uranium samples.

Mao purportedly spurned Kim's proposal, though
Tsukamoto also asserts that the Chinese leader suggested Beijing
could provide a fuller security guarantee to North Korea.[40] A
former Chinese Foreign Ministry official confirmed some of the

particulars in a July 1993 interview with American journalist Don Oberdorfer. According to this retired official, following the first Chinese test Kim Il-sung sought Chinese assistance for a North Korean programme. The Chinese supposedly spurned Kim's request, believing that the expense of such an effort was unwarranted for 'a very small country [like the DPRK]'.[41] But the Cuban missile crisis also prompted Pyongyang to ponder longer-term nuclear goals paralleling Chinese objectives. In North Korean eyes, Moscow's failure to ensure the security of another small, distant socialist state meant that the DPRK stood alone, and could depend on no one to uphold its fundamental strategic interests. Kim may have also believed that China's nuclear-weapons development provided some protective political cover for a covert programme of his own.

Following Khrushchev's ouster from power in October 1964, Kim Il-sung hoped that Moscow would reconcile with Beijing as well as provide Pyongyang with increased military and technological support. But these hopes evaporated quickly. A DPRK party and government delegation led by Vice Premier Kim Il visited Moscow in November 1964, during which Kim sharply attacked Soviet policy in a meeting with Prime Minister Alexei Kosygin. An East European ambassador later described the substance of these heated exchanges:

> The Korean leaders were distrustful of the CPSU and the Soviet Government, [and] they could not count on that the Soviet Government would keep its obligations related to the defence of Korea it [had] assumed in the Treaty of Friendship, Cooperation, and Mutual Assistance … and therefore they were compelled to keep an army of 700,000 and a police force of 200,000. These huge armed forces constituted enormous expenses for the national economy of the DPRK …

> Comrade Kosygin asked him what caused this distrust. In the view of Kim Il, the Soviet Union had betrayed Cuba at the time of the Caribbean crisis, and later it also betrayed the Vietnamese ... [and] the Soviet Union did not support the national liberation struggle of the Asian and African peoples.

In a January 1965 discussion between Kim Il-sung and the Soviet ambassador in Pyongyang, the North Korean leader conveyed comparable sentiments, though somewhat less laden with invective and directed specifically at his experiences with the now-ousted Soviet leader:

> Khrushchev had had big power ambitions, he, as the leader of a big party, wanted to force his will upon the smaller parties, Kim Il-sung said. They [the KWP leaders] pursued an independent policy, one could not make them go out of their way by putting pressure on them. Although Korea was a small power, they knew better than others which political line they should adopt and how the Korean people should be led on the path of revolution.[42]

A month later, reinforcing his insistence that North Korea would not be tethered to either of its allies, Kim told Kosygin that 'we ... implement the purest Marxism and condemn as false both the Chinese admixtures and the errors of the CPSU ... For all that we are still regarded as China's disciples, although we are only pursuing our own independent policy.'[43]

Kim had laid down important strategic markers, but the path had been set years before. North Korea would control its own fate, while also seeking maximal assistance from Moscow and Beijing. A nuclear programme, justified as an energy source and a touchstone of scientific advancement, would advance the autonomy and security of the North Korean system. North Korea was assembling the building blocks of an indigenous nuclear industry, with various facilities being completed over the next two decades.[44] Kim Il-sung may not have fully grasped the differences between the civilian and military applications of nuclear technology, but it is not likely that these mattered to him. He deemed accelerated development of nuclear technology a necessity, no matter what its ultimate purposes.

The impregnable fortress

Kim Il-sung wanted to control his own fate, but how? The treaties of alliance signed with Moscow and Beijing just weeks apart in July 1961 presumably provided Kim the external security guarantees that he had long sought from the Soviet Union and China, though Soviet pledges seemed more conditional. Moscow and Pyongyang pledged that they would 'continue to participate in all international action designed to safeguard peace and security in the Far East', with both affirming that they would render immediate 'military and other assistance' in the event of armed attack. The treaty was to be in force for ten years, with the treaty to remain operative for an additional five years and beyond should neither state give advance notice of an intention to withdraw from the treaty.[45] By contrast, China was obligated to a more explicit provision to collaborate with Pyongyang on measures to forestall prospective threats. Article 2 of the Treaty of Friendship, Cooperation and Mutual Assistance between China and the DPRK stated:

> The contracting parties undertake jointly to adopt all measures to prevent aggression against either of the contracting parties by any state. In the event of one of the contracting parties being subjected to the armed

attack by any state or several states jointly and this being involved in a state of war, the other contracting party shall immediately render military and other assistance by all means at its disposal.[46]

In addition, the treaty was open-ended, and would remain in force 'until the Contracting Parties agree on its amendment or termination'.

However, Pyongyang did not convey great confidence in regime security. Kim's anxieties were most probably rooted more in internal circumstances, leading him to reinforce the power of his ex-guerrilla loyalists within the Korean Workers Party. Following his return from his trips to Moscow and Beijing where the treaties were signed, Kim convened the 4th KWP Congress in September. A clear majority of those elected to the Central Committee membership were drawn from Kim's circle of Manchurian-era partisans or those linked to them, with dwindling numbers of those with Chinese or Soviet connections.[47]

Kim nonetheless still sought to curry favour with Moscow. In a series of meetings with the Soviet ambassador to Pyongyang in the summer and autumn of 1962, Kim praised past Soviet assistance, and declared the KWP as 'the younger brother of the CPSU', even claiming that 'as true friends, we do not have secrets from each other'.[48] In a meeting at the start of November, he even praised Khrushchev's handling of the Cuban missile crisis, declaring it 'the sole correct decision', and that 'the socialist camp does not need a war right now'. But Kim also signaled his intentions and needs. He alluded to his 'plans to attend to military matters [and] become acquainted with the state of defence of the country'. Kim was preparing to table major military aid requests above and beyond those he had sought during his 1961 visit to Moscow.

Kim's wish list arrived in Moscow two weeks later, immediately prior to the visit of a North Korean military delegation to Moscow. Warning that the DPRK's air defence was 'exceptionally weak' and much of the coastline undefended, Kim requested submarines, MiG-21s, and the expansion of surface-to-air missile divisions from two to 14.[49] Even as Kim expressed optimism about the North Korean economy, he asserted that 'at the present time we do not have [the] funds for such large-scale purchases', and urged that the entire military aid package be provided free of charge. Khrushchev, deeply offended by Kim's unabashed cult of personality and his overt challenge to the Soviet leader's anti-Stalin stance, refused. As a consequence, Kim sought increased Chinese military aid, resulting in heightened China–DPRK military collaboration during Khrushchev's final two years in power (1963–64).[50]

At a party plenum in December 1962, without disclosing his intentions in advance to any of the embassies in Pyongyang, Kim enunciated 'the four-point military guideline'.[51] Adrian Buzo describes these decisions as 'set[ting] in place a strategic and policy framework that Kim pursued for the rest of his life'.[52] Economic development and military enhancement, though depicted as coequal objectives under the new plan, were in practice decidedly unequal. The policy changes skewed investment patterns in favour of the military, with the manpower, financial and infrastructural demands severely hobbling the DPRK's economic development. Kim Jong-il's enunciation of a 'military first' policy in 1998 (to be reviewed in a later chapter) was thus not a new strategic conception: it ratified and enshrined steps taken by Kim Il-sung more than three and half decades earlier. As Hans Maretzki has argued, the military first policy is 'as old as the DPRK itself'.[53]

Developments in South Korea also influenced Kim's priorities. The overthrow of Syngman Rhee in April 1960 had prompted momentary optimism in Pyongyang. Kim possibly believed that the DPRK could finally achieve entrée into the ROK and might even heighten political support within the South for the withdrawal of American forces. In a conversation with the Soviet ambassador to Pyongyang, KWP Central Committee Vice Chairman Pak Kum-chol argued that the North Koreans still retained hopes in early 1962 that 'the students and intelligentsia' could successfully oppose the South's 'Fascist dictatorship', but Park Chung-hee's seizure and consolidation of power and his success 'in improving the country's economic situation to a certain extent' made any political inroads into the South impossible.[54] Kim Il-sung expressed similar sentiments in a conversation with Romanian dictator Nicolae Ceausescu nearly a decade later.[55] However, by sharply skewing investment in favour of military goals, Kim frittered away the North's extant economic advantage over the ROK, and it was never recovered.

The build-up of North Korea's military capacity was extraordinary. It encompassed widespread domestic mobilisation (including the militarisation of daily life), an independent national-defence doctrine, defence preparations on a nationwide scale (encompassing a vast expansion in the size of the armed forces), and maximal autonomy in weapons production. Buzo describes it thus:

> Arming the entire population ... established a military basis for daily life ... with weapons training, military drill and instruction from kindergarten to retirement age ... Fortification of the entire country meant the establishment of substantial strategic stockpiles and the construction of vast complexes of shelters, bunkers and underground facilities including whole armament factories. The modernisation process meant that the

proportion of total state investment devoted to military production rose from about 6 per cent to 30 per cent during the period of 1964 to 1967 as the military-industrial sector expanded to roughly four times the size of its Soviet model in proportional terms.[56]

As Buzo further observes, DPRK militarism had geopolitical, ideological, and psychological roots, and drew on Kim's formative experiences as a guerrilla leader. By 1962, the autonomous development of military power was fully entrenched in North Korean strategy and state policy; Kim also appeared increasingly reliant on military leaders for internal political support.[57] Though nuclear weapons were not yet a realistic possibility, Kim's longer-term vision presumed equivalence with the major powers. If nuclear capabilities were appropriate for others, then they could not be excluded from the DPRK's strategic future.[58]

The pervasive militarisation of the North Korean system in the early 1960s and the familiarity of senior North Korean officers with Soviet nuclear strategy suggest that some officers may have advocated the early pursuit of nuclear weapons. However, as Alexandre Mansourov observes, 'Kim Il-sung thoroughly repressed consideration of an autonomous nuclear programme within the North Korean military. Furthermore, he could not tolerate the decision of even secondary military matters related to the nuclear programme without his knowledge and prior approval. He considered the military nuclear programme his exclusive concern and guarded it fiercely.'[59] A decision of this magnitude would be Kim's alone.

Kim had sanctioned a highly risky military strategy in the late 1960s, simultaneously seeking to undermine the ROK and challenge the United States. According to Buzo, North Korean actions reflected the increased dominance of former guerrilla leaders in the Political Bureau, and perhaps a parallel belief that the US was far too preoccupied with the war in Vietnam to respond to North Korean provocations.[60] The strategy encompassed conventional and unconventional operations against the South, including at least three attempted assassinations of Park Chung-hee; repeated assaults against US and South Korean forces along the Demilitarised Zone (DMZ); the seizure of the USS *Pueblo* in January 1968 (only days after North Korean commandos came within several hundred metres of the Blue House in a failed assassination attempt against President Park); and the shooting down of a US EC-121 reconnaissance aircraft in April 1969, which killed all personnel on board.[61]

Kim possibly saw enhanced risk-taking as the best opportunity to destabilise the South and to legitimate the increasing militarisation of the North Korean system. The post-Khrushchev Soviet leadership, confronting the prospect of open-ended political and military tensions with China, had undoubted reason to improve relations with Pyongyang. Kim perceived a clear opportunity to heighten his demands for weapons, economic assistance, and nuclear technology transfer from Moscow. During the visit of Soviet Prime Minister Alexei Kosygin to Pyongyang in February 1965, Kim lamented his inability to meet the goals of the Seven Year Plan, and renewed his plea for free military aid that Khrushchev had spurned three years earlier. Senior North Korean generals also sought to exploit their close ties to senior Soviet counterparts, some dating from the period when the Manchurian partisans had fled to the Soviet Far East.[62] Pyongyang's renewed arms request encompassed new categories of weapons, with the estimated cost exceeding the previous aid package by half. Additional requests were made three months later. Anticipating the need for a regional ally in its growing face-off with China, Moscow accommodated Kim's expectations.[63]

Though Soviet leaders sought to meet Kim's demands, Pyongyang remained focused on plans and goals of its own. As Foreign Minister Pak Song-chol conveyed to his Russian counterpart Andrei Gromyko in April 1966, 'turning the country into an impregnable fortress' and 'arming the entire people' were intended to protect the North against vulnerabilities that the United States could exploit.[64] An adventurous military line was openly endorsed by Kim Il-sung. At a party plenum in October 1966, Kim declared the 'liberation of South Korea [a] national duty' and that the United States was preparing for a preemptive strike against the DPRK.[65] North Korea was deploying ever larger forces in forward positions near the Demilitarised Zone (DMZ) and was undertaking operations under nuclear-war conditions and had initiated plans for the relocation of large portions of Pyongyang's population. In response, Soviet leaders began to voice mounting disquiet about North Korean behaviour.[66] CPSU First Secretary Leonid Brezhnev directly chastised a senior North Korean official in November 1967, holding the DPRK responsible for heightened tensions and military incidents along the DMZ.[67]

Soviet reactions to the *Pueblo* crisis were even sharper. Pyongyang did not inform Moscow in advance of its plans to seize the vessel, and Brezhnev expressed unease about North Korean intimations of impending war, of which Moscow wanted no part. As the Soviet leader observed, North Korea 'sought to bind the Soviet Union somehow, using the existence of the treaty between the USSR and the DPRK [as a pretext] to involve us in supporting plans ... that we know nothing about'. Calling the North Korean actions 'steps that alarmed us', the Soviet leader pressed Kim to visit Moscow to explain himself. Kim insisted that he could not travel at a time of increased danger, opting to send Politburo member and Defence Minister Kim Chang-bong in his stead. A month later Kim Il-sung sought to reassure the Soviet ambassador to Pyongyang that 'we have no intention of raising military hysteria'.[68] But North Korean actions prompted growing Soviet wariness that persisted to the end of the Brezhnev era in 1982.

As Cold War historian Sergey Radchenko notes, 'Kim Il-sung wanted tension for tension's sake …. [he] was persuaded not to fight a war he most likely never intended to fight.'[69] But North Korean actions engendered growing doubts in Moscow about the DPRK's reliability and trustworthiness. All the while, Soviet and North Korean diplomats continued to debate the NPT. In late 1969, Soviet diplomats noted to Hungarian counterparts en route to assignments in Pyongyang that Moscow's efforts at 'patient and persistent persuasion' of the DPRK had yielded very few results. When Soviet officials raised the prospect of Japanese nuclear-weapons development should a non-proliferation treaty not be agreed to, North Korean officials conceded that it was an unwelcome prospect, but they refused to assent to non-proliferation as a broad goal, engendering added distrust of Pyongyang's intentions.[70]

Scholars continue to debate Kim's high-risk strategy of the latter half of the 1960s. Did Kim believe that active destabilisation of the ROK might trigger turmoil in the South, thus providing the pretext for a direct military intervention? Was he seeking to tether the Soviet Union to his own military plans, in a bold gamble reminiscent of the Korean War? Was he hoping to further solidify the growing militarisation of the DPRK economy and the enhanced power of the military within the system? Or did he see his defiance of Moscow as justifying pursuit of autonomous military capabilities so that no major power could ever again dictate to North Korea? Many of these factors may have part of Kim's larger calculus, but Kim would ultimately pay a major cost for defying his most important benefactor.

Fears of a two-front war

Additional dangers loomed for Kim in the latter half of the 1960s. China had embarked on the radicalism and xenophobia of the Cultural Revolution. According to a report from the Soviet Embassy in Pyongyang, in late 1964 the KWP leadership began to voice concern about the potential risks of close association with the CCP, 'grow[ing] alarmed over the obvious great Han nationalism and political adventurism of the Chinese leaders, and the possibility of ending up alone with only the Chinese'. In a meeting between Kim Il-sung and the Soviet ambassador in early May 1965, Kim candidly acknowledged the limitations of an autonomous strategy, 'taking into account that the DPRK borders two socialist countries – the USSR and China – and a capitalist country, Japan'. With growing US military involvement in Vietnam, North Korea also expressed mounting concern that Chinese policy was undermining Hanoi's interests.[71] In a report delivered to a party meeting in October, Kim conveyed his readiness to send Korean volunteers to the conflict in Southeast Asia if requested by Vietnam, reflecting the need for 'a unified anti-imperialist course of action on an international scale'.[72] In the aftermath of Prime Minister Kosygin's visit to Pyongyang in early 1965, Soviet arms deliveries began to increase, and a three-year trade agreement with Moscow was also signed.

Mounting tensions with China were reinforcing Pyongyang's need to avoid extreme alienation of the Soviet Union. In late 1966, Kim Il-sung and other senior leaders travelled incognito to Moscow, where they met with Brezhnev and Kosygin.[73] In a discussion with Brezhnev about developments in China, Kim characterised the Cultural Revolution as 'mass lunacy' that was endangering North Korea. But Kim also said that the DPRK would avoid identification with either Moscow or Beijing, informing Brezhnev that the KWP would 'neither participate with you, nor with the Chinese'.[74] According to a subsequent assessment from the Far Eastern Department of the Soviet Foreign Ministry, in a party meeting in October 1966 Kim reaffirmed that 'the KWP will never "dance to someone else's tune"', and that it would seek 'to maintain normal relations with both the PRC and the USSR'.[75]

Despite these assertions, relations with China continued to deteriorate throughout 1967.[76] Kim seemed increasingly worried, expressing mounting fears that China could pose an immediate threat to the DPRK.[77] He openly criticised China for 'big-power chauvinism, dogmatism, and "left" opportunism' and recalled all North Korean personnel then enrolled in Chinese military academies.[78] In response, China curtailed food deliveries and the supply of industrial commodities to the North. In confidential conversations with Soviet officials, Kim reaffirmed his previous characterisation of the Cultural Revolution as 'incredible madness'. China was reopening past border disputes with Pyongyang, and there were reported deaths of ethnic Koreans at the hands of Red Guard units near the Sino-DPRK border. Relations had deteriorated dangerously, but Kim feared that severing the alliance with China 'would mean we would have enemies at our back as well'.[79] Unlike his risk-taking propensities with South Korea and the United States, Kim showed caution and avoided needlessly provoking Beijing.

By mid-1968, however, things went from bad to worse. There were even armed incidents along the Sino-Korean border. Kim feared that a planned visit of senior North Korean officials to the Soviet Union entailed appreciable dangers for their personal safety. An air route over the water involved risks of interception by Chinese aircraft; and overflying PRC territory entailed the possibility of a forced landing in China and potential humiliation at Chinese hands. To avoid such possibilities, Pyongyang requested use of the narrow air corridor into Soviet territory.[80]

The Soviet Union (already in the midst of large-scale militarisation of the Sino-Soviet dispute) was the only country that could deflect Chinese pressure or encroachment against the DPRK. But Chinese troops crossed into North Korean territory at the time of the Sino-Soviet clashes along the Ussuri river in 1969, and Soviet forces were not able to defend the North; it is not even clear that Kim sought such protection. He decided to be patient and hope that Chinese forces would withdraw without major incident or lasting repercussions, and his caution was validated. However, the late 1960s underscored the potential dangers that Kim faced in dealings with far more powerful neighbours, even ones linked by a shared past and by treaty obligations. But in his darkest moments, Kim had never envisioned a two-front war.[81]

As China's domestic upheaval subsided, North Korea sought to restore normal party-to-party relations with Beijing. Senior DPRK officials requested a meeting with premier Zhou Enlai at the time of the Chinese Communist Party's 9th Party Congress in April 1969, and Zhou reciprocated with a 1970 visit to Pyongyang, his first trip abroad following the end of Cultural Revolution violence and mayhem. On his visit to Pyongyang, Zhou met twice with Kim Il-sung, during which the Chinese leader sought to repair the damage inflicted by the excesses of the Cultural Revolution.[82] The turbulence of preceding years – first with Moscow, subsequently with Beijing – underscored the inherent vulnerabilities faced by a small state sandwiched between far larger powers and already prone to paranoia.

Pyongyang was not yet able to break free from either the Soviet Union or China. These constraints became even more apparent in the 1970s, as the relations of both major communist powers with the United States warmed and North Korea's leverage with Moscow and Beijing diminished. The economic consequences of North Korea's militarisation were also increasingly apparent, with Seoul advancing while Pyongyang stagnated. Pressured on multiple fronts, while still retaining core convictions about his country's strategic independence, Kim Il-sung sought to escape from his mounting policy dilemmas. How could he construct an impregnable strategic fortress, and who was the principal threat that necessitated such efforts? The subsequent decade would compel Pyongyang to address these questions, with Kim turning increased attention to a nuclear-weapons option.

CHAPTER THREE

The nuclearisation of Korean strategy

At the beginning of the 1970s, there was increased political normalcy for the DPRK, at least as leaders in Pyongyang might have defined it. Sino-North Korean relations were recovering from their deep decline and near-crisis of the Cultural Revolution, and Soviet leaders (hoping to inhibit excessive risk-taking by Pyongyang) were resigned to open-ended subsidisation of the DPRK economy. In November 1970, the KWP convened its first Party Congress in nearly a decade. With economic performance in the North starting to flag under the cumulative weight of militarisation, Kim Il-sung urged accelerated scientific and industrial development, including calls for appreciably heightened investment in nuclear energy. Kim also hoped to parlay continuing animosities between Beijing and Moscow to garner increased assistance from both powers.

Unprecedented strategic realignments were also quietly under way in the communist world. Unbeknown to the North Korean leader, the United States and China had initiated confidential high-level contact, culminating in US National Security Adviser Henry Kissinger's secret trip to Beijing in July 1971 and President Richard Nixon's visit in February 1972. These profound shifts in major-power relations soon compelled both Koreas to reassess their respective strategies, beginning with unprecedented initiatives in inter-Korean relations, followed by efforts in nuclear-weapons development by both Seoul and Pyongyang. For the first time North Korea also pursued more diversified economic and diplomatic strategies, accepting loans from Western Europe, selling weapons to Middle Eastern and African states and establishing trading companies to undertake illicit commercial and technological activities for future military development.[1]

Kim Il-sung had also begun to ponder leadership succession. A nuclear-weapons programme (though not yet a realised capability) was now among his long-term objectives. He concluded that a nuclear-weapons option was necessary to maintain strategic autonomy, to counter the ROK's growing power, and to support impending plans for leadership transition in the North. The consequences of Kim's pursuit of a nuclear future continue to reverberate today.

The communist world transformed

The transformation in Sino-American and Soviet–American relations in the early 1970s sharply altered the DPRK's strategic calculations. No external change was more certain to generate North Korean suspicions of major-power collusion than simultaneous political-military accommodation of its two major allies with the United States. Moscow had long dealt with Washington, but Pyongyang saw Beijing's opening to America was seen as especially fraught with risk for Pyongyang. Somewhat surprisingly, however, Kim Il-sung initially treated the breakthrough in Sino-American relations as an opportunity rather than a danger, resulting in the first significant contact between the two Koreas since the establishment of separate regimes in 1948.

US–China rapprochement created the possibility of Beijing sacrificing North Korea's strategic equities to advance its own interests, and Beijing moved quickly to dispel Pyongyang's worst fears. Two days after Kissinger's departure on 11 July 1971, Zhou Enlai travelled to Hanoi for consultations with the Vietnamese leadership, followed immediately by a visit to Pyongyang for seven hours of discussions with Kim Il-sung.[2] Details of the meeting remain unknown, but weeks later Kim characterised Sino-American reconciliation as a singular political victory for the communist world. On 6 August, he delivered a speech containing direct overtures to the ROK, depicting Nixon's impending visit to Beijing as 'a trip of the defeated that fully reflects the declining fate of US imperialism'.[3]

If Kim harboured serious anxieties about the discussions between Washington and Beijing, Zhou's actions at least momentarily dissipated these concerns. Kim travelled to Beijing just before to the Nixon visit for additional consultations with the Chinese, and a DPRK diplomatic delegation followed later for further talks.[4] The DPRK's declared policy positions on Korea and Japan – including long-standing demands for dissolution of the United Nations Commission on the Unification and Rehabilitation of Korea (UNCURK), which was avowedly antagonistic to DPRK interests – are fully reflected in a paragraph about Korea drafted by the Chinese in the Shanghai Communiqué, the joint document presaging the normalisation of US–China relations in the late 1970s.

There were equally deep anxieties in Seoul about major-power relations. In November 1969, in the aftermath of his Guam Doctrine speech of the previous July – in which he called on US allies to take responsibility for their own defence, but assured them of US protection if needed – President Nixon ordered the US military to plan for 50% reductions in forces stationed in the ROK.[5] The ultimate decision, reached in late March 1970, scaled back the reductions to approximately one-third of total US force strength. The redeployments were scheduled for completion by June 1971, with the 7th Infantry Division to be fully withdrawn from South Korea. When US officials informed the ROK government of its plans in the spring of 1970, President Park Chung-hee's resistance was unequivocal, prompting him to send angry, anguished letters to President Nixon. Washington sought to mollify Park by parallel US assistance for ROK force modernisation, including a commitment that 'the United States reaffirms that in case a nuclear power threatens the freedom or security of the Republic of Korea, it will provide a shield against such a threat'.[6] Park subsequently acceded to the US troop withdrawals, but his acute unhappiness with US policy decisions would not be eased by subsequent decisions.

The disclosure of US secret diplomacy with Beijing very possibly stimulated Park's decision to pursue covert nuclear-weapons development. In July 1972, Park announced plans for 'self-reliant defence'. Park's acute feelings of vulnerability and abandonment following the US–China rapprochement were palpable. He expressed private fears that other unilateral US moves could undermine ROK interests and security comparable to those faced by leaders on Taiwan. His primary anxieties concerned potential Sino-American understandings over the peninsula, not worries about a direct US approach to Pyongyang.[7]

The Korean peninsula was the topic of exchanges between Zhou Enlai and President Nixon in February 1972.[8] Zhou acknowledged recent US withdrawals from Korea, also noting that 'the official policy of … President [Nixon] is that he is prepared to finally withdraw [US] troops from Korea in the future, and also to prevent the entry of Japanese troops into South Korea'. Drawing a clear parallel with relations between Beijing and Taipei, he added: 'How does one promote contacts between North and South Korea? How does one promote peaceful unification? That question will take a long time.' President Nixon urged that 'both of us exert influence to restrain our allies'. He referred to personal experiences with Syngman Rhee in 1953, when as vice president he informed Rhee that Washington would not allow ROK forces to advance northward. As Nixon further observed in his exchange with Zhou:

> The Koreans, both North and South, are emotionally impulsive people. It is important that both of us exert influence to see that these impulses, and their belligerency, don't create incidents that would embarrass our two countries … [or] to have the Korean peninsula be the scene of a conflict between our two governments. It happened once, and it must never happen again. I think that with the Prime Minister and I [sic] working together we can prevent this.

Zhou did not respond directly to Nixon's characterisations, instead focusing on inter-Korean relations and urging a reduced role for all major powers on the peninsula. It is possible that Zhou based his arguments on earlier understandings with Kim Il-sung. He urged the promotion of contact between the two Koreas and the cessation of UN institutional arrangements staunchly opposed by the DPRK. In a subsequent meeting, Zhou renewed his earlier reference to President Nixon's commitment to 'the gradual reduction of [US] forces on the peninsula', with the US assuring Beijing that Japan would not assume a direct military role in Korea. Zhou thus argued that Sino-American rapprochement provided an opportunity for inter-Korean accommodation. The People's Republic of China (PRC) had been seated at the UN for the first time in the autumn of 1971. Beijing quickly supported efforts to revoke the Security Council resolution legitimising the presence of US forces.

A US military withdrawal from the ROK had long been among Kim Il-sung's foremost strategic objectives. As he remarked to Romanian leader Nicolae Ceausescu only a month before the Kissinger visit, '[I]n the absence of the Americans in South Korea or of any other foreign forces, the South Korean people could install a democratic progressive government, through its own forces, and the establishment of such a government would draw us very close to each other, so that, without fighting, we could unify the country.'[9] Kim thus deemed US political-military support to the ROK essential to Seoul's existence as a separate system and to the sustainment of the South's adversarial relations with the North. Less than three years after North Korean commandos had nearly assassinated Park Chung-hee, Kim was abruptly pursuing political inroads with the same leadership.

The two Koreas moved quickly to establish direct communication. Seoul and Pyongyang initiated preliminary contacts through Red Cross channels in the summer of 1971, the first significant interactions between the two Koreas since the establishment of rival regimes in 1948. These culminated in meetings between senior leaders, including unprecedented discussions involving representatives of Kim and Park and their closest subordinates (though not between the two leaders), including Kim's younger brother and fellow Political Bureau member Kim Yong-ju. (Constitutional revisions in late 1972 designated Kim Il-sung as president rather than prime minister. This appointment was probably occasioned by the perceived need for equivalence with his ROK counterpart and with other heads of state.) Inter-Korean meetings took place in Panmunjom, Pyongyang and Seoul between late 1971 and the autumn of

1972. The talks produced the North–South joint declaration of 4 July 1972, the still-unrealised framework for a 'Korea only' approach to peninsular accommodation. Though the North–South exchanges ultimately foundered and collapsed in mutual recrimination, the meetings revealed abiding mistrust from the great powers on both sides of the 38th parallel.

Documents from ROK Foreign Ministry archives underscore the deeply held nationalistic sentiments in both Koreas. The two leaderships expressed parallel suspicions about major-power manipulation. In extolling the virtues of *juche*, Kim Yong-ju objected strongly to

> worshipping the powerful … Flunkeyism is a painful lesson in our nation's history … The South and the North together should put an end to Flunkeyism. We notice that you [the ROK] are promoting a policy to distrust the powerful states. It is a great effort. The strong powers pretend that they support you. However, ultimately they promote their own good … We do not have the Soviet Union or China [backing us].[10]

In his first meeting with Kim Il-sung, Lee Hu-rak, director of the Korean CIA and Park Chung-hee's closest aide, emphasised that 'reunification is not a matter for the four big powers to intervene. It is a matter for us to voluntarily decide … we must leave a unified motherland as a heritage to our descendants.' Some of Lee's views were even more intensely felt than those voiced by Kim Il-sung: 'It cuts to my heart having outsiders intervening in our matters. It's a huge disgrace being unable to resolve our own issues and greatly humiliating. How would the outsiders view us?' As Lee also observed, 'About 100 years ago, we had no choice but to cringe to the great powers because we were not strong enough. However, in the future, the great powers of today will cower before us ... the great powers wanting our reunification is only a lie they tell on the outside. In fact, they do not wish for it in the inside.'

Responding to Lee's comments, Kim Il-sung observed that

> our stance is to be against foreign reliance in the issue of reunification ... The great powers and the Imperialists are keen to divide a nation and split them into many [small groups] ... We shouldn't depend on foreigners ... [It] seems President Park and I have complete agreement in thoughts ... we must show the world that our nation is strong and is capable of uniting ... In other words, no one, including Nixon, China, and the Soviet Union, is obligated to any decision in the issue of Chosun.[11]

In a subsequent meeting, Kim Il-sung spoke at length on 'the three principles of national unification'. He declared that

> the most important factor which characterises a nation is the community of language and culture ... some people are now trying to solve the reunification problem with guarantees afforded by big powers. This is a great mistake ... We should not tolerate foreign interference in the internal affairs of Korea under any circumstances ... At present, the north and the south say their armies are for self-defence. However, they should not undertake self-defence against each other. They must work together to defend themselves against foreign invasion.

He then characterised the January 1968 seizure of the USS

Pueblo as 'a legitimate self-defence measure of our People's Army', adding:

> but instead of apologising to us, the Americans threatened us by bringing large forces ... to the East Sea. It was a flagrant infringement of and a grave challenge to our nation's sovereignty. We did not yield to the Americans' threat and pressure.[12]

The documents highlighted the existential vulnerabilities of both leaderships, albeit from different strategic vantage points. Senior officials in North and South sought to outbid one another in their expressions of intense nationalism and suspicions of the major powers. It is impossible to know how far inter-Korean relations might have proceeded had the talks been sustained. Kim Il-sung had concluded that South Korean leaders were increasingly uneasy about the Guam Doctrine, US force reductions on the peninsula and the impending American withdrawal from Vietnam, where ROK forces were still deployed in significant numbers. Kim, ever attentive to the opportunities to exploit fissures among adversaries, sought political inroads in the ROK that had long eluded him. Rather than sustaining mutual accommodation, both Seoul and Pyongyang soon opted for strategic autonomy, premised in equal measure on inter-Korean rivalry and fears of great-power domination. Neither had yet ratified the NPT, and both now initiated steps in nuclear development to free them from external control.

The ROK, then at an early stage of industrialisation, formulated ambitious, highly secretive nuclear goals. Scientists from the Agency for Defence Development (first established by Park Chung Hee in 1970) presented a full plan to the ROK president in late 1973. Following the Indian nuclear detonation of 1974, US intelligence was increasingly attentive to the possibilities of a covert weapons programme linked to civilian nuclear development. (South Korea was seeking to import two Canadian-designed CANDU heavy-water reactors at the time.) American officials detected South Korean activities at an early date. Washington sought to shut down the programme before it achieved major results. The ROK had signed the NPT in 1968 but had not ratified it. Under intense US pressure, Seoul formally acceded to the NPT in April 1975. Nevertheless, research and development activities linked to nuclear-weapons potential, including South Korea's pursuit of a complete nuclear fuel cycle, persisted into the late 1970s.[13] Park also continued to display interest in a weapons programme, including in an on-the-record interview in the *Washington Post* in the summer of 1975: 'If South Korea were not provided with a nuclear umbrella, South Korea would do anything to protect its security, including the development of nuclear weapons.'[14]

It seems probable that the DPRK's nuclear aspirations were triggered at least in part by the South Korean programme. Unlike the ROK, North Korea's weapons-development plans remained in largely gestational form, primarily because of technical and industrial limitations. In the late 1960s, Pyongyang had sought to enhance its nuclear industrial base by appeals for large-scale assistance from the Soviet Union and the GDR.[15] Moscow, deeming such appeals premature when the Soviet experimental research reactor had only begun operations, was highly wary of North Korean demands. But the DPRK was undeterred and repeatedly lobbied Moscow to undertake major new reactor projects. Soviet planners had to respond to incessant demands from Pyongyang, described by a Hungarian diplomat as 'crude and insulting'. Moscow asserted that it could not undertake any additional nuclear projects in the 1976–80 Five Year Plan. Soviet officials informed North Korea that it would defer any consideration of additional nuclear technology transfer until the 1980s, though such statements were well short of the pledges that Pyongyang sought.[16]

North Korea, already in arrears on debt repayment to Moscow and highly dependent on Soviet economic and technological support, had motives but not the means for rapid nuclear advancement. Comparing the major strides in ROK nuclear development to the North's persistent prodding for enhanced support from the Soviet Union, China and East European states, the Hungarian ambassador to the DPRK presciently outlined future possibilities. As he observed in an early 1979 diplomatic cable: 'The DPRK … wants [socialist countries] to provide it with equipment for nuclear power plants or even to build a nuclear power plant. It tries to make up for its lag behind South Korea in this way, with the hidden intention that later it may become capable of producing an atomic bomb.'[17]

Kim ponders a nuclear future

The precise date when Kim Il-sung decided to initiate pursuit of nuclear weapons remains unknown. Indeed, to the very end of his life Kim repeatedly denied that North Korea even had a programme or the intention and capability to begin one.[18] No document attests to Kim's nuclear decision. His convictions about a weapons option were likely maintained within a very small circle and may have been imparted cryptically. As Alexandre Mansourov has observed: 'It is likely that the DPRK's nuclear intentions were never written in any DPRK military regulations or developed in the Great Leader's works on military matters. Instead, they were hidden away inside Kim Il-sung's head, and he might have shared only reluctantly his thoughts and intentions with his close associates.'[19] But any instructions or explicit guidance from Kim would have irrevocably obligated his subordinates. If there was an explicit nuclear decision, it probably dates from the early to mid-1970s.[20] As noted earlier, some observers contend that Kim made the decision in the early 1960s. But this would have been more of an aspiration than a viable weapons option. Moreover, the precise timing of Kim's nuclear decision matters less than the major factors that shaped his thinking, and how the parallel pursuit of civilian and military development advanced North Korea's quest for an independent strategic identity.

During the 1960s, the enhancement of the North's nuclear infrastructure and the training of increased numbers of scientists and engineers made nuclear weapons a more practicable option. But the technical and engineering requirements for an actual weapons programme remained gestational.[21] The DPRK as yet lacked the full spectrum of technologies, project designs, and industrial materials needed to build a reactor for fissile-material production or the ancillary facilities to reprocess spent fuel. In a six-year plan adopted in November 1970, new policy guidelines stated that 'we must step up research work on the development of a nuclear industry on the basis of our own raw materials and technology.'[22] At the same time, North Korea continued to solicit support from the Soviet Union and Eastern Europe for training of technical experts and for large-scale technology transfer.

Evidence of a weapons programme, however, remained limited and indirect. The lead time on a covert weapons option was substantial. In addition, Kim had reason not to disclose his plans to the Soviet Union and to conceal any such information as long as possible from the United States. According to a Russian expert with many years experience in North Korea, by the early 1970s, 'the North Korean leadership ... all but ceased to invite Soviet scientists for practical participation in projects involving the development of the material and technological bases for research in the nuclear field'.[23] Pyongyang also continued to purchase substantial instrumentation and equipment from the Soviet Union for both theoretical and experimental research. North Korea was assembling the building blocks for a dedicated nuclear-weapons effort, but a meaningful weapons potential was still well in the future.[24] During the 1970s, the DPRK concentrated on uranium milling, conversion and fabrication; as discussed later in this chapter, it also initiated efforts to acquire technical data on reactor design and the needed industrial materials in the latter half of the decade. As early as 1974, North Korean scientists had also increased the thermal capacity of the Soviet-supplied research reactor to 8 megawatts.[25]

Three principal considerations shaped Kim's thinking about nuclear weapons. Firstly, even if Kim was momentarily reassured of Chinese and Soviet strategic intentions, any such assurances were at best conditional. Kim maintained profound doubts that Beijing or Moscow would indefinitely support his ambitions or military plans. In the immediate aftermath of the fall of Saigon and the end of the Vietnam War in April 1975, Kim undertook a two-month trip to China and Eastern Europe, his longest trip away from the DPRK since 1956. He was seeking heightened political, economic and military support, with a stop in Moscow conspicuously absent from his itinerary. During his visit to China, Kim delivered a fiery banquet speech extolling North Vietnam's victory, but Beijing was unprepared to endorse any comparable risk-taking by Pyongyang.[26] Though in a parallel banquet speech Chinese leader Deng Xiaoping characterised the DPRK as 'the sole legal sovereign government of the Korean nation', Beijing sought to deny Pyongyang any possible pretext to justify the renewed use of force against the South.[27]

During an early 1976 visit of senior North Korean officials to Moscow, Soviet officials were comparably circumspect in deflecting Pyongyang's renewed demands for construction of a nuclear power plant.[28] Kim also sought to diversify his international ties. He saw links to the non-aligned movement as essential to the growing diplomatic competition with South Korea, including impending battles on UN representation. Relations with the capitalist world provided a new source of economic aid and enhanced possibilities for acquisition of advanced technology, including whole plant purchases from Western Europe and Japan, financed mainly on credit.[29] Kim even made overtures to the United States, including letters sent to members of Congress proposing improved relations.[30] In addition, North Korea for the first time opted to market weapons in the Middle East and Africa, rather than provide them gratis.[31] In 1974, the KWP Central Committee also established Bureau 39, whose front companies engaged in smuggling, drug-trafficking, and counterfeiting to garner foreign exchange for the central leadership's programmes and needs.[32]

Secondly, Kim was envious and fearful about the South's covert nuclear activities. He was increasingly discomfited by South Korea's economic and military advances, which threatened his plans to dominate the peninsula and may have even triggered fears that the DPRK might ultimately be subordinated to the power of the ROK.[33] The South's cancellation of its nuclear-weapons programme and Seoul's highly ambitious plans for nuclear energy must have been intrinsically upsetting to Kim, all the more so as ties between the ROK and Japan deepened. (Tokyo and Seoul established diplomatic relations in 1965, and their political and economic links advanced steadily in subsequent years.) Moreover, Kim probably assumed that a programme once begun could be resumed, or could continue in secret. Equally or more perturbing to Kim, the South had launched its weapons programme before the DPRK had an equivalent capability.

Thirdly, Kim Il-sung was increasingly concerned about the regime's longer-term prospects. Though he was still vigorous and active in the 1970s, he was already turning his attention to leadership succession. This was very possibly the decisive factor influencing his calculations about weapons development. Kim concluded that the prospects for his successor would be better assured with nuclear weapons than without them. In a revealing discussion with visiting Romanian leader Ceausescu in June 1971, Kim observed:

> People [in North Korea] living nowadays don't know how capitalists look like. They don't know what Japanese imperialism means, they are not aware of American imperialism … All these are [significant] issues for us. Those who carried out the revolution in the past are old now. We have new elements in the system who did not have to confront the same hard-ships and whose life is relatively easy … the younger cadres in the army are not well trained for direct confrontation … These young cadres don't know how Americans look … they saw them in movies, [but] they don't know much and haven't lived in hardship.

As Kim further lamented, 'we are a divided, dismantled country … we have liberated half the country but the other half is still under occupation … geographically we are surrounded by the Japanese, the Chinese, the Americans, and the Soviets. We are surrounded by three great powers and their influ-ence can be felt.'[34] Kim's pointed reference to 'young cadres' who understood American military power primarily through movies might well have been directed at the individual he soon selected to succeed him.

The succession

Kim Il-sung lived in a world devoid of enduring external relationships, with multiple enemies and far more powerful allies who distrusted his intentions and actions. The identity and very existence of the North Korean state was threat-based. His neighbours to the north were major powers whose intentions Kim did not trust, and his neighbours to the south were a rival, ideologically antagonistic Korean state and the loathed former colonial overseer of the peninsula, both close allies of the United States. Most importantly, Kim was deeply invested in a family-centred regime, something that had never been undertaken in a communist state, and which generated considerable disquiet, even among his allies.[35] Believing that the North Korean system's prospects for survival were best assured by retaining power within his immediate family, Kim decided that his successor would come from his own bloodline. His younger brother Kim Yong-ju was one potential candidate, as were several sons by a later marriage. In the early 1970s, however, the elder Kim chose Kim Jong-il as his successor and elevated him to party secretary in 1973. He first revealed his decision internally at a Party Plenum in February 1974, though the selection of Kim Jong-il was not disclosed publicly until the 6th KWP Congress in October 1980. Throughout much of the 1970s, an esoteric propaganda campaign persisted to build up Kim Jong-il's stature as the leader most qualified to succeed his father, though he was never mentioned by name.[36]

Kim Il-sung knew that his son would not be nearly as imposing a leader, but his goal was to maintain the system, not to change it. His eldest son seemed a more plausible candidate than any other family member, let alone any of Kim's close associates within the ruling elite. This necessitated a sustained propaganda strategy to depict the younger Kim as boundlessly loyal and uniquely qualified to assume power. In 1982, the elder Kim purportedly told Deng Xiaoping that selection of a senior colleague within the leadership would run the risk of factionalism and in-fighting within the elite, whereas the leadership would concur to the selection of a member of Kim's immediate family.[37] Though the younger Kim was described as his father's virtual equal in brainpower and strategic vision, these characterisations were for political effect, and were not a representation of his actual skills. A senior North Korean official once told an Eastern European diplomat that Kim Jong-il's strengths were organisation and control; he was not considered to be a daring or innovative leader.[38] Unlike his father, Kim Jong-il was far more reserved in his demeanour, and he seldom spoke at length in public settings.

The senior Kim believed that a dutiful, loyal son was best suited to maintain extant policies and power relations within the system. As Adrian Buzo notes:

> [A] distinguishing feature of Kim Jong-il's career is that he has left no mark or trace of influence on major state policies independent of his father after many years in senior positions. Father and son seemed to share almost a seamlessly complementary relationship bound by the filial tie, the strong influence of Kim Il-sung's personality on his son, common ideological commitment and clear functional differentiation. The father set the major ideological, economic and diplomatic parameters while the son attended to mobilisation work that flowed from the ideological parameters ... aimed at improving the citizens' quality

of life-aesthetically through direction of the 'arts' and
prestige public architecture, and materially through
construction of major leisure facilities and distribution of bounty to individuals.[39]

Though Kim Jong-il later displayed awareness of the failings of
the North Korean economy, he seldom addressed these acute
shortcomings in sustained fashion. If Kim Il-sung was intent on
preserving the system he had built, then he chose the appropriate successor.

Kim Il-sung envisioned the leadership transition as an
extended apprenticeship for Kim Jong-il, one that would
continue during much of the 1980s and into the early 1990s,
with the elder Kim progressively transferring more responsibilities to his son. This transition also provided an opportunity for
Kim to elicit fuller acceptance for the succession within party
circles and also to garner support (or at least acquiescence)
from Beijing and Moscow. He had more success at home than
abroad. According to a Chinese diplomat with many years of
service in Pyongyang, in Kim's final meeting with Mao Zedong
in 1975, Kim failed to gain Mao's support for a dynastic succession, with the aged Chinese leader supposedly deeming it a
violation of Leninist principles.[40]

Deng Xiaoping proved more supportive of the succession
than Mao. As Deng argued in a speech in May 1980:

> [T]he actions of a foreign fraternal Party ... [should
> not be] judge[d] according to some rigid formula ...
> Conditions vary greatly from country to country [and]
> the level of political awareness varies from people to
> people ... How can a fixed formula be applied mechan-
> ically despite all these differences? ... The correctness
> of the domestic principles and line of a Party in a given

country should be judged by that Party itself and by
the people of that country.'[41]

China (or at least Deng) was making a virtue out of necessity.
When Deng delivered this speech, Kim Jong-il's succession to
power was already an accomplished fact; the announcement
and formal ratification at the 6th Party Congress was only
months away. But the elder Kim was seeking to solidify the
family succession at the precise time when the Chinese were
subjecting Mao's political record (including the cult of personality) to a withering critique. According to commentaries
appearing in the Hong Kong press, some CCP leaders found
the transfer of power from father to son particularly offensive.[42]

According to an official involved in Sino-DPRK relations
at the time, in 1982 Kim Il-sung travelled with Deng to the
Chinese leader's native province of Sichuan, a principal laboratory for many of China's early reform policies. According to
this official, Kim gave assurances to Deng that his son would
visit China annually to study China's reforms. The Ministry of
Foreign Affairs established a preparatory group to oversee this
process.[43] By endorsing the succession, Deng believed that he
could nudge the North Korean system towards changes equivalent to those undertaken in China. He also calculated that he
could create opportunities for a breakthrough in US–North
Korea relations.

Both assumptions proved grievously mistaken. In a meeting
with Secretary of Defence Caspar Weinberger in September
1983, Deng (with Kim's evident concurrence) openly broached
the possibility of trilateral talks and tension reduction measures
among the US and the two Koreas, with China serving as host.[44]
Beijing's probable advice to Pyongyang entailed two elements:
the need for political and military restraint to facilitate relations with the United States and to advance unification; and

reliance on Beijing's growing ties with Washington and Tokyo to communicate with the United States and Japan.

The devastating bombing in Rangoon, Burma, less than three weeks later on 9 October shattered Deng's expectations. The attacks, by North Korean agents, killed 17 senior South Korean officials and narrowly missed ROK President Chun Doo-hwan. The attack occurred only a day after Beijing had passed a message from North Korea to Washington seeking direct diplomatic contact with the United States.[45] North Korean actions unambiguously undermined Beijing's repeated assurances to the United States and Japan that North Korean intentions were entirely peaceful and oriented toward economic construction.

Deng viewed the Rangoon bombing as a personal affront, purportedly demanding (and receiving) an apology from Kim Il-sung. Deng allegedly concluded that Kim Jong-il was responsible for ordering the terrorist attack, resulting in a long estrangement between Deng and the younger Kim that never healed during Deng's years in power. Kim Jong-il's abiding suspicions of China did not dissipate in subsequent years, in particular as China pursued and consolidated relations with the United States and with the ROK.[46] Unlike his father, who travelled to China almost annually, Kim Jong-il's June 1983 visit was his sole sojourn to China until 2000, more than three years after Deng's death.[47]

Kim Il-sung may have secured the succession for his son, but it entailed substantial costs in relations with China. As Deng remarked with decided understatement to a visiting Japanese delegation in late 1984, 'we do not necessarily agree with some policies made by North Korea'.[48] Public comments, including from the party leader Hu Yaobang, cautioned that 'whatever actions are likely to aggravate tension [in Korea], no matter where they are from, should be avoided'.[49] Beijing's private comments may have been even sharper, probably warning

Pyongyang of more severe consequences should North Korea again act contrary to its repeated professions of peaceful intent.

Although China continued to express periodic support for tripartite talks, Deng was not prepared to remain protective of the DPRK if Kim Il-sung's designated successor could not be trusted. In the aftermath of the Rangoon bombing, China began to move towards informal relations with the ROK. Equally significant, a Chinese official for the first time sought to limit Beijing's security obligations to Pyongyang. In a meeting with a delegation from the Japan Socialist Party in June 1984, Zhang Xiangshan, an adviser to the CCP International Liaison Department, stated that 'if the DPRK strikes the first blow and starts a war, China would be in no position to support her'. Though he reiterated that China would not 'remain a specta-tor with its arms folded [if] the South expands its army and invades the North', Zhang's disassociation from North Korea's highly destabilising actions was unmistakable.[50] By contrast, Yuri Andropov, Leonid Brezhnev's successor as CPSU general secretary, rendered strong support to North Korea, sending a high ranking delegation to Pyongyang for the 35th anniver-sary of the DPRK's founding shortly after the bombing.[51] When Andropov died in February 1984, Kim Il-sung and Kim Jong-il made a joint condolence call on the Soviet Embassy; both Kims made a comparable gesture when Konstantin Chernenko died in March 1985. There was no condolence call by either Kim to the Soviet Embassy following Leonid Brezhnev's death in November 1982. Even more telling, Kim Jong-il did not make a condolence call on the Chinese Embassy following Deng's death in February 1997.[52]

Opening the nuclear door

Kim Il-sung had concluded that a nuclear-weapons option would enhance Kim Jong-il's consolidation of power.[53] But the senior Kim also did not want to endanger Soviet alliance commitments or put Soviet industrial and technological assistance at risk. However, it is not certain how Moscow conveyed a pledge of extended deterrence to Pyongyang. As noted in Chapter Two, Soviet security obligations seemed more committal in response to an attack on the DPRK, and less explicit in seeking to deter potential hostilities. Even as it signed the 1961 treaty, Moscow seemed uneasy about becoming overly obligated to Pyongyang. There was also no explicit evidence of a Chinese nuclear commitment to North Korea, in as much as the PRC was not a nuclear-weapons state when Beijing and Pyongyang signed the alliance treaty. But the Soviet Union remained the most active external benefactor of the North. Given the scale of Moscow's economic and technical involvement in the DPRK, it would have been very difficult to hide all evidence of the development of the North's nuclear infrastructure from Soviet officials. But the first major construction projects unambiguously linked to weapons development (including ground breaking for an indigenous nuclear reactor) were not undertaken until the very end of the 1970s, so Kim may have been able to keep Moscow at least partially in the dark for a few years.

North Korea was also seeking to build a civilian nuclear-power industry, explaining Pyongyang's repeated lobbying for Soviet light-water reactors (LWRs). The 5th KWP Congress in 1970 had enunciated the goal of building 'nuclear power plants on a large scale in order to sharply increase the generation of electrical power', which North Korean officials regularly cited as the principal impediment to accelerated modernisation.[54] These ambitions remain wholly unrealised four decades later. The oil crisis of the early 1970s gave additional impetus to development of domestic energy resources. The abundant supply of natural uranium (though fuel for LWRs would require uranium to be enriched) made nuclear energy a leading candidate.[55]

In January 1974, the DPRK passed an Atomic Energy Act, creating a larger policy and research infrastructure for future nuclear activities.[56] Amidst mounting economic difficulties, the nuclear industry was a highly favoured industrial sector. Though Pyongyang may have tried to differentiate its civilian and military programmes, to the Soviet Union they were inseparably connected.[57] In the early 1980s, North Korea continued to push for major civilian nuclear assistance from the Soviet Union and different East European states, but Moscow remained very skittish about additional nuclear assistance to Pyongyang.[58]

Following the death of Leonid Brezhnev in November 1982, Kim Il-sung renewed demands for additional Soviet nuclear assistance, first with Brezhnev's successor Yuri Andropov and subsequently with Andropov's successor Chernenko. Brezhnev had become far warier of close alliance ties to the North in light of the DPRK's risk-taking in the latter half of the 1960s and early 1970s. Senior Soviet officials had repeatedly deferred consideration of major new aid requests from Pyongyang, including Kim's renewed push for nuclear reactors. Pyongyang was already in major arrears on its obligations to repay its debts to the Soviet Union, and Brezhnev was unprepared to enter into new deferred payment arrangements. At the same time, any serious consideration of North Korean requests for nuclear-energy assistance presumed that the DPRK would explicitly pledge to forgo nuclear weapons.

Chernenko proved much more pliant and accommodating to Kim Il-sung's appeals. In October 1984, Kim embarked on an extended trip to the Soviet Union, Poland and the GDR. Chernenko assented to a plan to build four VVER-440 light-water reactors with a projected electrical capacity in excess of 1700 MWe, opening a line of credit for the DPRK to cover the costs incurred in this hugely ambitious project.[59] The Soviet leader also undertook extensive new weapons transfers to the DPRK, and agreed to defer North Korean debt repayments then totalling $11.2 billion. In return, Kim granted overflight rights for Soviet reconnaissance aircraft and renewed access for the Soviet Navy at Wonsan for the first time since 1953.[60] But Chernenko's successor, Mikhail Gorbachev, made approval of the reactor project contingent on the DPRK's signing of the NPT, which occurred on 12 December 1985. The reactor contract was signed 13 days after North Korea's accession to the NPT. For the first time, Pyongyang had formally adhered to non-proliferation goals, but it did so under duress, and the regime's readiness to comply with the treaty remained very uncertain.

North Korean non-nuclear assurances had already been rendered largely moot by its own actions. At the end of the 1970s, the North undertook an indigenous reactor project that would ultimately provide the fissile material for nuclear-weapons development. The 5 MWe graphite-moderated reactor, modelled on the design of a Calder-Hall research reactor first designed and built in the UK in the 1950s, soon triggered suspicions among US intelligence experts about its ultimate purposes.[61] The available evidence suggests Pyongyang under-took construction of the reactor without substantial Soviet knowledge or involvement. By characterising the reactor's output as electrical rather than thermal output, North Korea sought to obscure the reactor's purposes as much as possible.[62]

In September 1974, the DPRK joined the IAEA, which enabled access to a wealth of technical data that proved pivotal to nearly all of Pyongyang's subsequent nuclear efforts. Choe Hak-kun, among the nuclear specialists trained first at Moscow University and subsequently at Dubna, was a pivotal actor in this process. (In 1986, Choe was named the first director of the

General Department of Atomic Energy, then newly constituted as a department under the Administration Council.) Between 1975 and 1979, Choe served as the DPRK's primary liaison with the IAEA. North Korea was now a member of the nuclear agency, providing Choe access to the IAEA's library of technical information, including data on reactor design and construction from countries already possessing operational reactors.[63] This included information on Calder-Hall and Marcoule gas–graphite reactor designs. The much larger plutonium-production reactor projects initiated though never completed at Yongbyon and Taejon in 1984 and 1986 utilised a French, rather than a British, design.[64]

The Yongbyon reactor was not a turnkey project. Though it drew on available designs, it was more a 'do it yourself' undertaking, constrained by limits in available industrial materials and by North Korea's lack of experience in reactor construction. Indeed, its external appearance and size was closely akin to the Tokai reactor in Ibaraki Prefecture, Japan's first power reactor that was also based on a Calder-Hall design.[65] It is possible that the Korean Association of Science and Technology, the organisation of ethnic Korean scientists in Japan, provided design data on the Japanese reactor.[66] The North may also have been intent on demonstrating symbolic equivalence to Japan in its technological aspirations. But any explicit comparison between the two facilities is dubious: in the estimate of one Japanese physicist, the prospective electrical output of the Yongbyon reactor was about 3% that of the Tokai facility.[67] Moreover, Tokai was unambiguously designed for power generation, not for weapons production.

A Calder-Hall reactor had numerous advantages for North Korea. It was a relatively simple and proven reactor design that utilised natural uranium for fuel and graphite as the moderator, both of which resources were readily available in the DPRK. There was no pressing need for Soviet engineering assistance, which would have quickly revealed the purposes of the project. Although there are two electrical generators at the reactor, the capacity and purposes of the generators were minimal, and the facility was optimised for production of weapons-grade plutonium.[68] Since plutonium production reactors do not need to maximise efficiency for electrical generation by operating at higher temperatures, this enabled a more simplified design.[69] The completion of the project in little more than a half decade (the reactor went on line in 1986, though there appear to have been start-up problems in the earliest years of operation) was a substantial engineering accomplishment. In approximately six years, a country with no previous experience in reactor construction had acquired and assembled the requisite technologies, industrial materials and natural resources for a functioning reactor. In another three years, North Korea had also largely completed a major reprocessing facility at Yongbyon – unambiguous proof that the reactor's purpose was military, not civilian.

As Alexandre Mansourov has observed, the military dimensions of the nuclear programme (reflecting various economic, financial and scientific constraints) 'developed in a wave-like fashion. Its occasional temporary freezes alternated with revivals time and again.'[70] The evidence of a military-oriented programme continued to grow during the 1980s, generating increased suspicions on the part of Soviet experts. All the while, Pyongyang continued to press Moscow for major increases in Soviet nuclear assistance. In fits and starts, with the outside world denied access to the project, a weapons programme was taking shape in North Korea. Kim Il-sung's two known visits to Yongbyon, first in August 1981 and again in March 1989 (in the latter instance accompanied by Kim Jong-il), underscored the strategic importance of the weapons programme to North

Korea.[71] The nuclear-weapons door had opened in the DPRK, and it has not closed since.

But Pyongyang was facing other unprecedented challenges. Adrian Buzo has described the DPRK's increasingly grim economic circumstances in the mid-1980s:

> The country possessed a stagnant economy, high foreign debt, an enormous burden in military expenditure, few value-added exports, little access to foreign technology and capital, few students or technicians with foreign training or experience, rapidly aging and inefficient plant, machinery, and infrastructure, and an obsolete, highly centralized command system of economic management'.[72]

Despite such daunting circumstances, neither Kim Il-sung nor Kim Jong-il appeared to waver from long-entrenched policies, and the warming in Moscow–Pyongyang relations in the mid-1980s tethered Pyongyang even closer to a Soviet system then in terminal decline.

Following Gorbachev's election to leadership of the CPSU and China's expanded economic reforms, the political and economic centre of gravity in both the Soviet Union and China irrevocably shifted, placing North Korea at an acute disadvantage. The normalisation of Sino-Soviet relations in the late spring of 1989 and the moves by both Moscow and Beijing toward full relations with South Korea severely undermined North Korean strategy. Pyongyang's determined efforts to disrupt the Seoul Olympics of 1988, most brazenly by blowing up a Korean Airlines flight in November 1987, ended in failure, and the Soviet Union and China were both full participants at the games. Leaders in Moscow and Beijing were no longer prepared to set aside their larger political, diplomatic and economic interests to protect their past ties with the DPRK. Soviet economic subsidies had sustained the North Korean economy for decades, but they were in increasing jeopardy as the DPRK experienced mounting economic stagnation, including its default on approximately $6bn in loans from Western Europe in 1986.

The ultimate upheaval and disintegration of East European communism at the end of the 1980s and the collapse of the Soviet Union shortly thereafter placed North Korea's well-being and security at unprecedented risk. As German reunification became a reality, Kim defiantly argued to Berlin's ambassador that East Germany's accommodation with its Western neighbour had doomed the GDR, and that North Korea would never suffer the same fate.[73] But Kim Il-sung would soon be without the economic subsidies and formal security guarantees that the Soviet Union had long provided, and China's parallel commitments were also now less binding. At the very time that North Korea was nearing completion of the nuclear fuel cycle, Kim Il-sung's long-standing support from (and dependence upon) Moscow and Beijing largely ceased. Equally important, at this point was the growing urgency of leadership succession. Kim Il-sung and the system he had built had entered uncharted territory, with sharply diminished options and little time to waste.

CHAPTER FOUR

From Kim Il-sung to Kim Jong-il

The late 1980s and early 1990s were an acutely testing time for the ageing Kim Il-sung. He remained deeply involved in major domestic and international issues, but his physical capacities were increasingly limited and grim domestic and international circumstances challenged his fundamental strategic assumptions. Kim was running out of time and out of options. The collapse of communist regimes across Eastern Europe, especially the GDR, with which Kim Il-sung had maintained especially close relations, was deeply disquieting to the North Korean leader, even as Kim had repeatedly warned Erik Honecker that the regime's links to West Germany would result in the GDR's inevitable ruination. The overthrow and execution of Nicolae Ceausescu in Romania, whose grandiose and highly personalistic regime bore immediate comparison to the DPRK, was also very jarring. Kim now transferred the full range of military responsibilities to his son, even though he had minimal military experience. At the same time, a weakened Soviet Union, fatigued by decades of support for Pyongyang, ended its subsidies to the North and demanded hard-currency payments for all future economic transactions. Amidst its own mounting economic woes, Moscow also actively cultivated relations with South Korea.

In September 1990, Soviet Foreign Minister Eduard Shevardnadze informed Pyongyang that Moscow would establish diplomatic relations with the ROK. North Korean officials viewed this as a lasting affront that invalidated prior security guarantees and compelled pursuit of an independent nuclear capability. China formally opened diplomatic relations with the ROK two years later, though Beijing (unlike Moscow) sought to avoid a sharp break in bilateral relations. When Beijing informed Pyongyang of its impending recognition of Seoul, the Soviet Union – North Korea's most important economic benefactor and its primary source of industrial technology and military assistance – had ceased to exist, and Boris Yeltsin showed little interest in long-term relations with the DPRK.

The end of communist rule in Eastern Europe and in the Soviet Union and the ROK's major political and diplomatic breakthroughs turned North Korea's world upside down. Multiple pressures and potential crises were impinging on the DPRK. The cessation of Soviet aid had worrisome internal reverberations, starting with an agricultural crisis that would, by the mid-1990s, result in a major famine. Kim Il-sung hoped to garner support from the capitalist world that his erstwhile allies were no longer willing to provide. A breakthrough with the United States held the greatest allure for Kim, but this was a dim prospect so long as the DPRK was unwilling to fully disclose its nuclear history to the IAEA. With the United States seeking to impose Security Council sanctions on Pyongyang as well as weighing the use of force against the DPRK to forestall additional nuclear development in the North, events were moving towards a major crisis and (quite possibly) overt military hostilities. Acting largely on his own initiative and without any formal authority to obligate the United States, former President Jimmy Carter travelled to North Korea in June 1994 and met with Kim Il-sung. Carter reached understandings with Kim that halted the slide into outright conflict and placed the basic provisions of a negotiated agreement on the table, which culminated with the signing of the Agreed Framework in Geneva four months later. The US–DPRK accord left the North's nuclear past unresolved and its nuclear-weapons potential frozen but intact. Kim was able to gain a measure of international affirmation, if not outright validation, through his discussions with Carter, but a larger political breakthrough eluded him. He died weeks after the meeting, leaving the DPRK's internal economic crisis unaddressed.

Kim Jong-il had been preparing to assume power throughout the 1980s. Following his father's death, there was a three-year period of official mourning, after which he formally assumed all top leadership posts. Kim's leadership was wholly untested, and the DPRK was in economic freefall. There was also the challenge of upholding his father's legacy (including the nuclear truce arranged with Carter) while still accommodating powerful domestic constituencies closely identified with the weapons programme.

Strategic abandonment

Mikhail Gorbachev's efforts to disengage the Soviet Union from its Cold War inheritances sharply diminished Pyongyang's leverage with Moscow. China also no longer attached pride of place to relations with the DPRK. Pyongyang had long demanded and received large-scale economic subsidies and military assistance from the Soviet Union; China also made significant contributions in both areas. But neither capital had any interest in sustaining the military rivalry between the two Koreas or in continuing to compete for Pyongyang's fleeting loyalties.[1] Moscow sustained the light-water reactor project (signed in 1985), but the undertaking was full of uncertainties. In early 1992, the agreement to provide North Korea with four VVER-440 reactors was renegotiated, with the Russian Ministry of Atomic Energy (Minatom) now pledging to build three newer MP-640 reactors. Site selection and technical design work proceeded during the early 1990s, but the DPRK failed to honour its debt obligations for the project, leading to suspension of the project in May 1992. Moreover, North Korea declared that, with the dissolution of the Soviet Union, it was no longer required to provide repayment to the Russian successor state. The project was definitively halted following the DPRK's announced withdrawal from the NPT in early 1993.[2]

Moscow's relationship with Seoul was an even larger source of the North's mounting dissatisfaction with Soviet leaders.[3] ROK President Roh Tae-woo's Nordpolitik policy, first promulgated in a speech in July 1988, was an explicit invitation to communist states to open ties with South Korea. Though Roh also urged the United States and Japan to pursue relations with Pyongyang, neither Moscow nor Beijing was prepared to make initiatives towards Seoul contingent on parallel steps by Washington and Tokyo towards the DPRK. (Japan and North Korea did initiate heightened if ultimately unsuccessful efforts at normalisation in the early 1990s.[4]) Mikhail Gorbachev was intent on making major changes in Soviet Asian strategy, and the DPRK was the odd nation out. The glaring contrast between the two Koreas (especially given Seoul's major economic assistance to the Soviet Union) made Moscow's relations with North Korea expendable.[5] Pyongyang tried to convince Gorbachev to visit the DPRK when the Soviet leader travelled to Beijing for the Sino-Soviet summit in the spring of 1989, but Gorbachev offered multiple excuses to avoid a visit.[6] No supreme leader of the Soviet Union would ever set foot in the DPRK.

In September 1990, Shevardnadze travelled to Pyongyang to inform the North Korean leadership of Moscow's decision to open diplomatic relations with Seoul. His counterpart Kim Yong-nam offered an especially bitter response. Kim claimed that diplomatic recognition of the ROK guaranteed the permanent division of the Korean peninsula, would embolden Seoul to undermine the North, and invalidated the 1961 treaty between the two countries. Shevardnadze was left in no doubt that North Korea no longer felt obligated to inform or consult with Moscow on its future policy actions, though Pyongyang's fealty to this pledge had long been highly dubious. In Kim Yong-nam's view, Moscow's actions had 'take[n] away any meaning' from the treaty of alliance. He asserted that the DPRK now needed to 'produce different kinds of weapons', which Soviet officials saw as barely disguised code language for nuclear-weapons development.[7] Shevardnadze departed early from Pyongyang without meeting with Kim Il-sung and (at a meeting with the South Korean foreign minister at the United Nations weeks later) advanced the onset of diplomatic relations with Seoul by three months.

A week after the Shevardnadze visit, Kim Il-sung made an undisclosed trip to Shenyang, meeting on successive days with Jiang Zemin and Deng Xiaoping.[8] Kim, deeply perturbed by the collapse of East European socialism and by Moscow's recognition of Seoul, hoped for increased support from Beijing in the aftermath of the Tiananmen crisis, asking Deng 'How long will the red flag fly?' Though Deng purportedly sought to reassure Kim, he again tried to coax North Korea into undertaking internal economic changes that he had encouraged as early as 1978, when Deng spent a full week in North Korea.[9] China's leaders drew a direct connection between North Korea's isolation and economic retrogression and its longer-term survival, but Kim was not prepared to draw comparable conclusions.

Beijing was attempting a measured and consultative approach towards future relations with Pyongyang. Though there were some calls within China to renegotiate the 1961 alliance, the formal provisions of the treaty remained intact. But China had also opted for a 'two Koreas' policy.

In his memoirs, China's former Foreign Minister Qian Qichen describes Beijing's efforts to remain respectful of the DPRK, without wavering from the major decisions China had taken in its Korea strategy.[10] The latent divergence between Beijing and Pyongyang that began with Sino-American rapprochement had deepened with the onset of China's economic reforms and the opening to the outside world. It sharpened further as the Chinese moved towards de facto relations with South Korea. According to Qian, Deng Xiaoping first raised the possibility of relations with the ROK to internal audiences as early as 1985; he first discussed this prospect with foreign visitors in the spring and summer of 1988.[11] Notwithstanding the Tiananmen crisis of 1989 and the sharp deterioration in US–China relations, Beijing and Pyongyang were heading in starkly different directions. As one leading Chinese expert subsequently acknowledged, relations between China and North Korea 'were at an all-time low at the beginning of the post-Cold War years'.[12] In May 1991, Prime Minister Li Peng visited Pyongyang, informing Kim Il-sung that China would no longer block simultaneous admission of the two Koreas at the next UN General Assembly session. Six months later, Qian visited Seoul for the first time, and planning for China–ROK diplomatic relations accelerated following his return to Beijing.

Qian presents a relatively seamless picture of his discussions with Kim Il-sung, claiming that Kim expressed understanding of China's shifting policy calculations. However, as China–ROK normalisation approached, the former foreign minister hinted elliptically at growing tensions with Pyongyang. During an April 1992 visit to the North to mark Kim Il-sung's 80th birthday, State President Yang Shangkun informed Kim that China was contemplating full relations with Seoul. According to Qian, Kim retorted that 'the situation on the Korean peninsula was precarious'.[13] Three months later, Qian informed Kim Il-sung of China's impending decision on the normalisation of relations with the ROK, acknowledging that this 'was not an ordinary foreign visit'.[14] Travelling to Kim's mountain retreat by helicopter, Qian had his shortest meeting ever with the North Korean leader, without the customary banquet to follow, and he returned to Beijing the same day. Qian asserts that Kim showed understanding of China's decision and insisted that he would work to maintain friendly relations with China. But Kim no doubt recognised that his enduring strategic nightmare was at hand.

Kim Il-sung had insisted for decades that the DPRK would make its own choices and be answerable to no external power. Less than two years before his death, these conditions fully materialised, at virtually the same time that long-simmering disputes over North Korea's nuclear activities portended a major international crisis. Kim Il-sung had to decide whether, when and how to place nuclear weapons on the political and diplomatic table.

Nuclear reckoning

At the beginning of the 1990s, nuclear progress at Yongbyon and nuclear diplomacy converged. A decade after initial construction of an indigenous reactor, North Korean capabilities in reprocessing and accumulation of fissile material had made major headway. There was increasing evidence of North Korea's ability to reprocess spent fuel into weapons-grade plutonium for a nuclear device. The DPRK's nuclear advancement triggered growing international attention, all the more so as nuclear reductions and non-proliferation were now central agenda items in US–Soviet relations. President George H.W. Bush on 27 September 1991 announced that the United States would unilaterally withdraw all remaining US tactical nuclear weapons from the Korean peninsula and from US surface ships in the western Pacific.[15]

Although President Bush's decision derived primarily from relations with the Soviet Union, it had major repercussions on the peninsula. On 8 November, ROK President Roh Tae-woo proposed principles for a non-nuclear peninsula, and called upon North Korea to agree to them.[16] On 25 November, Pyongyang declared that it would sign the long-delayed IAEA safeguards accord 'if the United States begins the withdrawal of nuclear weapons from South Korea', also proposing 'DPRK–US negotiations to discuss simultaneous inspections and removing the nuclear threat against us.'[17] Pyongyang also declared its readiness to enter into separate nuclear talks with South Korea. On 13 December, the prime ministers of North and South signed an Agreement on Reconciliation, Nonaggression, and Exchanges and Cooperation, which more closely approximated a peaceful coexistence accord than anything negotiated between the two Koreas previously or since.[18] Five days later, President Roh declared in a televised address that 'As I speak, there do not exist any nuclear weapons whatsoever, anywhere in the Republic of Korea.'[19]

On 26 December Seoul and Pyongyang initiated discussions on an inter-Korean nuclear accord, culminating with the signing on 20 January 1992 of a Joint Declaration of the Denuclearisation of the Korean Peninsula. Both stated that they would not 'test, manufacture, produce, receive, possess, store, deploy nor use nuclear weapons', and that neither would 'possess nuclear reprocessing and uranium enrichment facilities'.[20] The ROK agreed on 7 January to cancel the annual *Team*

Spirit exercises, the largest combined exercises with US forces, to which North Korea had long strenuously objected. But the ROK premised the cancellation of the exercises on the North's early assent to safeguards arrangements with the IAEA and satisfactory fulfillment of nuclear inspections. In response, North Korea signalled its readiness to sign a safeguards agreement 'in the near future'.[21] In a subsequent round of North–South nuclear talks, the two sides agreed to the creation of Joint Nuclear Control Commission that would oversee de-nuclearisation, but disputes over verification stymied further agreement, and no inspections took place. On 22 January, US Undersecretary of State for Political Affairs Arnold Kanter met in New York with Kim Yong-sun, the KWP secretary for international affairs, the highest-level exchanges ever between the respective governments. The US reiterated that an inspections agreement would need to precede the political and economic benefits that Washington might offer the North.

North Korean officials sensed the growing pressure for nuclear disclosure, aimed initially at ensuring the DPRK's assent to a safeguards agreement with the IAEA. Though the DPRK ratified the NPT in December 1985, its obligation under the treaty to sign a full-scope safeguards agreement had long been mired in confusion and delay. The agency mistakenly provided Pyongyang with a INFCIRC-66-type agreement for individual nuclear sites such as the smaller research reactor at Yongbyon, as distinct from a more comprehensive INFCIRC-153-type agreement required of NPT signatories.[22] North Korea had no incentive to call this error to the IAEA's attention, and this may have reinforced beliefs in the North that assent to a safeguards agreement was a formality which it could stymie or ignore. Even when the IAEA corrected its oversight in June 1987, it had no leverage to hold North Korea accountable to the 18-month period for submitting the requisite documentation.

The agency's failure to uncover Iraq's nuclear activities prior to the Gulf War of 1991 led to stricter reporting requirements and more intrusive inspection demands on other states, and North Korean compliance was the immediate test case.[23] It is not certain that leaders or technical personnel in the DPRK grasped the full implications of a safeguards agreement, though Pyongyang did respond to the IAEA's initial requests for information. On 10 April 1992, another five years beyond the stipulated deadline, the DPRK formally assented to full-scope safeguards, followed on 4 May by its declaration of nuclear activities and facilities, including an admission that it had reprocessed miniscule amounts of plutonium in the late 1980s.[24] The IAEA professed surprise at the scope of the North's nuclear activities, including the Yongbyon 5 MWe reactor, parallel construction of a reprocessing facility (described in the declaration as a 'radiochemical laboratory') and initial construction of larger Magnox reactors at Yongbyon and Taechon.[25] An IAEA delegation led by its then director, Hans Blix, undertook an initial visit to the DPRK one week later. Blix's interlocutors included Choe Hak-kun, then the director of the General Department of Atomic Energy and previously North Korea's representative to the IAEA in the mid- to late-1970s, when he acquired the design data needed to build the Yongbyon reactor.

A binding safeguards agreement would have obligated the North to open its nuclear facilities. Access by international inspectors to the North's nuclear plants, verification of North Korean claims of peaceful nuclear intentions, and ensuring the DPRK's adherence to its non-proliferation commitments were all on the table, posing unprecedented challenges for a state that had long walled off nearly all its nuclear activities. North Korea sought to provide sufficient information to mollify the inspectors, but its disclosures were incomplete and unsatisfactory, generating demands for additional information and increased access. Initial IAEA measurements revealed evidence of previously undisclosed shutdowns of the Yongbyon reactor during 1989, 1990 and 1991, increasing suspicions that spent fuel had been removed and the reactor reloaded with fresh fuel rods. There were also reports of multiple high-explosive tests presumably linked to development of an implosion device.[26]

The IAEA's inspection efforts have been extensively analysed in earlier studies, so there is no need to address this history in any detail.[27] It is more important for our purposes to understand North Korea's presumed expectations of the inspections, the lessons that Pyongyang learned from these experiences, and the resultant consequences for its nuclear programme. The visits of the IAEA during 1992 and 1993 were without precedent in North Korean history. Beyond fulfilling its existing safeguards obligations for the Soviet-supplied research reactor, the DPRK had never before allowed scrutiny or measurement of any of its declared nuclear sites, much less permit access to undisclosed facilities. It seems plausible that Pyongyang did not fully appreciate the technical competence of IAEA personnel, who were able to identify discrepancies and gaps in the DPRK's nuclear declarations. As various anomalies and suspicious activities became apparent, the North began to defy and to stall. Seeking to deflect IAEA demands for special inspections at two camouflaged nuclear-waste sites, North Korea deemed them military sites and declared them off limits to inspectors. The IAEA asserted that the continuity of safeguards was at risk, and on 12 March 1993 (less than a year after assenting to full-scope safeguards) the North announced its withdrawal from the NPT, declaring that the IAEA's demands constituted an unacceptable violation of its sovereignty.

North Korea's initial experiences with the IAEA enabled its technical and diplomatic personnel to hone their skills for subsequent tests of will with international inspectors and with the United States. North Korea also asserted for the first time that its declared withdrawal from the NPT gave it 'special status' under the non-proliferation regime.[28] As characterised by Ambassador John Ritch, then the US representative to the IAEA, there was a need to weigh the relative importance of the 'ancestry' of the North Korean programme, as distinct from its 'destiny'.[29] For the Clinton administration, reconstructing nuclear history could wait, but nuclear potential (that is, the prospect of a major increase in the North's plutonium production capability if the DPRK were to complete much larger reactors then under construction) demanded immediate attention.[30] Nearly two decades later, the disputes that triggered the confrontation over North Korea's nuclear activities remain wholly unresolved, though North Korean officials subsequently asserted that Pyongyang's multiple reprocessing campaigns in the early 2000s rendered these earlier controversies moot.[31] By the North's logic, its accumulation of weapons-grade plutonium following the breakdown of the Agreed Framework meant that these past controversies were, for all practical purpose,s irrelevant, since its ability to reprocess plutonium was no longer at issue.

The early negotiations over inspections highlighted a recurrent pattern in subsequent diplomacy with North Korea.[32] Pyongyang assented to highly ambitious declaratory formulas, followed by prolonged contention over implementation of various pledges, repeated breakdowns in the procedures needed to fulfil agreements, and efforts to shelve or defer indefinitely clarification of the historical record. This pertained in particular to actions that would have required direct access to North Korean nuclear facilities. Nuclear diplomacy bought time and repeatedly raised expectations, which were then stymied by disputes over details or abrupt changes in the

North's negotiating tactics. North Korean officials may have believed that a tougher negotiating stance would elicit concessions and added inducements from the IAEA and others. But the DPRK's nuclear-weapons potential remained unperturbed, and extant obligations unfulfilled. Moreover, the DPRK had already achieved an initial reprocessing capability and had privately disclosed its nuclear-weapons plans to Moscow.[33]

The road to the Agreed Framework

The breakdown in negotiations between Seoul and Pyongyang and between North Korea and the IAEA generated mounting concern in the Clinton administration. Kim Il-sung was also weighing his responses to increased US political and military pressure. As long as Kim was alert and alive, his authority was presumably unchallenged, though he was in declining health. According to highly informed Russian sources, during a meeting with a visiting Bulgarian delegation in the summer of 1986, Kim suffered a massive heart attack. His life saved by the intervention of Soviet cardiologists flown to the DPRK at his son's urgent request.[34] Prompted by awareness of his increasing frailty, Kim Il-sung relinquished most leadership responsibilities to Kim Jong-il. But Kim Jong-il was involved primarily with various construction projects and with propaganda and cinematic activities. There was only minimal evidence of the younger Kim's direct involvement in external affairs, and his domestic portfolio focused primarily on issues of immediate personal interest, rather than on North Korea's increasingly dire economic circumstances.

Kim Il-sung seemed far more attentive than Kim Jong-il to the DPRK's looming internal crisis. According to a detailed account prepared by a former correspondent in Pyongyang, in late 1991 Kang Song-san, prime minister between 1984 and 1986 and then serving as governor of North Hamgyong Province, informed Kim Il-sung about the province's increasingly dire conditions as the agricultural crisis took hold. In response, Kim declared in his New Year's Day speech that 1992 would be 'the year of agriculture'.[35] Kang (reappointed to the prime minister's post in December 1992) reported at a Party Plenum the following year on the failure of the Seven Year Economic Plan (1987–93). As a consequence, the plenum announced a two to three year economic 'adjustment period'.[36] Weeks later in his New Year's Day address, Kim Il-sung announced priority would be given to agriculture, light industry and foreign trade, all supposedly geared to enhancing people's livelihoods, although these pronouncements did little to stave off the famine that materialised fully in the mid-1990s.[37]

Kim was also pursuing new avenues for economic assistance. On 28 September 1990, the KWP and senior representatives of the Liberal Democratic Party and the Japan Socialist Party signed a joint declaration, with the signatories agreeing that 'Japan should fully and officially apologise and compensate ... the Democratic People's Republic of Korea for the enormous misfortunes and miseries imposed on the Korean people for 36 years and the losses inflicted upon the Korean people in the ensuing 45 years after the war.'[38] An equally implausible benefactor was Moon Sun-myung, head of the Unification Church who had fled the North many decades earlier and was a fierce opponent of the regime. Moon travelled to North Korea as a state guest in December 1991 and met with Kim Il-sung, and subsequently invested in various projects, including a major hotel and an automotive joint venture.

Kim Il-sung also strengthened the power and role of the North Korean military. He realised that the political loyalty of the military and the internal security apparatus would be essential for North Korea to avoid the fate of East European socialism.[39] In addition, he recognised that the KPA constituted a crucial source of political support for Kim Jong-il. The younger Kim had been indirectly involved with military affairs since the early 1980s, but his father now assigned him formal defence titles and responsibilities. He was appointed vice chairman of the NDC in May 1990, supreme commander of the KPA in December 1991 (with Kim Il-sung relinquishing his long-held title), and marshal of the Republic in April 1992, one rung below his father's title of grand marshal.[40] The DPRK constitution was also revised for the first time in two decades, with control of the KPA transferred from the state president to the NDC chairman. When Kim Jong-il was named chairman of the NDC in April 1993 the process of power transition appeared complete. He was now entrusted with nearly all critical defence responsibilities, presumably including the nuclear programme.[41]

Kim Il-sung nevertheless continued to retain near exclusive control of the nuclear negotiations and of US–DPRK relations. Kim's involvement in nuclear diplomacy was evident well before President Carter's visit. During the early 1990s he repeatedly met with US media representatives, legislators and researchers. In June 1993, the US and North Korea undertook bilateral talks, and Pyongyang suspended its unilateral withdrawal from the NPT. When negotiations resumed days later in Geneva, Senior Vice Foreign Minister Kang Sok-ju unveiled what he termed 'bold, new instructions' from Pyongyang to replace the 5 MWe reactor and the larger graphite-moderated reactors then under construction at Yongbyon and Taechon. Only two months following Moscow's cancellation of the MP-640 reactor agreement, Kang's proposal presumed that the US would now supplant Russia as a provider of light-water reactor technology to the DPRK. Kang conditioned the proposal on US guarantees for the project. He also stated that additional consultations with the IAEA would be 'inconceivable' without a US commitment to reactor development. Kang also gave explicit credit to Kim Il-sung for the proposal.[42] These interactions culminated with the meetings between Kim and Jimmy Carter in June 1994 and the subsequent negotiation of the Agreed Framework.[43]

Under the terms of the Geneva agreement, the DPRK was required to freeze its extant nuclear programme and ultimately dismantle the facilities associated with the 5 MWe reactor at Yongbyon. But such measures were contingent on the US assembling an international consortium (the Korean Peninsula Energy Development Organisation, or KEDO) to finance and construct two 1000 MWe light-water reactors. The US also agreed to provide heavy fuel oil to North Korea to offset the energy production presumably forgone by the suspension of building work on the larger graphite-moderated reactors. Upon completion of a 'significant portion' of the LWR project, the DPRK would be required to 'come into full compliance' with its safeguard obligations and to reach agreement with the IAEA on verifying 'the accuracy and completeness' of its reporting of nuclear materials. (However, there was no explicit obligation under the Agreed Framework for North Korea to rejoin the IAEA.) Other measures under the Agreed Framework focused on security assurances to the DPRK and measures to advance normal economic and political relations with the United States. Full implementation of the Agreed Framework was expected to require ten years or more. Despite the IAEA's obvious dissatis-faction that it was unable to verify the DPRK's previous nuclear reporting or to undertake inspection of the suspect waste sites that had triggered Pyongyang's announced withdrawal from the NPT in 1993, the agency grudgingly consented to an agree-ment that appeared to forestall an acute crisis. As the IAEA's official history concluded: '[I]f the "Agreed Framework" had, in fact, persuaded the DPRK to abandon a nuclear-weapons

Table 1 **Joint Activities of Kim Il-sung and Kim Jong-il, 1980–1994**

1980	4
1981	4
1982	12
1983	8
1984	19
1985	31
1986	19
1987	12
1988	15
1989	19
1990	14
1991	11
1992	25
1993	17
1994	1

Source: Data compiled from information provided by the Open Source Center.

programme, and if the concessions made had averted a proliferation chain reaction in North East Asia, the price seemed worth [the] concessions.'[44]

Questions nevertheless remain about relations between Kim Il-sung and Kim Jong-il in the spring and summer of 1994,.[45] As highlighted in Table 1, Kim Jong-il's frequent joint appearances with his father reached near-peak levels in 1992 and 1993, only to abruptly halt in 1994. Though the elder Kim continued to meet regularly with domestic audiences and foreign visitors, father and son were seen in public together on just a single occasion (a late April event commemorating the founding of the KPA). With North Korea facing its most acute crisis in decades, the younger Kim's appearances were limited to a few ceremonial events. The United States also received intelligence reports that Kim Il-sung was dissatisfied with Kim Jong-il's management of the nuclear crisis.[46]

Kim Il-sung grasped that without an agreement to defer the nuclear impasse, North Korea would not be able to halt its economic implosion. According to President Carter's accounts of his meeting with the Korean leader, Kim did not seem fully aware of the events that had precipitated the nuclear crisis, in particular North Korea's threatened expulsion of IAEA inspectors. (However, Stephen Linton, an American deeply involved in medical relief in the DPRK who met with Kim Il-sung on multiple occasions, observes that Kim was very hard of hearing near the end of his life, which helps explain why subordinates had to repeat information and instructions to him.[47]) The meetings with Carter assumed symbolic significance as well as major policy import. Carter also held discussions with Kang Sok-ju, whom Carter found 'not as forthcoming' as Kim. According to Carter, Kang relented from more strongly asserted positions when the former president retorted that Kang's policy preferences diverged from those that Kim Il-sung had conveyed in an earlier meeting.[48] However, the basics of the agreement had surfaced in 1993 in a previous round of the US–North Korea talks and in earlier meetings with American visitors.[49]

Officials in Pyongyang saw the Agreed Framework (in particular the LWR accord) as the means to achieve a diplomatic breakthrough with the United States; it may also have helped assuage North Korea's perceived grievances with its former ally in Moscow. As noted in previous chapters, Kim Il-sung had pursued a Soviet commitment to a nuclear power reactor without success for decades until gaining Konstantin Chernenko's assent in 1984, only to see the project cancelled following the DPRK's announced pullout from the NPT in 1993. Kim now sought to make his long-term American enemy the guarantor of a revived project, and (by implication) the DPRK's primary political and economic benefactor.

A relationship with Washington (replete with US obligations to assist the North) represented a major prize for Pyongyang; the question was, what if anything did North Korea needed to do to realise it. In his discussions with the former American president, Kim Il-sung stated that (in return for a US commitment to helping to build LWRs, American assurances that it would not attack North Korea, and US willingness to pursue diplomatic relations) North Korea would not unload spent fuel from the Yongbyon reactor or reprocess more spent fuel. He also pledged that the DPRK would forgo additional work on the larger reactors then under construction. Equally significant, Kim (possibly anticipating provision of economic assistance by Seoul) responded immediately and favourably to Carter's urging that Kim invite ROK President Kim Yong-sam to the DPRK. The first face-to-face meeting between the presidents of North and South was scheduled for late July 1994.

Kim Il-sung's agreement with President Carter thus staved off the most acute security crisis in Northeast Asia since the Korean War. Carter's pledge that he would urge the Clinton administration to negotiate with Pyongyang was highly validating to Kim. The outcome represented an aged leader's final legacy; it also obligated Kim Jong-il to uphold his father's commitment, at least for a time. The elder Kim died three weeks later, reportedly from a heart attack induced by advanced arteriosclerosis and by 'repeated mental stress'.[50] It was not until 2005 that Kim Jong-il characterised denuclearisation as Kim Il-sung's 'behest', which he presumably aired with President Carter and possibly with Deng Xiaoping.[51]

Kim Il-sung's life ended without closure on North Korea's nuclear intentions, and at the precise moment when the system's economic implosion was at hand. From North Korea's perspective, the Agreed Framework had two principal virtues. Pyongyang, not Washington, had proposed the essential accord, and it bore Kim Il-sung's personal imprimatur. All subsequent denuclearisation initiatives were proposed either by Beijing or Washington, thus requiring North Korea's assent to formulations over which it did not claim authorship or ownership.

From the US perspective, the Agreed Framework prevented a rapidly deteriorating situation descending into an uncontrollable crisis. It also deferred the possibility of Pyongyang appreciably expanding its nuclear-weapons potential. The completion of two larger gas–graphite reactors would have greatly enhanced North Korea's fissile-material production capabilities.[52] The United States decided that their possible completion posed unacceptably high risks to US interests. The 5 MWe reactor, admittedly a much smaller facility, was completed in six years. Washington therefore decided to buy time. Regardless of the uncertainties and imperfections of the Agreed Framework, it was preferable to any of the alternatives.[53]

The DPRK characterised the Agreed Framework as a major victory. The KWP daily newspaper *Rodong Sinmun* published a full text of the accord as well as President Bill Clinton's separate letter of assurance to Kim Jong-il on its front page. In his letter, Clinton pledged to 'use the full powers of my office to facilitate arrangements for the financing and construction of a light-water nuclear-power reactor project within the DPRK ... subject to the approval of the US Congress.' A major breakthrough with Washington seemed within Pyongyang's grasp, without North Korea having to forgo its nuclear-weapons potential or disclose its prior nuclear history until a much later point.

However, American and North Korean definitions of denuclearisation were highly divergent, and the gap between their interpretations has not narrowed in the intervening years. To the United States, the term presumed the North's forgoing its technical and industrial capacity to build nuclear weapons and the relinquishing of any fissile material or completed devices and weapons. The DPRK's more expansive definition posited the cessation of US nuclear commitments and alliance obligations to the ROK before North Korea would contemplate or undertake the actions sought by the United States. We do not know whether the elder Kim was prepared to definitively forgo nuclear weapons, but he at least broached this possibility. Without his direct involvement, it is very doubtful that denuclearisation would have been placed on the policy agenda. Despite subsequent negotiated agreements and (at times) halting progress to limit North Korea's weapons programme, Kim's abrupt death may have effectively ended the possibility of definitive denuclearisation.

Kim appeared to grasp the stakes in an agreement with the United States. North Korea remained wholly excluded from the strategic realignments in Northeast Asia at the end of the Cold War, and the DPRK was on the edge of a horrific economic contraction. A US pledge to facilitate construction of two LWRs would commit Washington to open-ended collaboration with Pyongyang, without the latter being obligated to clarify its prior nuclear history until an appreciable portion of the project had been completed. The agreement therefore bought time for Pyongyang. The DPRK's paths to nuclear power and nuclear weapons could be maintained indefinitely, with the US facilitating the reactor project to the extent that financial arrangements and the protection of sensitive technologies allowed.[54] Even as Pyongyang in the late 1990s began to object to the desultory pace of the project, the United States had already emerged as a primary source of food aid and humanitarian assistance to the North, in addition to provision of heavy fuel oil stipulated under the Agreed Framework.[55]

Kim Il-sung's decisive intervention in the nuclear crisis revealed his awareness of the North's increasingly dire circumstances. Kim had the internal stature and authority to undertake audacious moves, including the prospect of North Korea ultimately forgoing nuclear-weapons development. He would not live long enough to see completion of the under-standings reached with Jimmy Carter, but he alone was able to broach such possibilities.

Following the Carter visit and only days before his death, Kim convened an economic planning conference at his Mount Myohyang retreat, with Kim Jong-il conspicuous by his absence. The elder Kim acknowledged that the North's energy needs were crucial:

> Above all, we must resolve the problem of electrical power. Since electricity is inadequately produced, factories and companies cannot function. Unable to produce fertiliser [without electricity], agriculture has also suffered considerably. *It will take too long to construct an atomic power plant to resolve the power shortages.* We do not have the materials to produce a hydro-electric power plant, and … coal production is also insufficient for thermal power plants. *Crude oil-power plants are optimal.*[56]

In view of the understandings with Jimmy Carter reached only weeks earlier, Kim's admission that LWRs were not a realistic answer to the North's acute energy woes was extraordinary. Moreover, Kim had made comparable remarks to the KWP Central Committee meeting in December 1993, asserting that the nuclear power plants 'would take at least six and up to ten years to construct. We cannot wait for so long to resolve the electricity problem.'[57] By implication, he understood that the LWR agreement was primarily symbolic and aspirational, and more a signal that the US was prepared to assist the DPRK over the longer term. The deliveries of heavy fuel oil (as stipulated under the Agreed Framework) presumably mattered far more to Pyongyang.

In the late spring or early summer of 1994, Kim also made an undisclosed visit to China to meet with Deng Xiaoping. This would be their final meeting.[58] Since the late 1970s, Deng had urged Kim to begin the wrenching process of internal economic change, but without evident success. But dire circumstances now appeared to compel the North Korean leader to weigh these possibilities far more carefully. He was aware that the North Korean economy was already on the edge of collapse and China seemed the only potential source of major assistance outside the capitalist world. He also needed to reassure Deng on North Korea's longer-term intentions.

Deng posed the fundamental question that hovered over the entire crisis: was North Korea prepared to irrevocably forgo nuclear-weapons development? Kim Il-sung offered Deng his personal commitment to denuclearisation, but he did not guarantee a comparable commitment by his successor. Kim's response must have been disquieting to Deng. There was no evidence of a major increase in Chinese economic assistance following Kim's visit. Chinese exports to North Korea continued at modest levels during much of the late 1990s, and North Korean exports to China plummeted throughout this period, before beginning a modest recovery in 2001.[59] It was only in 1997 and 1998, with North Korea in the depths of famine, that Beijing delivered substantial emergency food assistance.[60]

Deng Xiaoping believed that a denuclearised North was the only way that the DPRK could build normal relations with the outside world. He had maintained a decidedly negative view of the younger Kim ever since the Rangoon bombing. As noted previously, Kim Jong-il had travelled to China in the summer of 1983, but he then showed no interest in ties with Beijing for nearly two decades. No ranking Chinese official visited the DPRK from the onset of China–ROK diplomatic relations in 1992 until September 2000, when a CCP delegation led by senior foreign policy official Dai Bingguo (then affiliated with the Party's International Department) travelled to Pyongyang and met with Kim Jong-il. Kim did not visit China until 2000.

North Korea had bought time, but time for what? Quite apart from the nuclear issue, Pyongyang confronted an immediate and hugely debilitating internal crisis, described for the first time in the New Year's editorial of 1996 as an 'arduous march'. The economic collapse had at least five primary components: a severe agricultural crisis resulting in part from major summer floods in the North; the stunning deindustrialisation of the DPRK (especially in 'rustbelt' locations in the Northeast)[61]; the breakdown of the Public Distribution System (PDS) upon which the North's citizens depended for their day to day livelihood; a major contraction of the DPRK's admittedly very modest foreign trade relations; and a parallel curtailment of energy supplies to the North, especially oil. The consequences included horrific food shortages and a famine that resulted in the deaths of hundreds of thousands of North Korean citizens, with some estimates running as high as several million. Several hundred thousand 'economic refugees' also crossed into northeastern China in search of food and jobs.[62]

For the first time, North Korea sought food and humanitarian relief from international organisations and from capitalist countries, including the United States. Beginning in 1996, the World Food Programme (WFP) as well as other international donors began to provide meaningful food assistance to the North, with WFP and non-WFP deliveries peaking at approximately 1.5 million tonnes of food aid in 2001.[63] An aid-based strategy was now integral to North's Korea's survival. In an internal speech on North Korea's economic crisis delivered in 2001, Kim Jong-il addressed the country's parlous economic circumstances. According to Kim, the DPRK's economic implosion reflected 'the collapse of the world's socialist market and the imperialists' severe isolation and suffocation maneuvers [against us], as well as natural disasters that repeatedly descended upon us.'[64] He also laid blame on the failings of economic functionaries in the North. But Kim did not acknowledge the cumulative results of decades of militarisation and the walls that the regime had built to insulate the DPRK from external influence. Deeply entrenched habits and policies explained Pyongyang's dire circumstances, not the tentative, halting responses of a vulnerable and threatened regime in the midst of acute crisis.

The ascendance of Kim Jong-il

When Kim Jong-il assumed formal leadership in the DPRK in 1998, he still remained virtually unknown to the outside world. It was only in 2000 that foreign interlocutors began to have meaningful contact with the North Korean leader, and even these interactions remained episodic. Russians, Chinese, Japanese, South Koreans and Americans who subsequently met Kim depicted him as capable of straightforward, rational conversation. Though not deeply inquisitive, he often posed detailed queries based on personal knowledge and observations.[65] As characterised by former Secretary of State Madeleine Albright, Kim 'was an intelligent man who knew what he wanted. He was isolated, not uninformed. Despite his country's wretched condition, he didn't seem a desperate or even a worried man. He seemed confident.'[66] A Chinese expert deeply versed in North Korean affairs also described Kim as an intelligent person, but someone consumed by abiding personal interests and 'lacking political imagination'.[67]

Though not extroverted like his father, Kim could be animated in private conversations. This seemed especially true in meetings with fellow Koreans and with Russian interlocutors.[68] He generally remained more circumspect in meetings with Chinese and Americans. As noted by a scholar with access to tape recordings of Kim from 1985, he was often 'a boisterous, high-pitched fluent talker. Contrary to his public shy image, he is quickly aroused by his own rhetoric and laughs unreservedly at his own perceived humour ... Kim ... seems to ignore other parties and conducts an enthusiastic monologue with frequent changes of mood and tone to reflect his emotional response to his own rhetoric.'[69]

Kim Jong-il was not Kim Il-sung. Upon assuming power he undertook changes in decision-making procedures suited to his own personality, abolishing various positions and ensuring his unquestioned supremacy atop the system.[70] Unlike his father, he did not favour speeches to larger audiences and seldom spoke at any length in public settings. Whereas Kim Il-sung delivered a major radio address each New Year's Day, Kim Jong-il instead relied on a joint editorial in the North's leading newspapers. He was also obsessed with personal security, with his movements disclosed only after the fact, and without specifying the precise dates or location of his travels. None of his trips to China, for example, have ever been characterised as official visits, and by mutual agreement his visits were never disclosed until after Kim returned to North Korea, even when there was already widespread information about his movements in China.

Kim Jong-il was a highly guarded individual. Even when Kim broached possible policy changes (for example, in the early 2000s when he appeared to encourage shifts in economic policy), he often pulled back or reversed course, reflecting indecision, his own conflicted beliefs, or a response to presumed pressures within the North Korean system.[71] He also allowed individuals appointed by his father to retain their formal leadership positions.[72] Over time, this resulted in the virtual atrophy of certain decision-making bodies. No Party Congress has been held in the DPRK since October 1980, when the younger Kim was first designated his father's successor, and meetings or decisions of the Political Bureau have very seldom been reported. Membership in the Political Bureau under Kim Jong-il has been defined by attrition rather than by appointment. No full or alternate members were elected to this body between April 1993 and September 2010, when 17 members were named to the Political Bureau at a Party Representatives Conference. But the composition of the body, with ten members over the age of 80, four in their seventies, and three in their sixties (including Kim Jong-il and his sister Kim Kyong-hui) attested to longevity and loyalty, not to new leadership arrangements.[73]

Internal decision-making under Kim Jong-il derived from highly centralised mechanisms for information transmittal, with documents flowing upward to Kim for approval, modification or subsequent transmittal by the leader. According to a detailed assessment by a South Korean analyst, this hierarchical process assigns responsibility to various departments within their specified areas of competence, but with no latitude or ability to share information or undertake consultations with other departments.[74] The power of decision was and remains rigorously controlled by Kim and his closest subordinates. Policy making under Kim Jong-il was highly compartmentalised, with Kim often relying on telephone conversations or brief written instructions to convey major decisions.

Kim also exhibited contradictory behaviour in his views of the United States. In an essay written in August 1997, Kim declared that 'we do not intend to view the United States as our 100-year sworn enemy, and we are hoping for the normalisation of relations with the United States.'[75] Little more than a year later, however, Kim spoke at the Sinchon Museum, which included various displays from the Korean War. The graves of large numbers of Koreans killed in the war are located near the museum. Kim described the museum as 'vividly show[ing] the US imperialists' bestial massacre … [and] the enemy's savage atrocities … surpassing the crimes committed by the Hitler fascist ring … [all citizens] may come to endlessly hate the US imperialists and the class enemy and have a determination to seek revenge upon them a thousand fold.' Kim also argued that the plans of 'the US imperialists and reactionaries to crush our Republic become more atrocious with each passing day.'[76] His remarks did not suggest that he was seriously intent on pursuing reconciliation with the United States, even though the United States was already a principal provider of food and energy assistance to the North.

Kim Jong-il was also increasingly reliant on support from the military ranks.[77] Though he had been named KWP general secretary following his father's death, he became ever more enveloped in military titles and responsibilities. In a revealing discussion with Russian special envoy Konstantin Pulikovsky during Kim Jong-il's train trip across Russia in 2001, Kim noted that his relationship with the KPA 'gives me pleasure. I like to visit military units, meet with officers and generals, and see how they are prepared for defence of the country. When I see that they are performing their duties conscientiously and serving the interests of the motherland, I derive true satis-faction as leader of the state.'[78] The relationship was one of codependence. Kim had elevated the military to ever higher status within the system, but the KPA's authority and weight remained principally in its designated areas of responsibility. Moreover, Kim also employed his power of appointment at the senior officer level to ensure unquestioned loyalty among key military subordinates.

At a meeting of the Supreme People's Assembly in September 1998 where major constitutional revisions were announced, Kim Jong-il was elected NDC chairman, simultaneous with the abolition of the post of state president. The timing of North Korea's first attempted satellite launch of 31 August 1998 was closely linked to Kim's elevation to top leadership. With the North Korean economy hitting rock bottom in 1998, Kim Jong-il sought to legitimate his power and authority beyond his blood ties to his father. A long-range rocket launch attested to Kim's personal imprint on policy, and the affirmation of his leadership within the DPRK. As his 1999 New Year's Day editorial, he claimed:

> The past year was a proud year in which the national power of Socialist Korea was forcefully displayed. By successfully launching our first earth satellite ... we demonstrated to the entire world our Republic's greatness and might. For our country to join the ranks of those who possess satellites in the midst of a severe ordeal is a miracle in history.[79]

The slogans of 'military first' (songun) and 'a powerful and prosperous nation' (kangsong taeguk) also appeared for the first time in the editorial. Kim's leadership was thus conjoined with the power and prerogatives of the North Korean military. Military-first politics and Kim Jong-il's consolidation of power coincided with the Clinton administration's efforts to revive relations with the North. There had been some partial agreements in the mid-1990s, mainly involving implementation of the agreements stipulated under KEDO, which was overseeing the LWR project, but more contentious issues met with little or no success, and the Agreed Framework was already in deep trouble.[80] Washington and Pyongyang openly disagreed on fulfillment of various milestones, and North Korea complained repeatedly about slippage in delivery schedules for the LWR project.[81] Other complaints focused on laggard oil shipments, and the North repeatedly demanded economic compensation for energy and economic losses. In August 1998, US allegations of a reputed secret nuclear site at Kumchangri (which subsequently proved unfounded) and the North's attempted long-range rocket launch underscored that support for the US–DPRK relationship in both capitals had appreciably dwindled.

As bilateral relations grew increasingly tense, President Clinton designated former Defence Secretary William Perry as special coordinator for North Korea policy. Perry's travels and consultations included a May 1999 visit to the DPRK, enabling the first-ever meeting between senior US officials and top KPA leaders. In a major report issued the following October Perry sought to revive support for US policy.[82] It was highly validating to leaders in Pyongyang, and led to the visit of North Korea's ranking military officer (Vice Marshal Jo Myung-rok) to the White House in October 2000. In a joint communiqué, both governments pledged that they would 'fundamentally improve their bilateral relations ... the two sides stated that neither government would have hostile intent towards the other and continued the commitment of both governments ... to build a relationship free from past enmity.' Both countries also reaffirmed their commitment to the Agreed Framework and North Korea pledged that 'it will not launch any long-range missiles while the [US–DPRK] talks continue on the missile issue.'[83]

Only weeks following Jo's visit to Washington, Secretary of State Albright visited Pyongyang, becoming the first US official to meet with Kim Jong-il. At these talks, Kim imposed major constraints on possible agreements with the United States. In discussions over a proposed moratorium on North Korean missile testing, Kim informed Albright that the DPRK's extant inventory of deployed missiles would be outside the purview of any possible missile agreement, since 'you [the US] can't go inside the units and inspect them'. He asserted that North Korea would be willing to agree to a ban on future missile exports, but the US made clear that any agreements would be contingent on credible verification arrangements. As Albright concluded, 'I ... found Chairman Kim prickly and unreceptive to any questioning of North Korea's trustworthiness or any perceived violation of its sovereignty. He would fight the idea of on-site inspections, yet we had no faith in his word. No agreement was possible unless we had the ability to make sure the DPRK was complying.'[84]

Albright's visit focused principally on missiles rather than nuclear weapons. With KEDO proceeding at a desultory pace, there was little to negotiate about. Moreover, North Korea's nuclear development was less a headlong rush, and more a deliberate, long-term pursuit. The North was not 'hell-bent on nuclear arming'.[85] It did not possess the technical and industrial capacities to sustain rapid nuclear development. The programme reflected the dogged persistence of its technical personnel, interspersed with technological opportunism when circumstances enabled more rapid progress, and defiance as required. As the Clinton administration drew to a close, North Korea remained unwilling to give up anything that mattered in relation to its weapons potential, especially its fissile material. Denial of direct access to the programme remained a defining element in North Korean strategy.

New political and economic possibilities were also emerging for Pyongyang. The November 1997 the election of Kim Dae-jung as president of the ROK, long an advocate of engagement and reconciliation with the North, soon led to unprecedented rapprochement between the two Koreas, culminating in the first ever presidential summit in June 2000. Two weeks prior to Kim Dae-jung's visit to Pyongyang, Kim Jong-il (accompanied by a group of senior KPA and KWP officials) travelled to China for the first time in nearly two decades, seeking to reestablish a relationship that had badly deteriorated during the 1990s. China had quietly facilitated the initial negotiations between Pyongyang and Seoul prior to the inter-Korean summit, and Kim at long last seemed prepared to deal with leaders in Beijing. In July, Kim Jong-il welcomed Vladimir Putin to Pyongyang on a visit laden with symbolism: no Soviet or Russian leader had been to the North Korean capital. For added measure, inside North Korea there was tentative exploration of economic change, including a willingness to permit limited marketisation.

But other issues loomed. The November 2000 election of a new US president contemptuous of Pyongyang and dismissive of the Agreed Framework would soon change the tone and substance of bilateral relations. There was also mounting evidence of North Korean acquisition of materials for uranium enrichment, raising the prospect of a separate means of fissile-material production. The possibility for sustaining an imperfect denuclearisation agreement continued to erode, injecting major changes in the nuclear equation that continue to roil Northeast Asia a full decade later.

CHAPTER FIVE

Nuclear breakout

The collapse of the Agreed Framework in the autumn of 2002 and Pyongyang's resumption of its plutonium-based weapons programme in early 2003 were definitive events in Korea's nuclear history, leading ineluctably to the North's first nuclear test less than four years later. The US–DPRK accords of 1994 had enabled Pyongyang to retain its weapons potential while energy assistance to the North and site preparation for the light-water reactors proceeded, albeit fitfully. But warning signs about the agreement's continued viability had already emerged as President George W. Bush took office. North Korea was conveying clear frustration over the laggard pace of oil deliveries and the slow progress of the reactor project. For added measure, President Bush and other US officials were harshly critical of the Agreed Framework and (when the agreement began to founder) few officials sought to sustain it.

Following the attacks of 11 September, 2001, the Bush administration's attitude hardened appreciably. This was apparent in the president's highly personalised criticisms of Kim Jong-il, his characterisation of North Korea as a member of the 'axis of evil'; public disclosure of the major conclusions of the Nuclear

Posture Review, including a reference to the potential use of nuclear weapons in a Korea contingency; and the official US national security strategy report emphasising the dangers of nuclear-weapons development by 'rogue states'. The 2003 invasion of Iraq, launched on the basis of US claims that a US adversary was covertly developing weapons of mass destruction, completed this strategic shift. It was difficult to imagine actions and policies more certain to reinforce North Korea's abiding suspicions of US strategy.

In the summer of 2002, US intelligence concluded that North Korea had undertaken equipment and material procurement for an industrial-scale uranium-enrichment programme. In the administration's view, these activities invalidated the primary rationale for the Agreed Framework. At US urging, KEDO suspended heavy fuel oil shipments to North Korea in November. Sensing urgency as well as opportunity, Pyongyang quickly breached red lines in US policy. It reactivated its long-suspended plutonium programme and withdrew from the NPT, becoming the only NPT signatory to formally renege on its treaty commitments. The Bush administration, intensely engaged in planning for the invasion of Iraq, refused to negotiate directly with Pyongyang and pressed China to rein in the North.

Beijing was deeply perturbed by North Korea's actions, but the Chinese were not prepared to undertake a highly coercive strategy. Though China briefly curtailed oil shipments to Pyongyang in early 2003, deliveries were soon resumed and then increased, helping alleviate the North's acute energy shortfalls. Beijing viewed the nuclear issue primarily as a test of wills between North Korea and the United States. Fearing an acute regional crisis, China was soon mediating between Washington and Pyongyang. Beijing hosted a trilateral meeting with the US and North Korea in April 2003 and then convened

Six-Party Talks between China, the US, the DPRK, the ROK, Japan and Russia in August. It also expressed open scepticism about US intelligence claims of an enrichment programme, and urged Washington to renew negotiations with the DPRK. But the US remained strongly opposed to bilateral diplomacy, which did not fully resume until after Pyongyang's first nuclear test in 2006.

North Korea was staking its claim to a nuclear-weapons capability in word and deed. During 2007 and 2008, North Korea curtailed some of its nuclear activities, including the shuttering and subsequent disablement of the Yongbyon reactor. The North also provided US officials with extensive documentation on the operating history of the reactor. But relinquishing its fissile material was never seriously up for consideration, and the North repeatedly balked at verifying either its nuclear claims or its nuclear denials, especially its uranium-enrichment activities. Having crossed the nuclear threshhold, it did not look back or turn back. Its claim to standing as a nuclear-armed state and its determination to retain its nuclear assets have defined regional strategic realities ever since.

The collapse of the Agreed Framework

The abrupt end of the Agreed Framework and the fitful course of nuclear diplomacy under the Bush administration have been extensively analysed in previous studies.[1] Scholars and practitioners continue to debate whether North Korea's shift from a recessed capability to overt possession of nuclear weapons was preventable, and whether a different US strategy might have led Pyongyang to defer its moves toward a weapons capability. In hindsight, the possibility of indefinitely forestalling North Korean nuclear-weapons development was remote. Pyongyang viewed the sharp departures in US policy as an open invitation to break its prior commitments. Moreover, the prospect of nuclear breakout was apparent well before the final collapse of the Agreed Framework. North Korean complaints about the slow pace of the reactor project began to accumulate in the late 1990s, and in early 2001 Pyongyang hinted at a possible exit from the 1994 accords. On 22 February, a DPRK Foreign Ministry spokesman stated: 'If [the US] does not sincerely implement the Agreed Framework ... we no longer need to be bound by the agreement. We cannot but regard the existence of KEDO as meaningless under circumstances in which we cannot estimate when the LWRs will be completed. The United States should clearly know that we cannot just keep waiting.' Pyongyang also asserted that 'we will no longer be bound by our proposals concerning the missile issue made during the previous administration. We agreed not to launch long-range missiles while missile negotiations were underway, but we will not be able to extend the missile moratorium indefinitely.'[2]

The United States was pursuing three primary denuclearisation objectives: to convince Pyongyang to relinquish its fissile-material inventory; to preclude the possibility of additional fissile-material production by the North; and to ensure the DPRK's full compliance with its non-proliferation commitments. In the 1990s the DPRK possessed limited quantities of weapons-grade plutonium that appeared sufficient for one or two nuclear devices; it also retained larger amounts of spent reactor fuel that (if reprocessed) would enable the manufacture of an additional six or more devices. But evidence also began to accumulate in the late 1990s that the North was pursuing uranium enrichment as a separate path to fissile-material development.

North Korea's interest in enrichment had a long lineage. German intelligence first detected evidence of North Korean acquisition of equipment and technical data for centrifuge development in the late 1980s.[3] Successive North Korean science and technology plans between 1988 and 1993 also identified uranium enrichment as a long-term R&D priority. The planning documents also made reference to development of a fast-breeder reactor, spent-fuel reprocessing and waste disposal as part of aspirations for a full nuclear fuel cycle. Such ambitious plans may have been more wish lists than ongoing projects, but they demonstrated Pyongyang's convictions about nuclear autonomy.[4]

The expanding relationship between Pakistani nuclear scientist Abdul Qadeer Khan and Pyongyang represented the pivotal turning point in the North's enrichment pursuits.[5] In the mid- to late-1990s, Khan transferred a few dozen gas centrifuges to North Korea; facilitated Pyongyang's acquisition of materials, equipment and design data for nuclear enrichment; and granted North Korean personnel access to his laboratories. In his official interrogation by Pakistani investigators, Khan asserted that North Korea first built a pilot enrichment plant in the early 1990s, several years before he purportedly undertook major transactions with the DPRK. He also claimed that North Korean scientists showed him six cores for three plutonium weapons in 1999, seven years before the DPRK detonated its first nuclear device.[6] Khan's long record of duplicity and Islamabad's refusal to grant the US or the IAEA direct access to the Pakistani scientist make it very difficult to prove or disprove his claims.[7] But the earliest known missile and nuclear transactions between the DPRK and Pakistan (extensively documented by David Albright and Paul Brannan) date from 1993, and directly involved then Prime Minister Benazir Bhutto. Jon Pyong-ho, the KWP's secretary for munitions since 1986, a full member of the Political Bureau since 1988, a member of the National Defence Commission since 1990, and director-general of the Second Economic Committee overseeing Pyongyang's covert technology acquisitions, was a lead participant in these transfers.[8]

In the summer of 2002, US intelligence concluded that Pyongyang had initiated a dedicated uranium-enrichment programme. The scope of these activities was uncertain and the location of enrichment work exceedingly difficult to pinpoint. But Khan's provision of enrichment technology apparently convinced Pyongyang to pursue centrifuge manufacture on its own, though Khan's network probably continued to facilitate these efforts. In a report to Congress in the summer of 2002, the CIA asserted that it

> did not obtain clear evidence indicating that North Korea had begun acquiring material and equipment for a centrifuge facility until mid-2002. In 2001, North Korea began seeking centrifuge-related materials in large quantities. It also obtained equipment suitable for use in uranium feed and withdrawal systems ... for a plant that could produce enough weapons-grade uranium [each year] for two or more nuclear weapons when fully operational.[9]

The earliest evidence of North Korea's transferring equipment and raw materials for nuclear development also dates from 2000 and 2001, notably transshipment through Pakistan of uranium hexafluoride gas to Libya, though some believe these intelligence claims were erroneous or overstated.[10] However, North Korea had also begun to collaborate with Syria in the late 1990s in construction of a graphite-moderated reactor. A senior North Korean technical specialist travelled to Europe on a purchasing mission for the project in 2001, and construction began soon thereafter.[11] (The reactor was destroyed in an Israeli bombing raid in September 2007.) North Korea was venturing into uncharted territory. At the very time that its own plutonium programme remained frozen, Pyongyang was facilitating the spread of nuclear technology to one or more countries beyond its borders.

There was also recurrent evidence of North Korean enrichment activity in subsequent years. In April 2003, French, German and Egyptian personnel intercepted a large shipment of high-strength aluminum tubes with dimensions matching the requirements for centrifuges already in North Korea's possession.[12] In 2007, Pyongyang provided the US with aluminum tubing purportedly used in conventional weapons programmes that contained traces of highly enriched uranium.[13] The 18,000 pages of documentation on reactor operations at Yongbyon provided to US officials in May 2008 also contained HEU traces.[14] Some analysts believe that these traces might have been explained by contamination in Pakistan, but the evidence of North Korean involvement was too pervasive to ignore.

It was only in the spring of 2009 (after years of denying American allegations) that Pyongyang announced experimentation with enrichment, purportedly to manufacture fuel for an indigenously designed LWR that North Korea stated that it planned to build, while also intimating the need to pursue a separate path for nuclear-weapons development.[15] North Korea had decided to disclose its enrichment activities only when it was confident about the programme's technical progress. In November 2010, Pyongyang finally revealed the location of an enrichment facility, built on the site of the fuel fabrication plant that had ceased operations in 2007.[16] North Korean technical personnel claimed that the enrichment facility had been constructed in slightly over 18 months, but (given the diverse and complex technologies involved in operating such a facility) Pyongyang had undoubtedly been engaged in covert centrifuge development over a much longer period. Moreover, the disclosure occurred only a few days after Pyongyang granted two American visitors access to the site where the DPRK had undertaken preliminary construction of its indigenously designed LWR.[17] North Korean personnel described it as an experimental project, thus explaining its smaller size. The project justified the need for centrifuges, but higher levels of enrichment would also serve military purposes.

The KEDO–DPRK Reactor Supply Agreement of December 1995 may have created an additional if inadvertent loophole for enrichment, even though the Joint Declaration of the Denuclearisation of the Korean Peninsula of January 1992 explicitly ruled out such activity. KEDO was obligated to provide 'LWR fuel for the initial loading for each LWR plant [and] to assist the DPRK to obtain LWR fuel'. But the agreement specified that subsequent supply contracts would be signed 'with a DPRK-preferred supplier'.[18] American officials probably assumed that an external vendor would furnish the reactor fuel, but the accord did not preclude reliance on a domestic supplier. According to Mark Hibbs, a leading authority on global nuclear commerce, in 2002 'the DPRK ha[d] let it be known that it was keenly interested in the front end of the [nuclear] fuel cycle and uranium processing, claiming to some Western officials … that [its] interest was prompted by a desire to supply fuel for the two [LWRs] being constructed under the Agreed Framework.'[19]

During the visit of US Assistant Secretary of State James Kelly to Pyongyang in October 2002, the US for the first time accused the DPRK of pursuing uranium enrichment.[20] Weeks later, the DPRK Foreign Ministry (quoting from remarks by Senior Vice Minister of Foreign Affairs Kang Sok-ju to Assistant Secretary Kelly) claimed that North Korea was 'entitled to possess not only nuclear weapons but any type of weapon more powerful than that so as to defend its sovereignty and right to existence from the ever-growing nuclear threat of the US'.[21] But plutonium constituted the more practicable path to weapons development, in as much as North Korea already possessed the facilities and technology for such a device, and its technical personnel had more than a decade of working experience with these materials.

A week following suspension of the heavy fuel oil deliveries, the DPRK Foreign Ministry declared that the Agreed Framework had collapsed.[22] It rejected an IAEA resolution of 29 November 2002 urging the North's immediate compliance with its non-proliferation obligations.[23] On 12 December, a DPRK Foreign Ministry spokesman, claiming acute energy shortages, declared that North Korea would end its commitment to the Agreed Framework, resume operations at Yongbyon and restart the larger reactor projects suspended since 1994.[24] The Ministry of Foreign Affairs announcement initiated a succession of audacious, unilateral actions that in a matter of weeks rolled back eight years of nuclear restraint. On 13 December, Pyongyang ordered the IAEA to withdraw its seals and cameras from its declared nuclear facilities. On 19 December the DPRK stated that the Agreed Framework now existed 'in name only … As long as the United States behaves this way, we do not intend to beseech the United States for dialogue. There is nothing we want from the United States. We will go our own way under the great military-first banner.'[25] Between 21 and 24 December, North Korean personnel removed or otherwise disabled the locks and monitoring equipment at the reactor, cooling pond, fuel-fabrication plant and reprocessing facility. On 27 December it announced the expulsion of the IAEA inspectors and informed the agency that it would resume spent-fuel reprocessing. On 29 December, the Foreign Ministry spokesman declared that American actions were 'compelling us to withdraw from the NPT'.

On 10 January 2003, the DPRK announced its 'automatic and immediate' withdrawal from the NPT and its 'complete free[dom]' from the restrictions of the safeguards agreement with the IAEA, simultaneously claiming that 'in the current stage, our nuclear activities will be limited to only peaceful purposes, including electricity production.' Pyongyang said that it would substantiate its claims of peaceful nuclear use 'if the United States suspends its hostile crushing policy on us and clears away the nuclear threat'. But North Korea was intent on changing facts on the ground as quickly as possible.[26] Its actions directly challenged the central tenets of the Bush administration's national security strategy.[27] American officials were caught flat footed by the speed and audacity of North Korea's moves. Senior Vice Foreign Minister Kang, who acted as the lead North Korean negotiator for the Agreed Framework, claimed that Pyongyang sought a bilateral agreement with both countries sitting 'knee to knee', but it is very doubtful that the DPRK anticipated or desired serious negotiations with the Bush administration.[28] Freed from negotiated constraints under which it had long chafed, Pyongyang moved quickly and decisively.

Fear and loathing in Pyongyang

The DPRK's withdrawal from the NPT, the reactivation of its long-dormant plutonium programme, and its covert pursuit of uranium enrichment irrevocably altered strategic realities in Northeast Asia. Had war in the Middle East not been imminent, the United States might have focused more intently on Pyongyang's nuclear defiance. But war *was* imminent, diverting US attention from events on the peninsula, even as it concentrated the minds of leaders in Pyongyang.[29] Given the North's well established record of worst-case pronouncements, it is easy to characterise the North's declared fears of attack as justifying measures it was already determined to undertake. However, the United States was preparing for preventive war in the Middle East, and the Bush administration had placed North Korea in the same category as Iraq and Iran. As Kang stated caustically to Kelly in October 2002, 'we are part of the axis of evil and you are a gentleman. This is our relationship. If we disarm ourselves because of US pressure, then we will become like Yugoslavia or Afghanistan's Taliban, to be beaten to death.'[30]

Kang was no doubt aware of the impending invasion of Iraq, even though he did not mention it. North Korean officials later referred to events in the Middle East to justify the DPRK's pursuit of nuclear weapons. In a meeting 11 days after US forces entered Iraq, North Korean diplomats informed US counterparts that 'we've watched what you're doing in Iraq … The lessons that we're getting out of that is that Iraq does not have weapons of mass destruction and you invaded them. So, we're going to reprocess the spent fuel rods, we're going to take them and create a nuclear deterrent so you cannot invade us.' [31]

Kim Jong-il was absent from public view during lengthy periods in 2003. His absence between mid-February and early April was his longest disappearance since 1994, immediately following his father's death. During the autumn, Kim was absent for two additional extended periods (40 and 39 days, respectively).[32] Kim's nearly two-month absence in the late winter and early spring correlated closely with US operations against Iraq. According to a foreign observer who visited the North during the Iraq invasion, the country seemed on a virtual war footing.[33] Kim Jong-il was reportedly preoccupied with contingency planning during much of the year. A copy of top secret April 2004 DPRK wartime guidelines, affixed with Kim Jong-il's official seal as chairman of the KWP Central Military Commission, was published in a South Korean newspaper in early 2005.[34] The document's length and specificity suggest that it had been in preparation for some time, very possibly encompassing the period of major US combat operations in Iraq. The document envisioned a total war scenario entailing a wide spectrum of military operations. The guidelines posited that hostilities would be imposed on the DPRK. The ultimate wartime goal was a 'do or die defence of the nerve centre of the revolution,' code language for Kim Jong-il.

During the spring and summer of 2003 Pyongyang repeatedly declared its nuclear intentions. Following the US call in early April for a Security Council meeting to discuss the DPRK's withdrawal from the NPT, a Foreign Ministry spokesman retorted:

> The UNSC's discussion of the Iraq issue was misused by the US as an excuse for war. The US intends to force the DPRK to disarm itself. The Iraqi war shows that to allow disarming through inspection does not help avert a war but rather sparks it … This suggests that even the signing of a non-aggression treaty with the US would not help avert a war. *Only the physical deterrent force, [a] tremendous military deterrent force powerful enough to beat back an attack supported by any ultra-modern weapons, can avert a war and protect the security of the country and the nation.*[35]

Two weeks later, North Korea claimed that its reprocessing activities were approaching a culmination point.[36] Li Gun, the senior MFA representative at trilateral talks held in late April, claimed that North Korea already possessed nuclear weapons and he threatened a 'physical demonstration' of its capabilities.[37] Li's remarks suggested that final assembly of a weapon had only been a matter of a few turns of the screwdriver. In early June, the DPRK Foreign Ministry spokesman warned that 'in the event that we judge that our sovereignty has been encroached upon, we will respond with an immediate, physical retaliatory measure. Neither sanctions nor pressure will work on us ... *as far as the issue of nuclear deterrent force is concerned the DPRK has the same status as the US and other states possessing nuclear deterrent forces.*'[38] This was the first time that North Korea posited nuclear equivalence with the US and other nuclear weapon states, though it had yet to test a device. Months later, Vice Minister of Foreign Affairs Kim Gye-gwan urged two professional staff members from the Senate Foreign Relations Committee to 'put your heads together ... and stop trying so hard to convince us to abandon our nuclear programme and start thinking about how you are going to live with a nuclear North Korea.'[39]

China was very troubled by North Korea's actions. Following Pyongyang's withdrawal from the NPT, President Jiang Zemin had chastised the North in especially harsh terms; Beijing also briefly curtailed energy exports to the DPRK.[40] The North's nuclear defiance initiated a debate among Chinese experts over North Korea policy that in various forms has persisted ever since.[41] China confronted unpalatable choices between a defiant neighbour from whom it was unable or unwilling to separate and a US administration whose declared national security doctrine reserved the right of unilateral action against a WMD-armed adversary. Though Beijing was not persuaded by US warnings that nuclear-weapons development by the North would trigger comparable pressures in Japan and South Korea, it considered the risks of passivity far too great.

During the late winter and early spring of 2003, Beijing (fearing that North Korea's withdrawal from the NPT might culminate in US military action on China's doorstep) became deeply involved in shuttle diplomacy with Pyongyang and Washington. In the words of an unnamed Chinese official, 'we have realised that we cannot let this situation alone'.[42] Hu Jintao's formal elevation to the Chinese state presidency during this period was an additional factor. A major crisis on the peninsula posed serious risks to the senior leadership's developmental priorities and its desire for an unperturbed regional environment. Beijing's intensive efforts during the spring and summer to coax North Korea into multilateral talks and its parallel communication with Washington were without precedent in the history of Chinese diplomacy.[43] Increased energy assistance to the DPRK was an additional element in Beijing's plans, helping ensure Chinese continued access to leaders in Pyongyang. Chinese energy exports to the North nearly tripled between 2002 and 2007 and other forms of Chinese assistance more than doubled between 2002 and 2006.[44]

In August 2003, the Six-Party Talks opened in Beijing, with China serving as convener and host. But the divergence between the US and the DPRK was evident from the outset. The United States insisted that North Korea had to undertake complete, verifiable and irreversible dismantlement of all its nuclear programmes and activities before the US would resume energy assistance or deal bilaterally with the DPRK. Pyongyang repeatedly denied the existence of an enrichment programme and insisted that bilateral agreements were essential to forestall a longer-term confrontation or an outright crisis. It also demanded major compensation for energy shortfalls resulting from the end of the Agreed Framework. But the United States had no intention of meeting Pyongyang's demands. In early 2004, the DPRK proposed a renewed freeze in weapons development, but the overture was laden with conditions that the United States deemed unacceptable. North Korea's nuclear goals were developmental, not diplomatic. Its repeated references to acquisition of a 'physical deterrent' and its display of plutonium metal to a US non-governmental delegation in January 2004 revealed Washington's inability to prevent the North's steady nuclear advancement.[45]

In February 2005, North Korea declared that it would suspend its participation in the Six-Party Talks. It also claimed to have manufactured nuclear weapons 'for self-defence to cope with the Bush Administration's policy of isolating and crushing the DPRK'.[46] This was the first time North Korea publicly announced that it had manufactured nuclear weapons. Pyongyang utilised its nuclear claims to redefine its expectations of any renewed negotiations:

> The time for discussing give and take type of issues, such as freeze and reward, at the Six-Party Talks has passed. Now that we have become a dignified nuclear weapons possessing state, the Six-Party Talks must naturally become arms reduction talks where the participating countries resolve the issue on an equal footing.[47]

Amid reports that North Korea was preparing for a nuclear test, a Chinese Foreign Ministry official stated that Pyongyang 'understands the consequences [of a test] very clearly', suggesting that Beijing had explicitly warned the DPRK not to detonate a nuclear device.[48] Chinese diplomacy, stymied at every turn, had been unable to prevent a deepening of the nuclear impasse, leading one prominent Chinese expert to describe the overall situation as grim and approaching a potential crisis.[49]

The truce and the test

At the outset of the Bush administration's second term, the failures and frustrations of nuclear diplomacy were readily apparent. American warnings to the DPRK and China's appeals to Pyongyang had elicited no meaningful responses from North Korea. The resumption of reactor operations at Yongbyon had enabled the North to augment its plutonium inventory, and the US seemed no closer to identifying the location or estimating the extent of North Korean enrichment activity. In the spring of 2005, Pyongyang completed additional downloading of spent fuel from the reactor and quickly reloaded the reactor with fresh fuel rods produced prior to the Agreed Framework.[50]

The Bush administration remained sharply divided over North Korea policy, but the prospect of open-ended plutonium production at Yongbyon was clearly disquieting to senior officials. Some US policymakers perceived an increasing need to address the known threat rather than dwell on the uncertainties of a nascent enrichment programme. These efforts resulted in intensive rounds of US diplomacy, led by Assistant Secretary of State Christopher Hill.[51] After a year-long absence from the Six-Party Talks, Pyongyang returned to the negotiations, culminating with release of the joint statement of 19 September 2005, with Beijing the principal drafter of the document.[52] All the signatories assented to the ultimate goal of 'the verifiable denuclearisation of the Korean peninsula in a peaceful matter'. North Korea also pledged that it was 'committed to abandoning all nuclear weapons and existing nuclear programmes and returning, at an early date, to the Treaty on the Non-Proliferation of Nuclear Weapons and to IAEA safeguards'.[53]

The joint statement featured generalised expectations among the six parties rather than a major shift in strategy. The document included the DPRK's insistence on 'the right to peaceful uses of nuclear energy' and a parallel statement that the other parties 'agreed to discuss, at an appropriate time, the subject of the provision of light water reactors to the DPRK'. However, the joint statement was laden with ambiguity on the precise terms, including whether North Korea had even tacitly agreed to ultimately disassembling the weapons it claimed to possess.[54] In contrast to October 1994, when the full text of the Agreed Framework was published on the front page of *Rodong Sinmun*, the joint statement appeared on the lower half of the newspaper's third page. Washington and Pyongyang quickly released unilateral statements with starkly different interpretations of their respective obligations. The US also froze North Korean financial assets at Banco Delta Asia, a bank in Macao which American officials believed was a principal conduit for North Korea's distribution of counterfeit US currency.[55] A brief and unproductive negotiating round took place in November, with the DPRK insisting that it would not return to the talks unless the financial sanctions were lifted. The September agreement had very likely staved off a nuclear test in the near term, but it seemed more a pause than a major negotiating breakthrough.

Despite the uncertainties or perhaps because of them, China persisted with its efforts to cultivate relations with Pyongyang. In late October, Hu Jintao undertook his first visit to the DPRK as CCP general secretary, with the DPRK providing a massive turnout of Pyongyang's citizens for the occasion. Hu urged Pyongyang to commit to ongoing communication with Beijing, but contrary to North Korean expectations the Chinese did not offer major increases in economic assistance. In mid-January 2006, Kim Jong-il paid a return visit to China, proposing a major expansion of economic collaboration with China, encompassing natural resources and energy, infrastructural development, tourism, telecommunications, agriculture and labour-intensive industries. With the imposition of sanctions on North Korea's bank accounts in Macao, its financial and economic needs had grown even more acute. But Kim returned home largely empty handed.[56]

Having failed to secure major new commitments from China and under increasing financial pressure, North Korea in the spring of 2006 shifted course, culminating with its first nuclear test in October. Preparations for multiple missile launches were first evident in mid-May, but there were also reports of planning for a nuclear test.[57] On 5 July, without informing Beijing or Moscow, North Korea undertook its most extensive series of ballistic-missile tests in three decades of development, firing variants of six unarmed missiles within four hours and a seventh test nine hours later. The most consequential (if unsuccessful) test was of a *Taepodong*-2 missile, the North's first long-range test since its failed satellite launch of August 1998. Pyongyang thus made good on previous statements that it was no longer bound by its earlier pledge to forgo long-range missile tests. Though the Chinese still resisted the formal imposition of sanctions, Beijing was increasingly exasperated with Pyongyang's behaviour.[58] With Beijing and Moscow both deeply involved in the drafting of the final document, UNSC Resolution 1695 condemned the launch, demanded that the DPRK suspend all ballistic-missile activities and required all member states to prevent transfer of materials and technology for North Korea's missile and WMD programmes.[59]

Pyongyang's response was an immediate and fierce statement declaring the resolution an 'extremely hostile act of the United States' and an infringement on DPRK sovereignty, it declared that 'we will have no option but to take stronger physical actions ... [to] strengthen its self-defensive war deterrent by all means and methods now that the situation has reached the worst phase.'[60] In August, there was further activity at the presumed nuclear test site in North Hamgyong Province, corresponding with oblique hints of an impending test.[61] On 3 October, the DPRK released a Foreign Ministry statement indicating that a test was imminent. Its tone was ominous and explicit:

> A grave situation prevails on the Korean peninsula today when our state's supreme interest and security are being seriously violated and our nation stands at the crossroads of life and death ... the United States' extreme nuclear war threats and sanction and pressure maneuvers have made it impossible for us to not carry out a nuclear test, a necessary requirement in the process of securing a nuclear deterrent.[62]

The test, undertaken six days later and with minimal advance warning to Beijing and Moscow, made good on Pyongyang's threat of a 'physical demonstration' first conveyed in the spring of 2003. According to a US non-governmental group from Stanford University, North Korea (in a communication with Chinese counterparts) informed the Chinese that it anticipated a 4 kiloton yield from the test. The test results were not as successful as Pyongyang had anticipated, with an explosive yield of less one kiloton.[63] DPRK officials informed this non-governmental delegation that Pyongyang provided the Chinese and Russian embassies two hours' advance notice of the test. A subsequent confidential Chinese account claimed that Pyongyang instructed its embassy in Beijing to provide China with 30 minutes' advance notice, but that the DPRK ambassador decided to provide only 20 minutes' notice.[64] The technical results and precise circumstances of the test were less important than the strategic consequences: in defiance of adversaries and allies alike, North Korea had unequivocally breached the nuclear divide.

Agreement and impasse

The North Korean nuclear test compelled all involved states, especially China and the United States, to reassess their prevailing strategies. There was little doubt that the Chinese took great offense at the North's nuclear defiance. China's characterisation of the test as 'flagrant' or 'blatant' (*hanran*) was a term generally reserved for highly antagonistic relations.[65] Following the issuance of the Security Council resolution condemning the test, China's Permanent Representative to the United Nations Wang Guangya described the test as 'irresponsible.'[66] A nuclear test on China's eastern doorstep had undermined fundamental Chinese political and security interests, leaving Beijing in a passive and diminished position.

Pyongyang's actions prompted China to reevaluate its policy options. Despite acute unhappiness over the test, China was the only outside power with regular access to leaders in Pyongyang, and it did not want to sever contact. Beijing's immediate priority was to communicate fully and openly with Washington (thereby avoiding the possibility that it might be blamed for North Korean actions), without triggering a fundamental break in relations with the DPRK. A report prepared by the CCP International Department in early 2007 acknowledged that China's use of North Korea as a strategic buffer had lost its relevance well before the nuclear test. But the report's authors cautioned against an avowedly 'pro-US, distant-DPRK' strategy. China sought to define a course that aligned with Washington on nuclear non-proliferation without inhibiting Beijing's continued freedom of action. As the report concluded, 'the most suitable course would be for the United States to take the main role and for China to cooperate by giving its tacit approval [to America's lead]', thereby 'allow[ing] China leeway to compromise and maneuver … [China] should not unnecessarily aggravate North Korea and force it to run into the arms of the United States.' But the report also advocated preparations for two worst-case scenarios: either a potential use of force by the US or internal upheaval in the DPRK.[67]

The shifts in US strategy were even more marked. Within weeks of the nuclear test, the United States and North Korea initiated bilateral talks in Beijing, followed by deeper discussions in Berlin in January 2007. Pyongyang had finally secured the bilateral channel it had sought unsuccessfully during President G.W. Bush's first term. To Pyongyang, the US willingness to undertake direct negotiations vindicated its decision to test. In the aftermath of the detonation, US officials expressed renewed awareness of the need to cap the DPRK's plutonium programme. Even though Pyongyang could not accelerate its weapons production in the near term, the prospect of open-ended nuclear-weapons development was clearly disquieting to the United States. The administration therefore sought tangible and verifiable steps in denuclearisation that would limit North Korea's plutonium production, without insisting on an immediate and unconditional dismantlement of Pyongyang's nuclear-weapons infrastructure. In return, the US was prepared to offer various forms of political assurance to North Korea and to resume energy assistance.

During 2007 and for a time in 2008, the administration's approach generated tangible results, producing the first evidence of North Korean nuclear restraint since the breakdown of the Agreed Framework. Under the terms of the denuclearisation action plan of February 2007 announced at the Six-Party Talks, the North agreed to 'shut down and seal for the purpose of eventual abandonment the Yongbyon nuclear facility' and to allow IAEA personnel to monitor and verify Pyongyang's compliance with its commitments. These steps were largely completed by mid-summer. The second phase action plan of October 2007 obligated the North to 'disable all existing nuclear facilities' at Yongbyon, that is, the 5 MWe reactor, the reprocessing facility and the fuel-rod fabrication plant, with the US directly involved in this process. The DPRK was also required to provide 'a complete and correct declaration of all its nuclear programs' by the end of 2007. In addition, Pyongyang 'reaffirmed its commitment not to transfer nuclear materials, nuclear technology, or nuclear know-how.'[68] These measures appeared to limit the DPRK's capacity to expand its plutonium potential and weapons inventory. However, unlike the Agreed Framework and the September 2005 joint statement, texts of the 2007 agreements were never published in *Rodong Sinmun*. At best, the DPRK's commitment to the 2007 agreements was hedged.

The steps specified under the accords were nonetheless sequenced, explicit and reciprocal. As the North undertook disablement measures, the United States and other participants in the negotiations resumed larger heavy fuel oil deliveries to the DPRK. US financial sanctions imposed on North Korean bank accounts in Macao were also eased. Parallel US pledges to initiate steps to remove the DPRK's designation as a state sponsor of terrorism and to end North Korea's inclusion under the Trading with the Enemy Act assumed additional significance to the DPRK, though neither designation involved the DPRK's nuclear-weapons activities. Such political compensation appeared to matter deeply to Pyongyang. Even more significant, the US appeared more willing to defer immediate attention to uranium enrichment. American officials had become far more cautious in their claims about centrifuge operations.[69] Unlike plutonium reprocessing, enrichment did not provide a telltale chemical signature, and centrifuge operations could be distributed across multiple locations. In the absence of detectable evidence of North Korean enrichment, Pyongyang implied that its programme had never approached an operational capability and that its activities were now largely dormant. Both assurances proved demonstrably false when Pyongyang unveiled the existence of a new enrichment facility at Yongbyon in late 2010.

The denuclearisation steps of 2007 and 2008 again posed the question of Pyongyang's larger strategic objectives. The DPRK had presumably decided to shut down reactor operations and cease plutonium production, but its steps remained well short of dismantlement.[70] By mid-2008, the DPRK had fulfilled numerous obligations under the 2007 agreements, including provision of an estimate of its plutonium inventory and transferring 18,000 pages of documentation detailing more than two decades of intermittent operations of the Yongbyon reactor, though the declared numbers were lower than most US estimates and the document made no mention of enrichment activities.[71] North Korea also destroyed the reactor's cooling tower in the summer of 2008, with Western television crews present to witness the event. Dismantlement in the absence of alternative means of fissile material production would have signaled that the DPRK's nuclear weaponry would be an essentially political deterrent, not a fully realised operational capability.

But the actions of 2007 and 2008 did not prefigure nuclear abandonment. In the immediate aftermath of bilateral talks with the US in Singapore in April 2008, a senior North Korean diplomat informed a US non-governmental delegation then visiting Pyongyang that disablement did not imply dismantlement:

> It is not correct to assume that dismantlement by us is the end. We are maintaining our deterrent. If we are relieved of the threat, we could give up our weapons. My country is divided in two, still technically at war. The US and ROK are armed with nuclear weapons and have a mutual defence treaty and a nuclear umbrella.

> The US could [deploy] nuclear aircraft carriers and
> ships. So we have to make sure what the nuclear-free
> status of the Korean peninsula would mean … Our
> principled position with regard to nuclear weapons is
> [that] when US-DPRK relations are fully normalised
> and no threat exists and mutual trust has been built,
> nuclear weapons will be eliminated.[72]

The North's plutonium stockpile and its actual weapons inventory were both left unaddressed in the 2005 joint statement and
in the 2007 accords. Having withdrawn from the NPT and
having tested a nuclear device, the DPRK sought to maintain
its claim to standing as a nuclear-weapons state, though its
capabilities remained limited. Disablement also did not constitute irreversibility; Pyongyang had not taken steps to render
the facility inoperative. Technical specialists who had visited
Yongbyon remarked on the facility's outright disrepair, encompassing major environmental damage and potentially involving
risks to the safety and well-being of technical personnel.[73]
Though North Korea was still able to produce weapons-grade
plutonium at Yongbyon, its actions and words suggested
that it might have been prepared to entertain an open-ended
leveraged buyout of the plutonium programme by the US,
possibly beginning with the prodigious tasks of decommis-
sioning and decontamination of various facilities at Yongbyon.[74]

US officials sought to pursue larger steps towards denuclearisation with Pyongyang in the waning months of the Bush
administration, but no such discussions took place. Continued
controversies over verification of North Korea's nuclear inventory repeatedly bedeviled negotiations during the summer
and autumn of 2008. In its nuclear estimate submitted in June,
Pyongyang had excluded two waste sites that it had first
declared off limits to IAEA inspectors in the early 1990s, trig-

gering the DPRK's 1993 withdrawal from the NPT.[75] Verification presumed detailed inspection of different facilities, access to documentation, and interviews with technical personnel, but facility access and collection of soil samples were the most contentious issues. US officials contended that (as part of a verification protocol purportedly reached in preceding months) the DPRK had 'basically agreed' to the removal of soil samples for testing in the United States, including soil samples from undeclared nuclear sites.[76] But a DPRK Foreign Ministry press statement in late August declared that US claims of a verification protocol were 'far fetched'.[77] The chasm between US and North Korean depictions of denuclearisation proved unbridgeable. In mid-August 2008, Kim Jong-il suffered a stroke, though US officials were initially unaware of his declining health. His evident physical incapacitation at the time made any diplomatic compromise exceedingly remote.

To the United States, interim steps in denuclearisation were appropriate and important, but true denuclearisation entailed definitive elimination of the North Korean weapons programme and infrastructure. To the DPRK, the technical specifics of various agreements were secondary to its enduring enmity with the US, and the legitimacy that Pyongyang believed these animosities conferred on its nuclear-weapon pursuits. The December 2008 session of the Six-Party Talks proved fruitless, with the DPRK balking at any commitment to written, binding pledges on verification. As the Bush administration drew to a close, Pyongyang felt no need to sustain the negotiating process of 2007 and 2008. It was intent on retaining the nuclear-weapons inventory assembled over the course of the preceding six years, while it contemplated next steps to enhance its weapons potential.

CHAPTER SIX

Nuclear assertion

In early 2009, North Korea forcefully expanded its claims to standing as a nuclear-weapons state. In abrupt, unequivocal fashion, the DPRK walked away from every denuclearisation commitment made during the latter years of the Bush administration. It asserted its right to possess nuclear weapons outside the NPT, declared it would enhance its plutonium-based programme, and announced plans to experiment with enriched uranium. The North carried out its second nuclear test six weeks later. Pyongyang showed no interest in diplomacy with President Barack Obama, who in his inaugural speech of 20 January 2009 pledged to 'extend a hand' to adversaries prepared to 'unclench their fist'. North Korea was determined to consolidate its existing capabilities and augment its longer-term weapons potential.

The DPRK claimed it was retaliating for a non-binding presidential statement issued by the UN Security Council in April 2009 following an attempted satellite launch earlier that month by North Korea. Its actions bore an obvious parallel to the events of the summer of 2006, when the UN Security Council imposed sanctions after North Korea carried out seven missile tests, with the first nuclear detonation following less than three months later. In early February preparations for the impending rocket test were detected by US intelligence. In mid-March, the DPRK announced its accession to the treaty on the peaceful uses of outer space, and informed relevant international organisations of its plans for a test. But it refused to comply with earlier UN Security Council resolutions forbidding it from undertaking additional long-range missile tests. Ignoring Chinese pleas and American warnings, Pyongyang launched the rocket in early April. The third stage failed to ignite, but the launcher's performance had improved significantly over previous tests.[1]

Only hours after the release of a non-binding UN Security Council presidential statement criticising this test, North Korea described the statement as 'an unbearable insult to our people and a criminal act never to be tolerated',[2] and threatening never return to the Six-Party Talks. Pyongyang insisted that it would 'strengthen [its] self-defensive nuclear deterrent in every way', weaponise its entire inventory of plutonium, resume operations at the Yongbyon nuclear complex and test intercontinental ballistic missiles. It summarily expelled IAEA inspectors and US government personnel involved in disabling the graphite-moderated reactor and other facilities at Yongbyon. By announcing that it would accelerate experimentation with uranium enrichment, the DPRK had finally acknowledged the existence of a programme it had long denied.

Leadership succession was a principal if unacknowledged reason for Pyongyang's actions. Though Kim Jong-il had resumed limited public appearances following his stroke of the previous summer, the DPRK did not want to display weakness or vulnerability with Kim still in very uncertain health. Rather than retreat, Pyongyang advanced. In early January 2009, Kim Jong-il designated his youngest son Kim Chong-un as his successor. Like his father, Kim Jong-il believed his son's (and the system's) prospects were better ensured with nuclear weapons than without them. North Korea appeared largely unconcerned with the reactions of outside powers. It was defying the United States and was again testing the limits of Chinese forbearance.

Defiance renewed

Pyongyang's decision to accelerate weapons development reflected careful advanced planning. Immediately prior to President Obama's inauguration, the DPRK had renewed its claim to equivalence with the US and other nuclear powers. North Korea had first enunciated this argument in early 2005, when it announced that it had manufactured nuclear weapons. On 13 January, the DPRK Ministry of Foreign Affairs dismissed the argument that 'the denuclearisation on the Korean peninsula ... would be realised if we alone were to give up nuclear weapons.' According to the ministry spokesman, the participants at the Six-Party Talks 'agreed to denuclearising not the northern half of the Korean peninsula but the entire Korean peninsula ... Our agreement to the 19 September [2005] joint statement started precisely from the principled position of *denuclearisation through the normalisation of relations, not the normalisation of relations through denuclearisation.*' As the press statement concluded, '*once US nuclear threats are removed and the US nuclear umbrella for South Korea disappears, we will not need nuclear weapons, either* ... [but] as long as the United States hostile policy toward the DPRK and nuclear threats are not fundamentally eliminated, we will never give up our nuclear weapons first, not even in a hundred years.'[3]

Four days later the Foreign Ministry warned the United States that it 'is committing a miscalculation if it thinks that normalisation of DPRK–US relations is a price for our nuclear abandonment.' The ministry spokesman asserted that North Korea 'can live without normalisation of relations with the United States but cannot live without a nuclear deterrent ... the normalisation of relations and the nuclear issue are completely separate matters ... if there is something that we long for, it is not the normalisation of DPRK–US relations but the strengthening of the nuclear deterrent in every way ... [to] more reliably protect our nation's safety.'[4]

Pyongyang made comparable claims to nuclear standing in private discussions between senior DPRK diplomats and American non-governmental interlocutors in the autumn of 2008 and early winter of 2009.[5] Senior North Korean diplomats declared that acceptance of the North's possession of nuclear weapons would be a condition for its participation in any future negotiations. In the view of these officials, the DPRK's first nuclear test and its accumulation of weaponised plutonium placed it on an equal footing with the United States and other nuclear powers. No matter how limited North Korea's nuclear capabilities were, these statements unambiguously revealed the political and strategic value that North Korea placed on its extant weapons. The North was insisting that the denuclearisation of the Korean peninsula would require the United States to disengage from its security commitments in Northeast Asia, remove its nuclear umbrella from South Korea, withdraw US military forces from the peninsula, and develop a US–DPRK strategic relationship paralleling the US–ROK alliance. Normalisation (presumably entailing a peace agreement to supplant the armistice accords of July 1953) needed to precede denuclearisation. North Korean officials also argued that dismantlement and final verification of the DPRK's nuclear inventory would only take place when the United States renewed and fulfilled its pledge to provide light-water reactors first specified under the Agreed Framework.[6]

Pyongyang probably believed that the United States would pursue bilateral diplomacy only when confronted by unambiguous challenges to fundamental US interests. However, if leaders in the North hoped to replicate prior breakthroughs with the United States, they miscalculated badly. The Obama administration openly cautioned Pyongyang not to undertake another long-range missile launch and warned of more severe consequences of a second nuclear detonation. It made good on both warnings. Washington quickly sought to deny the DPRK any political or strategic advantage it claimed from the nuclear test and pressed for additional sanctions at the UN Security Council. However, North Korea's immediate preoccupation was leadership succession, not relations with the United States. There had been elliptical hints in North Korean media about the succession for over a decade, but Kim Jong-il was not yet willing to make definitive decisions. The stroke he suffered in August 2008 necessitated steps that he had long tried to defer. He was absent from public view during the late summer and early autumn, most notably at the celebration marking the 60th anniversary of the founding of the DPRK in September. Kim's first post-stroke meeting with a foreign visitor (with Wang Jiarui, director of the CCP International Department) took place in late January 2009. Weeks earlier, Kim Jong-il had designated Kim Chong-un as his successor, with Kim's inner political circle expected to oversee his son's preparations for leadership.[7]

However, North Korea was not headless during Kim's absence. Preparations for the rocket launch and the second nuclear test were almost certainly under way while he was recovering from his stroke. Kim Jong-il visited the monitoring facility on the day of the rocket launch, signalling that the 'military first' line would remain dominant. His reappointment as chairman of the National Defence Commission (NDC) at the

Supreme People's Assembly in April 2009 only days after the rocket test affirmed his return to leadership, though his physical weakness was readily apparent in television footage. The SPA meeting also highlighted the enhanced role of the NDC, including the appointment to this leadership body of Kim's brother-in-law Jang Song-thaek, and of Ju Kyu-chang, a senior official closely identified with the DPRK's advanced weapons programmes.

Having openly declared in April its intention to pursue uranium enrichment, North Korea wasted little time in revealing R&D results that had long preceded its acknowledgment of these activities. On a 9 May visit to the Huichon General Machine Tool plant (a major facility for defence production), Kim Jong-il, accompanied by Jon Pyong-ho, Ju Kyu-chang and Jang Song-thaek, inspected what appeared to be four steel-alloy rotor segments required for the operation of centrifuges in the uranium enrichment process.[8] As noted in the previous chapter, Jon's involvement with weapons transactions and technology transfer with Pakistan (including the acquisition of centrifuges) dated from at least the early 1990s. Ju had accompanied Kim Jong-il when he visited the monitoring facility on the day of the rocket launch. North Korea had unambiguously resumed its missile and nuclear-weapons development, simultaneously signalling that its nuclear efforts would no longer be limited to plutonium. Two weeks following the factory visit, Pyongyang (again with a minimum of warning) undertook its second nuclear test.

The May 2009 test

The DPRK may have crossed the nuclear threshold in 2006, but the first test did not achieve its anticipated results. North Korea's weapons scientists presumably recognised that design and engineering deficiencies in the initial detonation would require additional testing. Pyongyang's decision to walk away from nuclear diplomacy provided the opening that the North's nuclear scientists presumably sought. According to US intelligence estimates, the May test had an explosive yield appreciably greater than the first nuclear explosion.[9] North Korean commentaries following the test implied that the second test validated a workable design for a warhead to be placed atop a missile. An assessment of the two nuclear tests by a leading Chinese physicist bears out this conclusion. Both tests appeared to have been undertaken with a projected yield of 4 kilotons, possibly indicating that North Korea had access to an existing weapon design. But the second test met its anticipated yield.[10] The simultaneous reactivation of the reprocessing facility at Yongbyon enabled completion of the third reprocessing campaign since the end of the Agreed Framework and replenished North Korea's plutonium inventory.[11] Equally important, the North's open acknowledgment of experimentation with uranium enrichment meant that centrifuge development could provide another means of fissile-material production, and possibly enable future testing of a different weapon design.

North Korea had reinforced its commitment to nuclear-weapons development in word and deed.[12] It already possessed a nuclear inventory estimated at between four to eight explosive devices, with enrichment diversifying the North's longer-term nuclear possibilities.[13] Pyongyang made clear that its nuclear capabilities were not negotiable. As a commentary in *Rodong Sinmun* noted a month following the second test,

> [w]e have never requested anyone to recognise our status as a nuclear weapons state nor have we entertained any idea of getting it recognised … our strengthening of the nuclear deterrent is an irrefutable exercise of our independent right and sovereignty for the defence of our dignity, system, and safety of the nation … our nuclear deterrent has nothing to do with someone's recognition of it and if it discourages the aggressors from provoking us randomly, its purposes are well served.[14]

However, these expressions of self-confidence obscured economic pressures impinging on Pyongyang. A month prior to the nuclear test, the DPRK leadership launched another of its periodic 'speed battles' (a mass-mobilisation economic strategies to spur heightened industrial production) designed to regain a measure of central control over productive resources. Initially scheduled to last for 150 days, it was followed by an additional 100-day campaign extending to year's end. The campaign concentrated on sectors deemed critical to North Korea's industrial recovery, notably steel production, coal output, the energy sector, rail transport and various industrial enterprises.[15] The consecutive speed battles may also have been intended to deflect economic pressures that the leadership anticipated following the second nuclear test.

Two days after the second detonation, Song Mi-ran, a political writer in *Rodong Sinmun* often entrusted with commentaries on highly sensitive political issues, published a lengthy political essay extolling the test. Song asserted that the North's nuclear capabilities were an essential bequest to future generations that justified major economic sacrifice: 'We [now] live in an impregnable fortress, on which no aggressor is able to pounce ... Our country ... is today firmly taking the complete initiative in the confrontation of power with aggressors, as a militarily powerful state ... Nobody will be able to turn our Korea into a weak and small state again; and Korea majestically declared over the world that Korea will rise over the earth and shine forever as a big and powerful country ... if we untie our belts [today], we will be the imperialists' slaves later, although we may be able to live comfortably at the moment'.[16]

US responses to the second detonation heightened the pressures on Pyongyang. On 12 June the Security Council unanimously passed Resolution 1874, which introduced additional sanctions designed to prevent or interdict nuclear, missile and technology transactions.[17] The thrust of the Security Council's actions were fourfold:

- to increase efforts to curtail Pyongyang's acquisition of technology and materials needed for its weapons programmes, including constraints on travel of key research and development (R&D) personnel and restrictions on financial activities related to weapons development;
- to carry out more rigorous monitoring, inspection and prevention of weapons shipments leaving North Korea;

- to stop all weapons exports by North Korea, thereby depriving the regime of revenue needed to sustain its strategic programmes; and
- to deny the DPRK any political acknowledgment of its claimed nuclear standing outside the NPT.

The Obama administration also reiterated that Pyongyang needed to halt its nuclear development, reaffirm its denuclearisation commitments at the Six-Party Talks, and take irreversible steps to preclude additional nuclear weapons development.

By mid-summer 2009 the DPRK acknowledged the increased effects of the Security Council's actions on the North Korean economy.[18] A Foreign Ministry statement in late July conceded that the sanctions were 'curbing the normal progress of the economy … [and] aim[ed] to disarm and incapacitate the DPRK so that it can only subsist on the bread crumbs thrown away by [others].' The statement hinted that 'there is a specific and reserved form of dialogue that can address the current situation', an oblique signal that Pyongyang grasped some of the political costs of its actions.[19] The statement echoed previous instances when Pyongyang had undertaken precipitate actions followed by tactical concessions, while trying to retain strategic advantage. This stance was evident during former President Clinton's visit to Pyongyang in August 2009. Clinton's brief visit included a meeting with a somewhat reinvigorated Kim Jong-il. Kim agreed to release two US journalists captured by North Korean security personnel during an unauthorised crossing of the China–DPRK border the previous March. North Korean media depicted the Clinton visit as a major victory, asserting that the United States had demonstrated a respectful attitude towards Kim that enabled 'a consensus of views … on resolving issues by way of dialogue'.[20] Though brief, the visit represented long-deferred vindication for Kim Jong-il following the former president's decision to forgo a visit to the DPRK in the final weeks of his presidency. It also bore obvious parallels to the visit of Jimmy Carter in 1994. Like his father, Kim Jong-il had now held a face-to-face meeting with an ex-US president, though the trip did not result in any shifts in US policy.

Renewed initiatives towards Seoul constituted another possible means to reduce the North's political and economic vulnerabilities. Following his inauguration as ROK president in early 2008, Lee Myung-bak had adopted a far more conditional approach to relations with the North. As the ROK began to restrict economic assistance, Pyongyang expressed mounting anger with President Lee. During a November 2008 visit to the Kaesong Industrial Zone, the showpiece of South Korea's engagement strategy with the North, senior military leaders made unambiguous threats to close the zone.[21] In late January 2009, Pyongyang nullified its assent to earlier inter-Korean political-military agreements, placing peninsular stability at increased risk.[22]

In the late summer, Pyongyang briefly curtailed its confrontational stance towards Seoul. In mid-August Kim Jong-il met with Hyun Chong-un, the chairwoman of Hyundai, the South Korean *chaebol* or industrial conglomerate that emerged as the DPRK's primary corporate benefactor in the ROK during the the presidencies of Kim Dae-jung and Roh Moo-hyun. (Hyundai's sunk costs in its investments in the North provided ample reason for Hyun to meet with Kim.) After the meeting, Pyongyang renewed its support for various income-generating activities that it had terminated in late 2008. Weeks later several of Kim's senior political lieutenants travelled to Seoul following the death of former president Kim Dae-jung and met with President Lee. The exchanges with Lee and other South Korean officials seemed devoid of overt hostility. But the overall tenor of North Korea's policies towardss the South remained adversarial, with little evidence of serious interest by the DPRK in closer inter-Korean relations and with no prospect for a heightened income stream from Seoul.

The China factor

Enhanced ties with Beijing represented Pyongyang's only realistic option to diminish its economic vulnerabilities and avoid even deeper international isolation. Over the previous decade, China had emerged as Pyongyang's primary economic and energy benefactor. As host and organiser of the Six-Party Talks, China's political investment in the diplomatic process also exceeded that of all other states. Its efforts to convince North Korea to forgo an initial nuclear test (in part by pledges of heightened economic assistance) persisted into the spring of 2006, but ultimately to no avail. Though the first detonation deeply angered Beijing, it treated the test as a one-off event, especially when nuclear diplomacy began to generate results in 2007 and 2008. The DPRK's denigration of the Six-Party Talks and its second nuclear test were thus another overt challenge to Chinese leaders. But Beijing again concluded that a highly coercive approach would reinforce North Korean truculence and potentially trigger even more severe consequences. The succession issue also induced additional Chinese caution. Despite ample frustration with North Korea (bordering on outright alienation among some experts), China sought above all to avoid a larger crisis.

In early 2009 Beijing sought to encourage North Korean restraint and remained unwilling to respond more forcefully to North Korean behaviour.[23] China repeatedly beseeched North Korea to refrain from the missile test, but without success. When China sought to soften the terms of the pending Security Council resolution, Pyongyang reacted with open hostility. To demonstrate its displeasure with the second nuclear test,

Beijing assented to additional Security Council sanctions. It also cancelled or postponed several scheduled visits to the North. Unprecedentedly sharp criticisms of North Korea appeared in Chinese media during the late spring and early summer. Some of these touched on highly sensitive internal issues, including information about the Kim family never before disclosed in Chinese publications.

But to what end? Though a few Chinese officials appeared to encourage alternatives to prevailing policy, the leadership consensus favouring restraint persisted, even as the US and others sought to impose additional costs on Pyongyang.[24] China was the only external power able to communicate regularly with the North, and it did not want to sever this link. Harsh critiques of North Korea continued to appear in Chinese publications, including some oblique criticisms of PRC policy. Some analysts expressed disquiet bordering on alarm over North Korean actions and their potential risks to China. But the essence of Chinese policy remained undisturbed.

China quietly acknowledged the liabilities in continued support of Pyongyang, whose adversarial politics and international isolation bore distinct echoes of Chinese policies and practices from the 1960s. To most Chinese policymakers, the North was a problematic inheritance which it could not readily separate. Some officials still appeared to believe that Pyongyang would ultimately move towards normal relations with the outside world, if not under Kim Jong-il then under a future leader or in a transformed system. Some also remained wary of US strategic intentions, arguing that continued ties with the North would inhibit US pursuit of more expansive strategic goals in Northeast Asia. Yet China faced the reality of an isolated, vulnerable nuclear-armed state still mired in the past: at best a needy and unreliable partner, and at worst a very dangerous neighbour.

The second nuclear test rekindled debates among Chinese analysts that had initially surfaced following the DPRK's first nuclear detonation. In a mid-June article in *Shijie Zhishi* [World Knowledge], a journal published by the Ministry of Foreign Affairs, Zhang Liangui of the Central Party School criticised unnamed Chinese experts from 'academic circles' who failed to grasp that 'developing nuclear weapons and becoming a nuclear state' was an 'unshakeable' DPRK objective. He faulted 'certain functional [government] departments' for ignoring the potential risks posed by North Korea's weapons tests, noting that the DPRK test site less than 100km from the Chinese border. He also disparaged 'the leaders of some countries' for paying high-level visits to the DPRK and extending invitations to Kim Jong-il for return visits. Such thinly veiled criticisms of Chinese foreign policy are extremely rare within the Beijing expert community.[25]

Other experts focused on the implications of Pyongyang's nuclear defiance for US–China relations. Some noted that North Korean strategy continued to inhibit economic development in China's northeastern provinces, which lagged behind the country's far more dynamic coastal regions. To Chinese skeptics, Pyongyang's depictions of dire security threats were attempts to justify its behaviour and longer-term goals, not an objective depiction of strategic realities. But Beijing did not want to foreclose the DPRK's possible return to negotiations or admit that the Six-Party Talks had failed. The more important question for China concerned the implications of North Korea's nuclear behaviour for Chinese regional interests. Beijing concluded that the price tag for assisting the North Korean economy warranted the costs, even given the negative repercussions for China's relations with the United States and the Republic of Korea. Economic and infrastructural links to the DPRK were also expected to indirectly facilitate the development of China's northeastern provinces.

In subsequent months, prominent Chinese analysts continued to revisit arguments that had first surfaced following the breakdown of the Agreed Framework. The July issue of *Xiandai Guoji Guanxi* [Contemporary International Relations] featured two major articles advocating divergent strategies. One assessment, co-authored by Wang Zaibang and Li Jun of the China Institutes of Contemporary International Relations, lamented North Korea's 'unprecedented diplomatic and strategic isolation'. The authors characterised North Korea's nuclear-weapons development as a means to compensate for its weakness. Since the US was the far superior power, Wang and Li urged Washington to reassure Pyongyang and offer inducements for the DPRK to return to negotiations. But the analysts faulted China for its own lack of initiative and insufficient attentiveness to the risks of a larger crisis: 'Chinese diplomacy must strengthen its awareness of peril, and resolutely avoid passive observation, getting nothing done … A big country that deals in passive and impotent fashion with hot and difficult issues on its periphery is not qualified to become a responsible world power.' The authors also objected to North Korea's 'unscrupulous' behaviour, stating that China 'cannot support in an unprincipled way the DPRK moves in stubbornly following its own course and heightening regional tension'.[26]

In a companion article, Zhu Feng of Peking University characterised North Korean actions in starkly negative terms.[27] Zhu argued that without imposing added costs on North Korea for its nuclear defiance, Pyongyang's behaviour would not change. In his view, North Korean actions were designed 'to completely subvert the existing mechanism for diplomatic resolution of the DPRK nuclear issue … the second nuclear test was not Kim Jong-il's "compromise" with the DPRK army, but was dictated by the need for the current DPRK system's survival.' Zhu faulted the 'consensus driven' approach at the

Six-Party Talks, arguing that multilateral diplomacy required a more credible enforcement mechanism. Implicitly criticising Chinese policy, Zhu asked: 'Today when the DPRK ... [seeks to] brutally impose its nuclear power status on the international community, should the Six-Party Talks build up an enforcement mechanism for unanimous cooperation, or should it sit idly by while the DPRK keeps possession of nuclear weapons for a long time to come?' Zhu characterised North Korean nuclear capabilities as an 'unchangeable reality' necessitating consideration of more coercive steps (though not the use of force) to advance a longer-term solution.

After the chill in bilateral relations that followed the test, Chinese policymakers renewed and enhanced ties with North Korea. In September 2009, senior foreign policy trouble shooter Dai Bingguo again travelled to Pyongyang and met with Kim Jong-il. Dai was soon followed by prime minister Wen Jiabao, the highest level Chinese visitor to the DPRK since before the first nuclear test. Kim Jong-il made the rare gesture of personally welcoming the Prime Minister at the airport. Wen's delegation included numerous senior Chinese officials, many with economic portfolios. China was attempting yet again to redefine its relationship with the DPRK, involving an uneasy balance among multiple Chinese policy goals.[28] Firstly, Beijing had decided to sustain its economic lifeline to Pyongyang. Wen Jiabao signed agreements on infrastructural collaboration, including construction of a new bridge across the Yalu that had been under discussion at least since 2005. Beijing still appeared to believe that it could indirectly promote internal change in the North, without triggering Pyongyang's fears of Chinese economic or political domination. The accords also solidified China's dominant position with various state-run trading companies that oversaw large-scale project activity in the North.[29]

Secondly, China sought to limit its long-standing, if largely dormant, security obligations to the DPRK. Bilateral ties were now described as 'friendly cooperative relations', not a military alliance. As a Chinese military researcher observed, the bilateral relationship entailed 'relations of friendship, cooperation, and mutual assistance', but 'there is no permanent body like a joint headquarters between China and the DPRK, nor is there any joint combat plan, and still less are [there] joint military exercises'.[30] Thirdly, Beijing reiterated that it would not accept the legitimacy or permanence of a North Korean nuclear-weapons capability. It still sought to induce Pyongyang's return to nuclear diplomacy, hoping to elicit sufficient gestures from Kim to convince Washington to renew high-level contact with Pyongyang.

There was an obvious imbalance among the three policy goals. Heightened economic and technical cooperation prompted immediate questions about China's readiness to enforce UN sanctions. Security Council Resolution 1874 had called upon all member states 'not to enter into new commitments for grants, financial assistance or concessional loans to [the DPRK] ... except for humanitarian and developmental purposes directly addressing civilian needs.' The sanctions were targeted against 'nuclear-related or ballistic missile-related or other WMD-related programmes or activities'.[31] China insisted that its actions were fully congruent with the resolution, but Wen Jiabao sounded unusually defensive following his return to Beijing. The prime minister declared that China's economic assistance was

> *mainly* used for developing the DPRK's economy and improving the people's livelihood. *This is line with the spirit of the resolutions of the UN Security Council.* All the efforts made by the Chinese side are to promote

the Six-Party Talks process, promote the realisation of the denuclearisation of the Korean Peninsula, and to help maintain lasting peace and stability in Northeast Asia.[32]

China's incentive-oriented strategy and America's constraint-based strategy highlighted the continued fault lines between Washington and Beijing. The dominant US policy objective was to limit North Korea's room for manoeuvre, constrain its options, and confront Pyongyang with an unambiguous strategic choice. The Obama administration also sought to broaden and deepen policy coordination among those directly affected by North Korean nuclear-weapons development. Enhanced Chinese economic assistance to the DPRK and a stronger political relationship between Beijing and Pyongyang undermined these goals, but China attached a higher priority to stabilising its immediate regional security environment than it did to pressuring the North. Beneath a veneer of cautious optimism, however, Wen conceded the tentativeness of any understandings with the North. Indeed, only a week before Wen's visit a DPRK Foreign Ministry spokesperson declared that dismantlement of the North's nuclear capabilities was 'unthinkable ... it is [also] unimaginable to expect the DPRK to return to the NPT as a non-nuclear state'.[33]

Beijing's emphasis on economic collaboration with Pyongyang continued after Wen's trip. This included visits by senior officials to both states, initial construction work on several hydroelectric dams along the Yalu, and increased Chinese investment in North Korea, including agreement on a ten-year lease on port facilities in Rajin, near locations that Kim Jong-il had visited for the first time in December.[34] Kim also endorsed the activities of a new State Development Bank that would oversee financing for various infrastructural projects. But the outright failure of the North's previous efforts to secure Chinese investment lent substantial uncertainty to Pyongyang's hopes for major economic assistance. When Kim Jong-il made a long-anticipated trip to China in May 2010, he tabled requests for additional economic aid.[35] But he offered tepid, equivocal support for the September 2005 denuclearisation accords, and there were no announcements of additional Chinese economic aid.[36]

Hu Jintao and other senior Chinese leaders extended every possible courtesy to Kim during his visit, including a turnout of the entire membership of the Politburo Standing Committee. Hu also put forward proposals for heightened contact between the two leaderships (including 'sending special envoys and messages'); reinforcing 'strategic coordination'; deepening collaboration on economics and trade; increasing personnel exchanges; and strengthening 'coordination in international and regional affairs'.[37] All had been conspicuously absent throughout the nuclear impasse, and were a continuing source of frustration to Chinese officials. Hu was again offering the DPRK meaningful political and economic support without explicitly insisting on changes in Pyongyang's nuclear stance. Though Kim presumably recognised the need to accede to China's minimal expectations, his commitment to return to nuclear talks was at best very hedged. Beijing had long claimed that North Korea's nuclear weapons were wholly unacceptable to China. Even though China elicited a grudging reference by Pyongyang to the Six-Party Talks (words that Kim reiterated during a second visit to China in August), the North's nuclear activities persisted without interruption, culminating with its November 2010 disclosure of its new uranium-enrichment facility at Yongbyon. Despite this added affront to Beijing, Chinese officials were powerless to prevent the building of the enrichment facility, and let its existence pass without notice.

Nor did China display any readiness to reassess its heightened engagement with Pyongyang.

The strategic outlier

The DPRK's second nuclear test further undermined years of effort to cap and reverse the North's nuclear-weapons development. Pyongyang continued to press for a peace treaty with Washington and the lifting of sanctions but without any commitment to halt its nuclear-weapons activities.[38] This stance was demonstrably unacceptable to the United States. As stated by US Secretary of State Hillary Clinton, 'Current sanctions will not be relaxed until Pyongyang takes verifiable, irreversible steps towards complete denuclearisation. Its leaders should be under no illusion that the United States will ever have normal, sanctions-free relations with a nuclear-armed North Korea.'[39]

Despite US warnings, the DPRK remained unwavering in its claim to status as a nuclear-weapons state. In the 2010 annual joint New Year's Day editorial in Pyongyang's major newspapers, North Korea reverted to language characteristic of earlier rounds of diplomacy: 'The fundamental problem in guaranteeing the peace and stability of the Korean peninsula and the region today is putting an end to the hostile relationship between the DPRK and the United States. Our position to provide a solid peace regime on the Korean peninsula and realise denuclearisation through dialogue and negotiations remains consistent.'[40] But North Korea was attempting to pocket its nuclear advances, while also trying to evade any consequences for walking away from its prior denuclearisation pledges.

Three principal factors were central to North Korea's nuclear future: the system's economic and industrial viability; its success in circumventing the sanctions that were designed to limit its weapons programmes; and the strategic value that the leadership attached to additional weapons development. The longer the DPRK retained its nuclear capabilities and advanced its weapons potential, the less likely it would be to see the need to forgo its programmes. Pyongyang's November 2010 disclosure of a uranium-enrichment facility reinforced this conclusion. A US non-governmental group the visiting the North observed an 'astonishingly modern' control room unlike any of the degraded facilities at Yongbyon. The members of the group were unable to verify North Korean claims that low-enriched fuel was already in production, but to nuclear scientist Siegfried Hecker the existence of a modern industrial operation involving as many as 2,000 second-generation centrifuges was 'stunning'.[41] It suggested technology acquisition on a major scale, indicating that North Korea had possibly found ways to circumvent at least some of the sanctions that the Security Council had imposed following the nuclear test. But it is possible that this R&D accomplishment largely antedated the second nuclear test; North Korea may have decided to relocate the facility only when the leadership deemed the timing propitious. Moreover, there was a strong likelihood that additional enrichment facilities existed in as yet undisclosed locations, underscoring the daunting impediments to comprehensive verification.

The Obama administration continued to argue that the North's retention of nuclear weapons would deny Pyongyang the potential benefits of fuller relations with the outside world. But Washington's message continued to fall on deaf ears in Pyongyang. With the singular exception of China, various neighbouring countries and the United States were engaged in deliberations and consultations *about* North Korea, not negotiations *with* North Korea. For its part, the DPRK was unprepared to conceptualise a strategic future without continued possession of nuclear weapons. China's willingness to strengthen bilateral relations with Pyongyang gave the DPRK little reason to act otherwise. But its nuclear aspirations reflected the isolation and vulnerability of the North Korean system. Authoritative statements described the DPRK's longer-term objective as 'the magnificent goal of opening up the gate to a powerful state in 2012', coinciding with the centenary of the birth of Kim Il-sung and the prospective date for the formal designation of Kim Jong-un as Kim Jong-il's successor.[42] However, 'opening up the gate' was more a slogan than a policy, and did not reflect the system's actual economic and political circumstances.

In December 2009, Kim Jong-il visited a North Korean steel mill, hailing the complex's purported technological break-throughs as 'a victory greater than [a] third successful nuclear test'.[43] Kim seemed to hint obliquely that the DPRK now possessed a proven design for a nuclear weapon, implicitly making it invulnerable to external coercion. Kim's visit to the steel mill also marked the beginning of a major campaign for economic advancement coinciding with the conclusion of the 'speed battles' of 2009. The New Year's Day editorial argued that the DPRK needed to focus on improving the living standards of its citizens. The editorial asserted that the country ('already a politico-ideological and military power') had to aspire to 'the status of an economic giant'.[44] An article in *Rodong Sinmun* cited an admission from Kim Jong-il: 'In the past, the leader [Kim Il-sung] always said he wished to feed our people with rice and meat soup, clothe them in silk, and let them live in tile-roofed houses. But we haven't yet fulfilled his wishes. I will do everything to let our people live a content life by improving their lives in the shortest period possible.'[45] These sentiments implicitly conceded profound systemic failure. But it seemed increasingly doubtful that the leadership would diverge from its bedrock convictions about strategic autonomy. North Korea continued to insist that it possessed 'independent guts ... on which no pressure or threat of any kind works', and that its people envied no one.[46]

Moreover, North Korea's nuclear weapons *did* exist, and (despite the shuttering of the gas-graphite reactor) the apparent completion of a centrifuge facility demonstrated longer-term potential for additional weapons development. US opposition to the DPRK's nuclear activities was unwavering. According to the April 2010 US Nuclear Posture Review, countries in default of their non-proliferation obligations would remain an exception to the announced shifts in American nuclear-weapons policy. In the US view, this necessitated 'maintaining a credible nuclear deterrent and reinforcing regional security architectures with missile defenses and other conventional military capabilities, [thereby] ... reassur[ing] our non-nuclear allies and partners ... of our security commitments to them and [to] confirm that they do not need nuclear weapons capabilities of their own'. These pledges were explicitly linked to 'reversing the nuclear ambitions of North Korea and Iran' and 'impeding illicit nuclear trade'.[47] But the North's durability and resilience was undeniable; the system could not be wished away. US officials spoke repeatedly of the need for 'strategic patience'. Washington continued to emphasise the opportunities for the DPRK if it displayed meaningful interest in denuclearisation, while reinforcing US security goals as long as it did not. By implication, a solution would require the emergence of leaders in the North who did not see the system's fundamental identity tied to retention of nuclear weapons. Under Kim Jong-il, this prospect was not imaginable.

Shortly after release of the US Nuclear Posture Review in April 2010, the DPRK Ministry of Foreign Affairs issued a detailed rebuttal of US policy. The conclusions were unequivocal:

As long as the United States' nuclear threat continues, we will, in the future, increase and modernize various types of nuclear weapons for deterrence as much as is deemed necessary. We have sufficient capability to do so. The United States is giving us the reason and justification to do as such.[48]

A separate assessment in a pro-DPRK newspaper published in Tokyo, which often prefigures official policy statements, raised the possibility of a 'third round' in the 'nuclear standoff' with the United States. It said that the DPRK would continue to 'build its economy on its own while maintaining its existing line of strengthening the nuclear deterrent', which it would do by developing uranium-enrichment technology. The article also noted that the United States 'may again take issue ... if the DPRK comes to have uranium enrichment technology ... [which] can be used as raw material for nuclear weapons'.[49]

An April 2010 DPRK policy memorandum revisited Pyongyang's past declaratory policy statements, covering its withdrawal from the NPT and the decision to undertake two nuclear tests. Asserting that 'nuclear threat is by no means an abstract concept [for North Korea] but a realistic and concrete experience', the document concluded that 'the unique position on the Korean peninsula ... required a special measure for a solution. The only and last option was to counter nuclear weapons with nuclear weapons.' The document continued:

The mission of the nuclear forces of the DPRK is to deter and repel aggression and attack against the country and the nation *until the denuclearisation of the Korean peninsula and the world is realised* ... We are ready to join the international efforts for nuclear non-proliferation and for the safe management of nuclear materials *on an equal footing with other nuclear weapons states.*

We will produce as many nuclear weapons as we need but will ... [not] produce more nuclear weapons than is necessary, and we will join the international efforts for nuclear disarmament on an equal footing with other nuclear weapons states.[50]

North Korea was pursuing its own version of strategic patience, insisting that 'the DPRK ... has [the] legitimate right to steadily bolster up its nuclear deterrent as much as it deems necessary'.[51] With this seemingly intractable evaluation of its status in mind, there is a need to consider longer-term possibilities and prospective steps to mitigate the risks and uncertainties posed by the DPRK's open-ended pursuit of nuclear weapons.

No exit?

For six decades, nuclear weapons have been deeply enmeshed in politics and security on the Korean peninsula. This book has tried to explain the why and how of this history, but the past does not tell us when or how the nuclear saga will end. It is also impossible to know the ultimate consequences of the North's nuclear capabilities and its accumulation of nuclear technology, knowhow and fissile material. The repeated diplomatic failures of the past two decades reveal the formidable impediments to definitive denuclearisation. North Korea's leadership shows no inclination to make realisation of this goal easy for the US or anyone else. The DPRK has detonated two nuclear explosions; it has sufficient fissile material to undertake additional tests; and it now possesses an incipient capability to enrich uranium. It has yet to demonstrate the capacity to deliver a nuclear weapon by missile or aircraft, though its development efforts persist. The DPRK is not a fully arrived nuclear power, and the United States and all of North Korea's neighbours want to prevent it from becoming one. The question is, how?

The outside world knows little about how the DPRK conceptualises its ultimate nuclear goals. If the North's objective is to develop a fully operational capability, as distinct from a symbolic or political deterrent, it confronts daunting industrial and technological impediments in achieving it.[1] But the North Korean leadership insists that it will pursue its own strategic path, not one postulated by others. There are sobering lessons from its nuclear history. A small, isolated, inward-looking regime confronting prodigious technical and industrial obstacles has successfully defied the world's most powerful states and sustained pursuit of nuclear weapons, first covertly inside the NPT and overtly following its withdrawal from the treaty. Pyongyang's nuclear breakout matters most in Northeast Asia, but the possibilities and troubling precedents extend well beyond the region.

The North Korean nuclear issue is also a misnomer. It is the history of North Korea and of Kim Il-sung, who built a system premised on exclusivity and adversarial nationalism and dominated it for nearly a half century; the leaders and institutions loyal to him; and of Kim Jong-il, who inherited power and has sustained the system following his father's death. Regardless of the precise number of North Korean nuclear weapons, their technical characteristics, or the size of the country's fissile-material inventory, the DPRK's nuclear capabilities are part of the legacy that Kim Jong-il plans to bequeath to his son, much as his father mandated the building of a nuclear infrastructure that he then passed to Kim Jong-il.

The DPRK long claimed that it pursued nuclear power for peaceful purposes, but this rationale became increasingly suspect as the weapons programme developed over the past two decades. The link between the North's extant nuclear facilities and its capacity to generate electricity is exceedingly tenuous. In the estimate of Siegfried Hecker and several colleagues at Stanford University, the Yongbyon reactor's total production of electricity during nearly 25 years of intermittent operations was equal to approximately 23 days' output of one modern light-water reactor.[2] Kim Il-sung first broached nuclear energy development with Soviet leaders in the mid-1950s, and (despite the training of large numbers of nuclear scientists and engineers and the priority devoted to the building of a nuclear infrastructure) this goal remains wholly unrealised more than a half century later. Lesser, non-nuclear ambitions could have long ago provided the DPRK with energy essential to its economic development, but Kim Il-sung and Kim Jong-il made very different choices.

At present, the DPRK has undertaken construction of an indigenously designed experimental light-water reactor at Yongbyon, claiming that it will be completed by 2012. However, the DPRK has no prior experience with designing and building a LWR, so the prospects for success remain very uncertain.[3] Regardless of whether North Korea is able to complete the reactor, it provides a justification for the production of low-enriched uranium. Completion of an industrial-scale centrifuge facility enlarges the North's future strategic possibilities, including the prospect of a new means of fissile-material production for weapons development. Even if North Korea defers pursuit of an HEU capability in the near term, it now has the potential for such a programme. Without an operational LWR, the only conceivable purposes for an enrichment facility would be for additional nuclear-weapons development, export of enriched uranium, or the threat to do one or both. All are highly disturbing possibilities.

The basic facts of North Korea's nuclear history are beyond dispute. A heavily armed, highly secretive regime minimally accountable to the outside world is now a de facto nuclear-weapons state. Other than South Africa, no country that undertook a covert nuclear programme and then tested a weapon has ever relinquished its nuclear capabilities, and South Africa's decision was directly linked to the end of apartheid and the cessation of white minority rule.[4] Barring major internal change in the North, Pyongyang seems almost certain to retain nuclear weapons for the indefinite future, and an enrichment capability will enable the DPRK to enhance and diversify its weapons options. Compared to other recent nuclear entrants, North Korea's nuclear capabilities still remain relatively modest. But the DPRK is located in the heart of Northeast Asia, a pivotal region in global economics and politics, and the North's strategic reach extends to all neighbouring states. It has long-standing political, technological and military ties to states with highly problematic nuclear histories, raising disturbing questions about the possible spread of weapons technology and nuclear knowhow.[5] With the exception of China, no major power has meaningful ties to senior leaders in Pyongyang, and China's influence and access is more limited than many assume.

The longer-term prospects for the North Korean system also remain very uncertain. Its economic freefall may have abated at the end of the 1990s, but the possibilities for meaningful recovery and renewed growth are still very doubtful. The DPRK's stunning deindustrialisation in the 1990s convinced many strategic analysts that the system was living on borrowed time. This expectation proved erroneous. Acute deprivation and major internal stress did not trigger the collapse of the political system or the end of its advanced weapons programmes. If anything, the relative influence of those advocating weapons development increased under conditions of isolation and severe economic vulnerability.

These observations have important policy implications. Kim Jong-il seeks to ensure political support for Kim Chong-un, his youngest son and designated heir, who officially assumed senior leadership positions (including his designation as a four-star general) in September 2010.[6] Kim Jong-il has entrusted his son's (and the system's) long-term fortunes to a small circle of family members, political loyalists, and the political, military and security elites and the organisations they oversee. Kim Chong-un's temperament and abilities remain wholly unknown and untested. Even assuming a relatively seamless transition from father to son and regardless of the younger Kim's personal disposition and political skills, he will be enmeshed in a system whose policies and practices have deepened and calcified across the decades.

The North Korean system is nevertheless very different from the one that Kim Jong-il inherited from his father. As Alexandre Mansourov puts it:

> The overwhelming process of late modernization [in recent years] began to change the substance of North Korean politics, create new social and political divisions in North Korean society, expand the policy issue areas, and propel new social forces, corporate concerns, and interest groups into the policy-making arena ... the [DPRK] ... is neither a monolith nor a 'black box.' It is a semi-privatised amorphous collection of rivaling immobile organizations and stove-piped bureaucracies that often act at cross purposes and are pressed hard and corrupted by the individual and group interests of competing clans, social and political forces vying for power, prestige and wealth.[7]

Is the existing system sustainable? Will the younger Kim reassess the regime's exceptionalist claims or will he reaffirm the nuclear programme's centrality in North Korean strategy? Will Kim Chong-un even be the genuine leader of the DPRK?

How do external powers leave open the possibility of future change in North Korea without validating the DPRK's claims to nuclear standing? If there is no exit from prevailing circumstances, external powers will have to consider the possible consequences and assess how to mitigate the dangers and risks. Answers must be sought at four levels: North Korea's internal evolution; and how South Korea, China and the United States conceptualise their respective long-term relations with Pyongyang. Japan and Russia could also play important roles in North Korea's future, but their involvement and influence on the peninsula is likely to prove much less decisive.

North Korea's future

Any assessment of the nuclear issue must begin with the future of North Korea itself. System preservation remains North Korea's defining imperative. Kim Jong-il views nuclear weapons as essential to holding a hostile world at bay. But could economic imperatives or external pressure compel a shift in strategy? Alternatively, has North Korea already absorbed most of the sunk costs of the nuclear programme, and do its leaders see the presumed value of nuclear weapons (in conjunction with China's enhanced political and economic support) outweighing the uncertainties and potential risks that they believe denuclearisation might pose to the system?

Some observers argue that economic opportunities and the requirements for closer links with the outside world will dictate the ultimate rollback of the DPRK's weapons capabilities.[8] This supposition has yet to be borne out. After briefly weighing a more permissive economic strategy in the early 2000s, North Korea reverted to a more self-protective stance.[9] Kim Jong-il decided that appreciable movement away from a centrally controlled (and military dominated) economy would undermine the regime. Kim also appears to have concluded that a

larger external economic presence (especially of the major capitalist economies) would be a direct threat to central control.
This made internal change (except on terms sanctioned by the
regime) impermissible.[10] But modern communications could
place the stability of the extant system at increased risk, should
elite loyalties attenuate, information disseminate within the
system, and popular disaffection mount.[11]

North Korea's leaders seek to deny information to all
but politically loyal core elites and to keep most trade and
investment within highly circumscribed channels. However,
significant portions of the citizenry operate outside the state-
managed economy, and the leadership has been unable to
prevent these activities.[12] The confiscation of private financial
resources in late 2009 momentarily curtailed 'marketisation
from below', triggering major public protests that compelled
a partial rollback of the original decision, an event without
precedent in North Korean history. But disaffection or outright
alienation does not automatically translate into 'exit' or 'voice'
within the system.[13] There are now approximately 20,000 North
Korean defectors residing in the ROK, but only a small portion
(estimated at 2–3%) are from privileged elite backgrounds.
The economic circumstances and opportunities of the moment
represent the primary factors influencing defection decisions.[14]

Military and security organisations remain the dominant
institutions within the North Korean system. Though some
policymakers in the DPRK appear to advocate increased
economic flexibility, their power base and influence remain
highly circumscribed. The Korean People's Army enjoys a
highly privileged position; it also benefits from the technological and financial resources procured beyond North Korea's
borders by various enterprises and trading companies. Despite
pronouncements urging industrial rejuvenation and increased
production of food and consumer goods, these appeals have

generated very modest results. Younger, more educated North Koreans may entertain growing doubts about the efficacy of the system and its prevailing strategies, but their ability to pursue alternative paths remains very limited. There is little evidence of overt alienation among elite groups, even if it almost certainly exists.

The DPRK's nuclear programme also reflects the enduring struggle between highly divergent visions of Korean national identity. The rivalry between North and South has repeatedly embroiled the major powers in peninsular affairs. The DPRK believes that nuclear capabilities provide it with substantial political, military and psychological advantage over the ROK as well as protection from external pressure, especially from the major powers. But nuclear weapons are more a symptom than a cause of these open-ended strategic antagonisms. The leadership has inculcated and upheld an exclusivist stance throughout its history. Without such beliefs and practices and the claims of the Kim dynasty to god-like authority, on what basis could the regime sustain its claims to absolute power?

More than 60 years since the founding of the DPRK, the country has been unable to escape its past; nor indeed, is there any indication that Kim Jong-il wants it to. Defying or deflecting the preferences of partners and adversaries alike, the DPRK has persevered in the face of circumstances that many observers long ago assumed would presage a major internal evolution or the system's outright demise. But neither outcome has transpired. At the same time, despite pursuit of nearly every imaginable approach to denuclearisation by the US and others, this goal is now farther from realisation than at any point since the signing of the Agreed Framework.

The leadership has put forward an idealised vision of North Korea's future, asserting that it will 'open the gate' to major economic change in 2012, coinciding with the centenary of Kim Il-sung's birth. The DPRK contends that it is already a full fledged ideological and military power; it only needs to emerge as a 'full economic power' to complete its transition.[15] Economic rejuvenation has been a recurrent theme in North Korean policy and propaganda, and with little to show for it. The modest encouragement of market-oriented policies evident in the early 2000s could reemerge, but past history should caution against undue expectations. Moreover, despite the prodigious costs associated with nuclear-weapons development, North Korea argues that the nuclear programme will enable strategic autonomy and economic development free from external pressure.

The DPRK also seeks legitimation by the major powers, in particular by the United States. There is a continuing paradox in Pyongyang's views of American power. The DPRK regularly condemns the US role on the peninsula and repeatedly accuses America of pursuing a 'hostile policy'. Though the leadership claims that a relationship with the US now matters less to the DPRK, Pyongyang still seeks American affirmation and acceptance. US standing as a global power and the enduring US relationship with the ROK ensure that the United States will remain central to North Korean strategic calculations.

North Korea asserts that it cannot envision relations with the US without American acceptance of its status as a nuclear-weapons state and the attenuation or outright cessation of America's alliances with Seoul and Tokyo. Both stipulations are inherently unacceptable to the United States. The US has repeatedly made clear that it will not countenance a normal relationship with North Korea without Pyongyang forgoing its weapons capabilities and without North Korea pursuing normal relations with the ROK and also with Japan. But the DPRK is not prepared to take steps sought by Seoul and Tokyo, or by Washington. As a consequence, there is stalemate.

Could North Korea ultimately emerge as a normal or quasi-normal state without nuclear weapons, and if so, how? Analysts have long conceptualised dichotomous possibilities, depicted either as a 'soft landing' (that is, an evolution of the system toward development-oriented policies and deeper ties with the outside world) or as a 'hard landing' (that is, the end, presumably quite abrupt and potentially quite violent) of the extant system.[16] A related scenario posits an acute humanitarian crisis that could trigger external involvement to contain an internal meltdown.[17] The leadership, however, posits a 'no landing' scenario – that is, the perpetuation of the existing system based on the unquestioned power and authority of the Kim family and of the ruling elites that support it, retention of its nuclear weapons capabilities, and a measure of economic recovery.[18]

These alternative characterisations of the North Korean future – evolution, extinction, instability or stasis – are not an academic exercise. Of the four possibilities, a genuine crisis or strategic instability seems avoidable only under the first scenario. The adaptability of the North Korean system (and the readiness of its leadership to conciliate with its neighbours and the United States) on terms acceptable to the outside world remain very questionable. Except for fleeting periods, North Korea has been unwilling to depart from the siege mentality that the leadership has long employed to legitimate its claims to absolute authority, and to legitimate the possession of nuclear weapons. Neither the imposition of added costs nor the prospective inducements of denuclearisation has resulted in long-term policy change.

The US counsels a policy of 'strategic patience', in the hope that a future leadership will ultimately recognise the necessity of nuclear abandonment. This would require leaders in the North to forgo possession of nuclear weapons and the means to produce additional fissile material, presumably in exchange for explicit commitments from the United States and others to peaceful coexistence with the North as well as explicit security assurances and sustained economic assistance. The United States and others have pursued variations of this outcome for close to two decades without lasting success. All powers with a major stake in the peninsula's future would prefer incremental change in the North – that is, change without major violence or a severe regional crisis. But an incremental transition without irrevocable steps towards denuclearisation is not acceptable to the United States.

Underneath the DPRK's rigid veneer, some long-time observers perceive a far more adaptable system.[19] Stephen Linton, whose on-the-ground experience in the North (primarily in provision of medical and humanitarian aid) almost certainly exceeds that of all other US citizens, contends that the DPRK is riven with internal fault lines that often inhibit major decisions. In his view, however, no state (especially one experiencing acute economic decline) can persist for more than six decades without functioning institutions and the capacity to adjudicate policy conflicts. Linton argues that understanding these internal cleavages requires sustained interaction and negotiation inside the system, and a willingness of outsiders to interject themselves in situations that North Koreans at times find overly messy or too dangerous to address. At the same time, powerful bureaucracies in the North must be convinced that the intent of foreign interlocutors is neither harmful nor deceitful.

Cultural forces will also continue to shape the system's future. Ethnicity and race constitute an enduring source of strength in both Koreas.[20] The DPRK views American power in all its forms as corrosive, threatening and almost inherently destabilising and Pyongyang's volatile experiences with democratic polities reinforce this judgement. Moreover, North

Korean officials responsible for negotiations with external powers must do more than uphold the regime's declared interests: their own careers and familial well being are also at stake in this most unforgiving of systems.

The nuclear issue thus seems sui generis. The Obama administration is not seeking another highly finessed diplomatic agreement or a placeholder for a longer-term breakthrough. Pyongyang has breached the nuclear threshold and insists there is no turning back. It repeatedly asserts that nuclear weapons – the forbidden fruit of global politics for non-nuclear states – enable it to punch above its weight. For added measure, the DPRK claims that the US–ROK and US–Japan security alliances and US extended deterrence guarantees confer quasi-nuclear status on Seoul and Tokyo, thus legitimating its own pursuit of nuclear weapons.

The DPRK also retains enduring memories of the Korean War; the past deployment of US nuclear weapons on the peninsula; periodic American consideration of highly coercive military actions; and the retention of nuclear planning options in US strategy. North Korean officials assert that the past is still the present, warranting continued war preparations and augmentation of the DPRK's nuclear capabilities. However, successive generations of US military planners have concluded that the use of force on the peninsula is imaginable only if North Korean actions give the United States no other choice. The DPRK may therefore be the only potential US adversary to achieve *conventional* deterrence of the United States.[21] The absence of major hostilities on the peninsula since the signing of the Korean armistice – even in the face of extreme North Korean provocations – attests to this fact. However, deep insecurity pervades the North Korean system. Warnings of imminent attack (including nuclear attack) seem almost ritualised, though it is impossible to judge whether the populace is largely inured to these characterisations. The repeated invocation of such threats reveals much about the exercise of power in North Korea. If different voices begin to be heard, the DPRK might well be on the cusp of major change, but that day has yet to arrive.

South Korea's strategic choices

The ROK has long confronted a deeply antagonistic rival in the North. The stark ideological and military divisions between the two Koreas during the Cold War made meaningful relations almost unimaginable. Despite being linked by a shared geography and a common cultural and linguistic identity, Seoul and Pyongyang inhabited separate worlds, sustained by their respective major-power benefactors.

As the ROK's development and international standing accelerated and as the DPRK experienced atrophy and decline, South Korea's political and diplomatic horizons shifted appreciably. Seoul's breakthroughs with Moscow and Beijing sharply altered the strategic geography of the peninsula, though relations between North and South remained largely frozen. Profound shifts in the balance of power between North and South and major realignments in ROK domestic politics injected new factors in inter-Korean relations. All South Korean presidents since the late 1980s have sought to devise preferred strategies toward the North. Their choices have reflected the political goals of individual leaders and their assessments of North Korea's strengths and weaknesses. These have clustered around three broad strategies: treating Pyongyang as a primary adversary; pursuing peaceful coexistence with North Korea; or extending a political and economic lifeline and safety net to the DPRK.

The largest shifts in ROK strategy occurred under Kim Dae-jung and Roh Moo-hyun.[22] Both leaders believed that political validation and economic compensation of the DPRK would facilitate a longer-term peninsular transition. Kim and Roh held summit meetings with Kim Jong-il (in June 2000 and October 2007 respectively), resulting in joint policy documents intended to govern inter-Korean relations in the longer term. Though the declarations were largely aspirational, they implied the readiness of Kim Dae-jung and Roh Moo-hyun to pursue integration of North and South without particular regard for the DPRK's pursuit of nuclear weapons. Both oversold the results of their meetings and agreements with Kim Jong-il, and dreams of unification leapfrogged the logic of coexistence.

Pyongyang had obvious incentives to collaborate with Seoul under these conditions. The 'sunshine policy' and the 'policy of peace and prosperity' were highly validating to Kim Jong-il, and the DPRK gave little and received much in return. The accommodation with the ROK was also a political breakthrough that Kim Il-sung never achieved, though the scheduled visit of Kim Yong-sam at the time of the elder Kim's death might have afforded an earlier opportunity. During the Kim and Roh presidencies, North Korea for the first time enjoyed meaningful entrée into South Korean politics. It was also able to evoke sympathy and proffer a shared concept of Korean identity that appealed to broad swathes of ROK public opinion, eroding US-ROK alliance ties in the process. Public perceptions of the North Korean military threat diminished under both presidents. Even as Pyongyang heightened its nuclear-weapons efforts, the North did not pay a major price in inter-Korean relations.

The sunshine policy also resulted in major South Korean economic assistance to the DPRK. The ROK's economic support was crucial to stemming the freefall in the North Korean economy. However, the subsequent revelation that Kim Dae-jung had provided $500 million through corporate channels to secure the visit to Pyongyang tainted his presidency.[23] For close to a decade, Pyongyang continued to receive substantial economic assistance from Kim Dae-jung and Roh Moo-hyun. The cumulative aid from ROK governmental and private sources between 1995 and 2006 has been estimated at 6.6 trillion won ($6.5bn).[24] For an economy of North Korea's size and in view of its acute vulnerabilities, these represented massive subsidies, with minimal accountability for how these resources were spent.

The engagement policies and national-security strategies of Kim Dae-jung and Roh Moo-hyun also created lasting fissures in South Korean internal politics. In decided contrast to the policies of his predecessors, Lee Myung-bak rejected unconditional reconciliation with the North, insisting that Pyongyang had to first demonstrate an unequivocal commitment to denuclearisation. Lee perceived few incentives and substantial liabilities in sustaining the North Korean system without tangible political returns. In the absence of policy change in the North, he was not prepared to continue the policies of his predecessors. In the early months of the Lee Myung-bak administration, Pyongyang deferred judgement on the new ROK president, but the DPRK subsequently launched extreme personal and political criticisms of the South Korean leader. With fleeting interruptions, these attacks have persisted ever since. More ominously, in 2010 the political attacks descended into military attacks.

Following the sinking of the *Cheonan* in March 2010, inter-Korean relations plummeted to their lowest level since the mid-1990s. An investigative report prepared by international experts under ROK auspices concluded that North Korea was responsible for sinking the ship. Seoul and Pyongyang soon halted cooperation in many of the remaining areas of inter-Korean accommodation. These included the interruption of most communications between the two Koreas and the ROK's suspension of many economic ties with North. The conspicuous exception – one that both Koreas seem prepared to retain – is the Kaesong Industrial Zone, which employs approximately 40,000 North Korean workers in South Korean industrial enterprises.[25] For a time, North Korea stated that there would be 'no dialogue or contact' with the South for the remainder of Lee Myung-bak's tenure. South Korean defence policymakers renewed attention to the dangers of military hostilities with the North. Though an improved atmosphere in inter-Korean relations still remains possible, North–South ties have again become predominantly confrontational, a conclusion reinforced by the November 2010 artillery attacks on Yeonpyeong Island.

South Korea has thus resumed a threat-based strategy towards North Korea. This approach could persist for the duration of Lee Myung-bak's time in office, which ends in early 2013. Seoul's political and strategic interests are again aligned closely with those of the United States, enabling much closer policy coordination with Washington and denying Pyongyang the opportunity to drive a wedge between the US and the ROK. The South Korean leadership also expects that its actions will deny the DPRK much needed foreign exchange and constrict its future strategic options. According to data from the Korea Development Institute, Seoul and Beijing account for more than 80% of North Korea's foreign trade and approximately 35% of the North's total GDP.[26] Even if the Kaesong zone continues to operate, the ROK's share of total trade will almost certainly decline during the remainder of Lee Myung-bak's presidency. But such economic strictures have not compelled the DPRK to reassess its strategic priorities, including its commitment to nuclear weapons.

North Korea has long grappled with major trade deficits, estimated at $1bn or more annually out of total foreign trade of $3–$6bn. Throughout the first decade of the twenty-first century North Korean exports have generally remained at approximately half the level of North Korean imports.[27] The DPRK has depended on loans; foreign aid and investment; and cash remittances to compensate for these shortfalls. But heightened Security Council sanctions have imposed limits on some of this assistance, constraining North Korea's economic opportunities.[28] The longer-term relationship between the two Koreas is thus unsettled and potentially very unpredictable. Though the ROK's well-being and viability does not depend on close relations with DPRK, the latent instability in relations with its nuclear-armed neighbour is dangerous and worrisome.

China's strategic choices

China's perceptions of the Korean peninsula and Beijing's primary interests derive from an amalgam of strategic, political, institutional and economic calculations.[29] Though many Chinese officials and experts remain deeply troubled by North Korean behaviour, this disaffection has not produced definitive policy reassessment, even when Pyongyang has openly defied Beijing. Over the past decade, China has helped sustain the North Korean system, and at present is its principal guarantor. China's leaders are playing for time and hope to minimise the potential risks of a larger crisis. But heightened Chinese assistance has not provided Beijing with meaningful influence over North Korean decision-making, especially with respect to nuclear weapons.

Past history also weighs heavily in Chinese strategic assessments. The Korean War had lasting consequences for PRC security.[30] Kim Il-sung's plans to attack across the 38th Parallel unsettled Mao Zedong. Kim was lobbying for Korean unification by means of war before the CCP had achieved full control over the Chinese mainland. Mao deemed Kim's plans militarily ill advised, but (fearing that Stalin would brand him another Tito) Mao ultimately acceded to Stalin's own reluctant consent to Kim's plans. Equally or more important, the American intervention in Korea and Washington's positioning of ships from the 7th Fleet in the Taiwan Strait renewed US embroilment in the Chinese civil war, compelling Beijing to abort plans for a final assault on Taiwan.[31] Sino-American estrangement defined East Asia's strategic geography for two decades, and major reverberations persist to the present day.[32]

China's intervention in the Korean War entailed enormous human and material costs. According to official data, China suffered 114,000 combat deaths; 21,000 died during hospitalisation; 13,000 died from disease; and 29,000 were missing in action, including 21,000 POWs sent to Taiwan; another 380,000 Chinese soldiers were wounded. Approximately 70% of the People's Liberation Army's total manpower (2.97 million soldiers) was deployed on rotational assignments to Korea at various points in the war, and 600,000 civilian personnel also served. China's total expenditure in the war was 6.2bn yuan, including a debt of $1.3bn to the Soviet Union.[33] Mao's eldest son, Mao Anying, was killed in an American air attack in the early weeks of the war; he is buried at the centre of the Chinese martyrs' cemetery 100km from Pyongyang.[34]

Chinese analysts continue to contest the legality of the US intervention in Korea. Yang Xiyu, former head of the Foreign Ministry's Office of Korean Peninsula Affairs, argues that the US intervention under Security Council auspices was 'under the manipulation of the United States' and in violation of the UN Charter. He characterises the US intervention as an 'act of war' and a direct interference into a sovereign state's internal affairs, resulting in a direct threat to China, thus necessitating Beijing's intervention.[35] The hostilities transformed a civil conflict into a US–China war, albeit one fought on Korean soil and one explicitly endorsed by the UN, in as much as Moscow was then boycotting the Security Council and Taipei still occupied the Chinese seat. Yang is not a defender of North Korean actions, least of all Pyongyang's pursuit of nuclear weapons. But he openly challenges US claims to the legitimacy of the UN Command in Korea, which he deems as 'lacking a basis in legal principle'. Under these circumstances, Yang perceives a clear need for a permanent peace regime that would replace the armistice agreement and resolve the 'security contradictions' that have rigidified since the signing of the armistice.[36]

Chinese experts do not challenge DPRK sovereignty or legitimacy. But Beijing's repeated toleration of egregious North Korean behaviour (including two nuclear tests undertaken in overt defiance of Chinese pleas) and its subsequent acquiescence to the sinking of the *Cheonan* and the artillery attacks against Yeongpyeong Island is very troubling. It suggests that the Chinese are unwilling to confront Pyongyang, and that the DPRK is prepared to directly challenge China's repeated calls for regional tranquility and heightened economic development in Northeast Asia. The traumatic events of the latter half of the 1990s, including the spillover consequences of the North Korean famine, when several hundred thousand North Koreans sought food, shelter, and income in northeastern China, were also very unsettling to Beijing. China has since installed fences along much of the border and has appreciably increased its surveillance and military patrols, and Pyongyang has also enhanced its border presence, sharply reducing the number of North Korean escapees.

China's anxieties run much deeper. Chinese experts view the DPRK system as similar to China in the late 1950s and early 1960s: beleaguered, isolated, dominated by the cult of personality, and unable to provide for its own citizens. Shortly after the first North Korean nuclear test, a senior Chinese diplomat noted that North Korean officials sought to defend their country's actions by emphasising the strategic parallels between China in the early 1960s and the DPRK in the early 2000s. Rebutting these claims, this official retorted that 'that was then and now is now'.[37] Few Chinese claim detailed knowledge of the contemporary North Korean system, and some obliquely indicate Beijing's lack of understanding of the DPRK and the North's unpredictability represent abiding Chinese fears. Beijing's attempts to conciliate the DPRK represent a risk minimisation strategy, and with no guarantee of lasting success.

Some Chinese officials also voice continued wariness of US intentions. There have been long-standing suspicions of malign American intent toward the North, especially within military circles and among officials responsible for party-to-party ties. These encompass fears that US actions in response to North Korean military provocations could trigger a larger regional crisis, that the US might move military forces north of the 38th parallel in a conflict, or that following unification, Washington could deploy forces in the northern half of the peninsula in a reconfigured US–ROK alliance. Some Chinese experts argue that sustaining the DPRK while seeking to inhibit its more extreme behaviour will enable Pyongyang to prevent US strategic encroachment and thus indirectly serve Chinese interests. But most Chinese experts recognize that Pyongyang's actions put major Chinese interests at risk, placing US–China relations under severe strain and complicating Beijing's growing ties with the ROK.

Characterisations of the DPRK as a buffer state or strategic asset for China thus miss the mark. Over the past two decades, China has pursued an explicit 'two Koreas' policy, enabling Beijing to pursue separate ties with Seoul and Pyongyang that far exceed those of any other external power with both governments. China asserts that it will pursue relations with

the two Koreas on their respective merits, and that it sees no
need to choose between South and North.[38] Periodic critiques
of US Korea policy (including Beijing's heated opposition to
US military exercises with the ROK following the sinking of
the *Cheonan*) are not an attempt to defend Pyongyang's actions,
but they are an effort to preserve China's options and avoid
an outright breakdown in relations with Pyongyang. Chinese
officials also worry that heightened isolation of the North will
reinforce the DPRK's worst tendencies, thus posing dangers to
regional stability and to vital Chinese interests.

China has no solution for Pyongyang's pursuit of nuclear
weapons. Beijing's calls for a resumption of the Six-Party Talks
no doubt reflect China's political and psychological investment
in this multilateral diplomacy, but this is an argument about
process, not about substance. From Deng Xiaoping to Jiang
Zemin to Hu Jintao, China's leaders have repeatedly urged
North Korea to accommodate with the outside world and to
move towards denuclearisation. But decades of cultivation and
compensation have yielded few lasting results. Chinese leaders
still appear to believe that Pyongyang will ultimately have to
undertake internal change paralleling Beijing's own policy
decisions of the late 1970s. Beijing continues to pursue opportunities in trade, investment and infrastructural development
in the North, viewing these activities as a down payment for a
post-Kim Jong-il internal transition. It also believes that such
actions will advance the economic development of China's
northeastern provinces, where the opportunities for growth
and international outreach have lagged well behind the more
dynamic coastal provinces.[39] Though party and military circles
still voice support for the extant regime in North Korea, the
credibility and force of these arguments have diminished. But
China does see value in maintaining a certain level of support
for the DPRK, less as a continued security guarantee and more

as relatively low cost means to prevent or defer far larger problems.

As noted previously, since the first nuclear test Chinese experts have diverged sharply in their assessments of the DPRK.[40] Many perceive North Korea as a burden and risk, and openly express these views. There is no other area of Chinese foreign policy where such dissent from official policy is so clearly evident. But geographic realities remain paramount in Chinese thinking. As a senior Chinese diplomat has observed, 'our mindset [towards North Korea] has changed, but the length of our border has not'.[41] China continues to avoid a definitive change in its North Korea policy, quite possibly reflecting indecision or debate among senior policymakers. There is also an unspoken fear that a more assertive Chinese strategy will trigger unpredictable reactions by Pyongyang, including higher levels of North Korean risk-taking. This has resulted in Beijing's acquiescence to North Korea's nuclearisation, even if Chinese officials insist that they do not accept the permanence or legitimacy of these capabilities. But China has no more of a solution to the nuclear issue than any other power; it seems prepared to buy time indefinitely. Pyongyang has repeatedly tested the limits of China's forbearance. Should the DPRK's continued nuclear development ultimately prompt a larger reassessment of Chinese policy, the consequences would be far reaching, but that day has yet to arrive.

America's strategic choices

The Obama administration asserts that its fundamental policy objective with the DPRK is 'a definite and comprehensive resolution' of the nuclear issue. How does the United States seek to inhibit and reverse programmes and activities that Pyongyang has pursued for decades, while protecting vital American interests and avoiding a repeat of past negotiating failures?

The United States has not yet deemed North Korean nuclear weapons a direct threat to US national security. But its nuclear and missile programmes remain a prospective threat against which the US continues to prepare, notably with respect to ballistic-missile defence. Independently of a potential explicit threat to US security, the DPRK's pursuit of nuclear weapons involves at least three fundamental American policy concerns. Firstly, the United States has an intrinsic, long-term interest in a durable regional order in Northeast Asia, with or without Korean unification. In the longer run, the US seeks to address the enduring abnormality between the two Koreas and between North Korea and Japan, while also reassuring Beijing of US strategic intentions on the peninsula, simultaneously seeking assurance from China about its longer-term peninsular goals. Nuclear-weapons development in North Korea directly challenges this fundamental US interest. It could also prove an enduring source of contention between the United States and China.

Secondly, the United States has a compelling interest in the integrity of the non-proliferation regime and preventing any transfer of nuclear weapons, technology or materials to states or non-state entities. Washington remains keenly aware of the deeply troubling precedents of North Korean nuclear development for non-proliferation as a whole. Unlike Israel, India and Pakistan, the DPRK was a signatory to the NPT. Pyongyang shredded its non-proliferation commitments, twice conducted nuclear tests, and engaged in highly problematic activities with several prospective nuclear aspirants. Some analysts see parallels to America's accommodation with a nuclear-armed China in the twilight years of the Cultural Revolution, but this analogy does not carry much weight. The strategic imperatives underlying Sino-American rapprochement do not apply to relations with North Korea. The ROK has vastly greater power and longer-term strategic potential than its beleaguered northern neighbour; it is also a vibrant democracy and a close American ally. Perhaps most important, Kim Jong-il seems unable or unwilling to make an enduring commitment to stable long-term relations with any outside power.

Thirdly, despite an abiding American interest in peaceful denuclearisation, the United States must remain prepared for all possible contingencies, requiring continued close security cooperation with the ROK and Japan. American policymakers do not accept the permanence or legitimacy of the North's possession of nuclear weapons. The United States believes that denuclearisation will require a binding, unequivocal diplomatic agreement and specific technical steps that would preclude any possibility of the DPRK resuming its weapons development. Some experts assert that the US should be willing to accept a shelved or recessed capability, akin to what was attempted under the Agreed Framework. One recent study, for example, advocates a gradual or phased approach to denuclearisation, arguing that the US should be ready 'to live with but not accept a de facto nuclear North Korea for some time'.[42] But the Agreed Framework is no longer the operative context for negotiations with the DPRK; the future of the Six-Party Talks is also at best highly problematic. The Obama administration is not prepared to reach major understandings with the DPRK that leave the North's nuclear capabilities intact. In the administration's view, North Korea must undertake steps that make denuclearisation irreversible.

Pyongyang contends that it wishes simply to be left alone, but its adversarial stance towards South Korea and Japan (including periodic threats to use force against both states) and its problematic dealings with Iran, Myanmar and Syria mean that it cannot be left to its own devices. The United States seeks to sharpen the policy choices faced by North Korea. American policy is based less on an expectation of near-term success, and more on the need to limit the risks to the US interests. So construed, the US is exhibiting strategic prudence as well as strategic patience.

Is failure an option?

The Korean nuclear issue has eluded resolution for a quarter century, frustrating US negotiators in successive administrations as well as policymakers across Asia. North Korea claims that its pursuit of nuclear weapons derives exclusively from US political, military and ideological animosities. Pyongyang insists that it will retain and if necessary enhance its nuclear capabilities for the indefinite future. It also asserts that its weapons capabilities ensure its treatment on 'an equal footing with other nuclear weapons states'.[43]

However, certain essential policy conclusions seem inescapable. North Korea does not treat nuclear weapons as a bargaining chip, and instead views these weapons as central to its identity and security planning. Periodic hints by the North that it might be prepared to exchange its nuclear capabilities for economic aid cannot be taken seriously. The DPRK has repeatedly (and increasingly) demonstrated a capacity for risk-taking, very likely believing that nuclear weapons provide an added measure of protection. It also believes that China's fears of the North's potential responses to heightened pressure inhibit Beijing from taking major measures against the DPRK, lest such steps trigger a far larger regional crisis. Despite the system's acute economic dysfunction, its capacity for enduring massive deprivation cannot be doubted, with the leadership prepared to make huge sacrifices to sustain its weapons programmes. The leadership thus remains locked in a nuclear mindset; it is unprepared to envisage longer-term survival of the extant system without retention and enhancement of its nuclear capabilities.

Moreover, North Korea's national strategy long predates recent decades. In a speech at a mass rally in Pyongyang commemorating the sixtieth anniversary of the outbreak of the Korean War, KWP Secretary Kim Ki-nam depicted the United States in highly antagonistic terms, characterising the US as the North's '100-year sworn enemy' and as an 'enemy with which we cannot live under the same sky'. Kim described US conduct as the 'most barbaric, murderous war unprecedented in history', deeming the US responsible for 'inflict[ing] intolerable misfortunes and agony on our nation while continuing its military occupation of South Korea and atrociously implementing [its] hostile policy toward the DPRK'.[44] The past and present combine in Pyongyang's perceptions of its place in the world, and in its unwavering commitment to strategic autonomy.

North Korea's words and actions do not suggest the intention or felt necessity to forgo its weapons capabilities. As stated in a DPRK commentary on the 2010 NPT Review Conference:

> Although some ... take issue with our possession of nuclear weapons ... we, as a country outside the treaty, pay no heed to them. [We] are not bound to any duty of not possessing nuclear weapons, and have the legitimate right to continuously expand and strengthen [a] nuclear deterrent necessary enough to defend the state's supreme interests. We neither want to be recognised as a nuclear state by someone nor feel the need to do so. Sufficient enough for our honour and pride alone that we have been able to reliably safeguard the country's sovereignty and the nation's security with our nuclear weapons.[45]

But US pursuit of denuclearisation is not a fool's errand. It is seeking to achieve a durable international consensus to constrict North Korea's weapons development and to mitigate the risks of even more worrisome possibilities. The continued dangers posed by the North's nuclear capabilities and nuclear knowhow remain uppermost in US policy calculations. The ultimate goal remains nuclear abandonment by the North, but a more practicable objective is risk minimisation, both in relation to the DPRK's extant weapons and in any potential transfer of technology and materials beyond North Korea's borders.

A different future for North Korea presumes a different leader and (even more fundamentally) a different type of system in which leaders do not believe that the survival or prosperity of the state depend on continued possession of nuclear weapons. The DPRK's capacity for grim endurance should caution policymakers and analysts alike about the allure of easy solutions. The fundamental policy challenges persist: How do the United States and others deny the DPRK any political claim to normal relations while it continues to pursue development of nuclear weapons? What can the US and other states do to limit the risks to international security if the future leadership of the North persists in its nuclear mindset?

The open-ended prospect of a nuclear-armed North Korea deeply alienated from its neighbours and unprepared to abide by its international obligations is very disquieting. But acquiescence to a nuclear-armed North is not acceptable in peninsular, regional or global terms. When, whether and how major change occurs in North Korea remains to be seen. Until such time, the United States, its regional allies and partners, and the international community as a whole must seek to ensure that this embattled system does not do larger damage to peace and security in Northeast Asia and beyond.

NOTES

Acknowledgements

1   For a thoughtful overview on the use of such materials, see Stephen C. Mercado, 'Sailing the Sea of OSINT in the Information Age', *Studies in Intelligence*, vol. 48, no. 3, 2004, pp. 45–55.

2   Jonathan D. Pollack, 'The United States, North Korea, and the End of the Agreed Framework', *Naval War College Review*, vol. 56, no. 3, summer 2003, pp. 11–49.

3   Correspondence with Jiun Bang, Korea Institute for Defense Analyses, June 2009.

Introduction

1   For an authoritative DPRK statement, see 'Memorandum of the DPRK Ministry of Foreign Affairs – The Korean Peninsula and Nuclear Weapons', Pyongyang, Korean Central Broadcasting System, 21 April 2010, http://www.kcna.co.jp.

2   For a full elaboration of this argument, see Leon V. Sigal, *Disarming Strangers: Nuclear Diplomacy with North Korea* (Princeton, NJ: Princeton University Press, 1998).

3   Joel S. Wit, Daniel B. Poneman, and Robert L. Gallucci, *Going Critical: The First North Korean Nuclear Crisis* (Washington, DC: Brookings Institution Press, 2004), pp. 11–13.

4   See Adrian Buzo, *The Guerilla Dynasty: Politics and Leadership in North Korea* (London and New York: I.B. Tauris Publishers, 1999); and Bradley K. Martin, *Under the Loving Care of the Fatherly Leader: North Korea and the Kim Dynasty* (New York: Thomas Dunne Books, 2006).

5   For pertinent examples, see the holdings of the Cold War International History Project and the North Korea International Documentation Project of the Woodrow Wilson International Center for Scholars (http://www.wilsoncenter.org). For two particularly revealing studies drawing on this documentation, see Shen Zhihua,

'Sino-North Korean Conflict and Its Resolution during the Korean War', in Kathryn Weathersby (ed.), 'New Evidence on North Korea', *Cold War International History Project Bulletin*, Issue 14/15, Winter 2003–Spring 2004, pp. 9–24; and Kathryn Weathersby, *Dependence and Mistrust: North Korea's Relations with Moscow and the Evolution of Juche* (Washington DC: US–Korea Institute at SAIS, Working Paper Series, WP 08-08, December 2008), http://www.uskoreainstitute.org.

6   See Hans Maretzki, *Kim-ismus in Nordkorea* [Kimism in North Korea], first published in 1991 and republished by Anita Tykve Verlag in 2003. Maretzki served as the last ambassador of the German Democratic Republic (GDR) to North Korea between 1987 and 1990, during which time he met frequently with Kim Il-sung. On the Soviet Union's early facilitation of North Korean nuclear development, see James Clay Moltz and Alexandre Y. Mansourov (eds), *The North Korean Nuclear Program: Security, Strategy, and New Perspectives from Russia* (New York and London: Routledge, 2000).

7   Evan Ramstad, 'Gulags, Nukes, and a Water Slide: Citizen Spies Lift North Korea's Veil', *Wall Street Journal*, 22 May 2009, http://online.wsj.com/… gulags-nukes-and-water-slide-citizen.html.

8   For a detailed comparative history of these dynamics, see Narushige Michishita, *North Korea's Military–Diplomatic Campaigns, 1966–2008* (London and New York: Routledge, Taylor & Francis Group, 2010). On the *Cheonan* sinking, see 'Investigation Result on the Sinking of the ROKS "Cheonan"', Seoul: Ministry of National Defence, 20 May 2010, http://www.mnd.mil.kr.; and 'Presidential Statement: Attack on the ROK Naval Ship "Cheonan"', United Nations Security Council, 9 July 2010, S/PRST/2010/13.

9   On the Yeongpyong Do shelling, see Mark McDonald, '"Crisis Status" in South Korea as North Shells Island', *New York Times*, 23 November, 2010, http://www.nytimes.com/2010/11/24/world/asia/24korea.html.

10 For an assessment of the failure of various predictions by a leading exponent of the collapsist school, see Nicholas Eberstadt, 'Why Hasn't the DPRK Collapsed?', in Jonathan D. Pollack (ed.), *Korea: The East Asian Pivot* (Newport, RI: Naval War College Press, 2006), pp. 143–70.

11 On the ROK's covert nuclear programme of the 1970s and US efforts to halt it, see Pollack and Mitchell B. Reiss, 'South Korea: The Tyranny of Geography and the Vexations of History', in Kurt M. Campbell, Robert J. Einhorn and Mitchell B. Reiss (eds), *The Nuclear Tipping Point – Why States Reconsider Their Nuclear Choices* (Washington DC: Brookings Institution Press, 2004), especially pp. 258–65; and Kang Choi and Joon-Sung Park, 'South Korea: Fears of Abandonment and Entrapment', in Muthiah Alagappa (ed.), *The Long Shadow – Nuclear Weapons and Security in 21ˢᵗ Century Asia* (Stanford, CA: Stanford University Press, 2008), especially pp. 375–8. On US intelligence and policy concerns related to North Korea's nuclear development dating from the early 1980s, see Robert A. Wampler (ed.), *North Korea and Nuclear Weapons: The Declassified US Record*, National Security Archive Electronic Briefing Book No.

87, 25 April 2003, http://www.gwu. edu/nsarchiv/NSAEBB/NSAEBB87/. See also Jeffrey T. Richelson, *Spying on the Bomb – American Nuclear Intelligence from Nazi Germany to Iran and North Korea* (New York: W.W. Norton and Company, 2007), pp. 346–51, 356–9, 517–37. For a valuable reconstruction of the IAEA's inspections of the early 1990s, consult David Albright and Kevin O'Neill (eds), *Solving the North Korean Nuclear Puzzle* (Washington DC: Institute for Science and International Security, 2000).

12 For accounts of nuclear diplomacy with the North (much of it drawing on the experiences of individuals deeply involved in the negotiating process), see Mitchell Reiss, *Bridled Ambition: Why Countries Constrain Their Nuclear Capabilities* (Washington DC: The Woodrow Wilson Center Press, 1995), pp. 231–319; Sigal, *Disarming Strangers*; Scott Snyder, *Negotiating on the Edge: North Korean Negotiating Behavior* (Washington DC: United States Institute of Peace Press, 1999); Yong-Sup Han, 'North Korean Behavior in Nuclear Negotiations', *The Nonproliferation Review*, vol. 7, no. 1, Spring 2000, pp. 41–54; Don Oberdorfer, *The Two Koreas: A Contemporary History*, Revised and Updated Edition (New York: Basic Books, 2001), pp. 249–368; Selig S. Harrison, *Korean Endgame: A Strategy for Reunification and US Disengagement* (Princeton, NJ: Princeton University Press, 2002); Pollack, 'The United States, North Korea, and the End of the Agreed Framework'; Wit, Poneman and Gallucci, *Going Critical*; Yoichi Funabashi, *The Peninsula Question – A Chronicle of the Second Korean Nuclear Crisis* (Washington DC: Brookings Institution Press, 2007); Charles L.

Pritchard, *Failed Diplomacy: The Tragic Story of How North Korea Got the Bomb* (Washington DC: Brookings Institution Press, 2007); Mike Chinoy, *Meltdown – The Inside Story of the North Korean Nuclear Crisis* (New York: St Martin's Press, 2008); and Michishita, *North Korea's Military-Diplomatic Campaigns*, pp. 93–116, 163–86.

13 Sigal, *Disarming Strangers*; Victor D. Cha and David C. Kang, *Nuclear North Korea: A Debate on Engagement Strategies* (New York: Columbia University Press, 2003); Mike Mochizuki and Michael O'Hanlon, *Crisis in the Korean Peninsula: How to Deal with a Nuclear North Korea* (Washington DC: The Brookings Institution, 2003); James L. Schoff, Charles M. Perry and Jacquelyn K. Davis, *Building Six-Party Capacity for a WMD-Free Korea* (Dulles, VA: Brassey's, 2004); Schoff, Perry, and Davis, *Nuclear Matters in North Korea-Building a Multilateral Response for Future Stability in Northeast Asia* (Dulles, VA: Potomac Books, 2008); Joel Wit et al., *US Strategy Towards North Korea: Rebuilding Dialogue and Engagement* (Washington DC: US–Korea Institute At SAIS, October 2009), http://www. uskoreainstitute.org.

14 See, in particular, Siegfried S. Hecker, 'Denuclearising North Korea', *Bulletin of the Atomic Scientists*, vol. 64, no. 2, May/June 2008, pp. 44–9, 61–62.

15 According to former North Korean diplomats, the DPRK in the early 1990s organised a Nuclear Management Team comprised of approximately 20 officials, charged with overseeing and coordinating all dimensions of nuclear policy. US interactions have been almost exclusively with the diplomatic wing of this group. For additional discussion, see Michishita, *North*

Korea's Military–Diplomatic Campaigns, 1966–2008, p. 110.

16 Peter Beaumont, 'Heir to the Dear Leader Appears from the Shadows', *The Observer Online*, 24 January 2010, http://observer.guardian.co.uk.

17 Interview, February 2010. There were, however, some exceptions to this policy, especially among some of the participants involved in humanitarian relief during the 'arduous march' period. See, in particular, Hazel Smith, *Hungry for Peace: International Security, Humanitarian Assistance, and Social Change in North Korea* (Washington DC: United States Institute of Peace Press, 2005).

18 Jacques E.C. Hymans, *The Psychology of Nuclear Proliferation: Identity, Emotions, and Foreign Policy* (Cambridge: Cambridge University Press, 2006). For his effort to apply the theoretical model to North Korea, see Hymans, 'Assessing North Korean Nuclear Intentions and Capacities: A New Approach', *Journal of East Asian Studies*, vol. 8, no. 2, May–August 2008, pp. 259–92.

19 Richard K. Betts, 'Universal Deterrence or Conceptual Collapse? Liberal Pessimism and Utopian Realism', in Victor A. Utgoff (ed.), *The Coming Crisis: Nuclear Proliferation, US Interests, and World Order* (Cambridge, MA: The MIT Press, 2000), p. 57.

Chapter One

1 Robert A. Scalapino and Chong-sik Lee, *Communism in Korea, vol. 1 – The Movement* (Berkeley and Los Angeles, CA: University of California Press, 1972); Bruce Cumings, *Korea's Place in the Sun: A Modern History*, updated edition (New York: W.W. Norton, 2005), pp. 86–184; Allan R. Millett, *The War for Korea, 1945–1950 – A House Burning* (Lawrence, KS: University Press of Kansas, 2005), pp. 16–42; Balazs Szalontai, *Kim Il-sung in the Khrushchev Era-Soviet – DPRK Relations and the Roots of North Korean Despotism* (Stanford, CA: Stanford University Press for the Woodrow Wilson Center Press, 2005); and Gi-Wook Shin, *Ethnic Nationalism in Korea: Genealogy, Politics, and Legacy* (Stanford, CA: Stanford University Press, 2006).

2 See Sydney A. Seiler, *Kim Il-song 1941–1948: The Creation of a Legend*, *The Building of a Regime* (Lanham, MD: University Press of America, 1994).

3 The quotation is from Kim San-ho, former head of the Higher Party School, who subsequently emigrated to the Soviet Union. Maria E. Trigubenko, 'The Role of the USSR in Liberating and Partitioning Korea', in Il Yung Chung and Eunsook Chung (eds), *Russia in the Far East and Pacific Region* (Seoul: The Sejong Institute, 1994), p. 41.

4 On Kim's early experiences in China and the Soviet Union, see Seiler, *Kim Il-song*, pp. 19–59; and Martin, *Under the Loving Care of the Fatherly Leader*, pp. 29–49.

5 *Ibid.*, p. 56.

6 Shin, *Ethnic Nationalism in Korea*, pp. 85–6.

7 Interview with Hans Maretzki, October 2008.

8 See, for example, *Kim Il-sung – A Condensed Biography* (Pyongyang:

Foreign Languages Publishing House, 2001).

9   In a revealing aside to Russian presidential envoy Konstantin Pulikovsky during Kim Jong-il's train trip across Russia in the summer of 2001, Kim stated that 'he liked his time in Khabarovsk best of all'. As Pulikovsky observed: 'It appeared to me that, in Khabarovsk, the head of the DPRK, was able to "rest his soul".' Pulikovsky, *Vostochnyi Ekspress: Po Rossii S Kim Chen Irom* [The Eastern Express: Across Russia with Kim Jong-il] (Moscow: Gorodets, 2002), pp. 139–40. Pulikovsky also notes that Kim was undoubtedly born very close to Khabarovsk. *Ibid.*, pp. 32–5. My thanks to Fiona Hill for a careful rendition of several passages from Pulikovsky's book.

10 Kim Jong-il's birth in 1941 has rarely been noted in published accounts, and has never been acknowledged by North Korean sources. However, Soviet records confirm the actual date of his birth. See Maretzki, *Kim-ismus in Nordkorea*, p. 36. For a reference in an authoritative Chinese publication, see Yang Yaqing, 'Kim Jong-il: The Still Mysterious Supreme Leader', *Shijie Zhishi* [World Knowledge], 1 July 2009, p. 21. As Yang notes, 'Kim Jong-il made his date of birth one year later in a bid to make people believe that he was born when his father was 30 years old. On the birth record card [of 16 February 1941], Kim Jong-il was registered ... as Yuri Irsenovich Kim.'

11 James M. Minnich, *The North Korean People's Army: Origins and Current Tactics* (Annapolis, MD: Naval Institute Press, 2005), p. 3.

12 Szalontai, *Kim Il-sung in the Khrushchev Era*, pp. 37–9.

13 On Kim's guerrilla loyalists, see Minnich, *The North Korean People's Army*, pp. 11–20. Estimates vary on the size of the group loyal to Kim; the core members likely numbered between 200 and 300. Interviews, February 2008 and October 2008.

14 Consult, for example, Carter J. Eckert et al., *Korea Old and New – A History* (Cambridge, MA and London: Harvard University Press, 1990).

15 See especially Seiler, *Kim Il-song*, pp. 43–71; and Andrei Lankov, *From Stalin to Kim Il-sung* (New Brunswick, NJ: Rutgers University Press, 2002), pp. 1–48.

16 See in particular, Charles K. Armstrong, *The North Korean Revolution, 1945–1950* (Ithaca, NY: Cornell University, 2003), p. 80. He describes North Korea's political essence as 'the "Koreanization" of Soviet communism, not the "Sovietization" of North Korea'.

17 Interview, January 2009.

18 Stephen Bradner, 'North Korea's Strategy', in Henry D. Sokolski (ed.), *Planning for a Peaceful Korea* (Carlisle, PA: US Army War College, Strategic Studies Institute, 2001), pp. 23–82.

19 Buzo, *The Guerilla Dynasty*, pp. 5, 20.

20 The recent literature on the history of the Korean War, as viewed by all three Communist participants as well as the United States and its allies, is ample, impressive and growing. On the Pyongyang–Moscow–Beijing triangle and how events on the battlefield shaped decision-making, see Chen Jian, *China's Road to the Korean War: The Making of the Sino-American Confrontation* (New York: Columbia University Press, 1994); Odd Arne Westad (ed.), *Brothers in Arms: The Rise and Fall of the Sino-Soviet Alliance*

(Stanford, CA: Stanford University Press for the Woodrow Wilson Center Press, 1998); Chen, *Mao's China and the Cold War* (Chapel Hill, NC and London: The University of North Carolina Press, 2001), pp. 49–117; Sergei N. Goncharov, John W. Lewis and Xue Litai, *Uncertain Partners: Stalin, Mao, and the Korean War* (Stanford: Stanford University Press, 2003); Shen, 'Sino-North Korean Conflict and its Resolution during the Korean War', pp. 9–24; *The Unforgotten Korean War: Chinese Perspectives and Appraisals* (Beijing: Western Returned Scholars Association, 15 August 2007); Weathersby, *Dependence and Mistrust*; and Shen, *Alliance of "Tooth and Lips" or Marriage of Convenience? – The Origins and Development of the Sino-North Korean Alliance, 1946–1958* (Washington, DC: US–Korea Institute at SAIS, Working Paper Series, WP-09, December 2008). On the US role, see William Stueck, *The Korean War – An International History* (Princeton, NJ: Princeton University Press, 1995); Millett, *The War for Korea, 1945–1950*; David Halberstam, *The Coldest Winter – America and the Korean War* (New York: Hyperion, 2007); and Millett, *The War for Korea, 1950–1951 – They Came from the North* (Lawrence: University Press of Kansas, 2010).

21 Kim's repeated efforts at pressuring Stalin to approve the war are carefully documented in Weathersby, *Dependence and Mistrust*, pp. 7–9.

22 For a map detailing the locations and strengths of the insurrectionary forces across the southern half of the peninsula in early 1949, see Millett, *The War for Korea, 1945–1950*, p. 180.

23 For a detailed account of US disorganisation during the occupation (especially as contrasted by the discipline and coherence of Soviet forces north of the 38th parallel), see *ibid.*

24 Telegram from Stalin to Kim Il-sung, 28 August 1950, as cited in Weathersby, *Dependence and Mistrust*, p. 8.

25 This paragraph draws extensively from Shen, *Alliance of Tooth and Lips or Marriage of Convenience?*, pp. 13–14.

26 Kim Il-sung's personal appeal to Mao Zedong urging a Chinese intervention is on permanent display at the Chinese Military Museum in Beijing.

27 Yao Xu, 'Kangmei yuanchao de yingming juece' ['The Brilliant Decision to Resist America and Aid Korea'], *Dangshi Yanjiu* [*Studies in Party History*], no. 5, 28 October 1980, p. 10.

28 This paragraph draws extensively on Shen Zhihua, 'Sino-North Korean Conflict and its Resoultion during the Korean War'.

29 Hans Maretzki, interview, October 2008.

30 Xu Yan, 'Chinese Forces and Their Casualties in the Korean War', *Chinese Historians*, vol. 6, no. 2, Fall 1993, pp. 45–58; and 'Korean War: In the View of Cost Effectiveness', Beijing, *Zhongguo Wang*, 29 July 2003, http://www.china.org.cn. Xu is a professor at the China National Defense University, and among China's leading historians of the Cold War.

31 See Szalontai, *Kim Il-sung in the Khrushchev Era*, pp. 43–45.

32 *Ibid.*, p. 45.

33 *Ibid.*, p. 46.

34 My thanks to Ezra Vogel for this information.

35 The estimate is from Erik van Ree, 'The Limits of Juche: North Korea's Dependence on Soviet Industrial Aid, 1953–76', *The Journal of Communist Studies*, vol. 5, no. 1, March 1989, pp. 57–8, as cited in Weathersby, *Dependence and Mistrust*, pp. 10–11.

36 Charles Armstrong, '"Fraternal Socialism": The International Reconstruction of North Korea, 1953–1962', *Cold War History*, vol. 5, no. 2, May 2005, pp. 161–87.

37 *Chaoxian Minzhu Zhuyi Renmin Gongheguo, 1948–1958* [The Democratic People's Republic of Korea, 1948–1958] (Beijing: Waiguo Wen Chubanshe, 1958).

38 Martin, *Under the Loving Care of the Fatherly Leader*, p. 96.

39 This story is well told in Tessa Morris-Suzuki, *Exodus to North Korea: Shadows from Japan's Cold War* (Lanham , MD: Rowman and Littlefield Publishers, 2007).

40 Eui-Gak Hwang, *The Korean Economies: A Comparison of North and South* (Oxford: Clarendon Press, 1993), pp. 120–121. Hwang's estimates of the North Korean gross national product are based on an exchange rate calculation, using North Korea's trade exchange rate (as distinct from its official exchange rate), then converted into US dollars.

41 Kim Il-sung, 'On Eliminating Dogmatism and Formalism and Establishing Juche in Ideological Work', as cited in Shin, *Ethnic Nationalism in Korea*, p. 87.

42 Charles Armstrong, *Necessary Enemies: Anti-Americanism, Juche Ideology, and the Tortuous Path to Normalization* (Washington DC: US–Korea Institute at SAIS, Working Paper Series, WP 08-3, September 2008), p. 3. See also B.R. Myers, *The Cleanest Race: How North Koreans See Themselves – And Why It Matters* (Brooklyn, NY: Melville House Publishing, 2010).

43 This history is carefully reconstructed in Andrei Lankov, *Crisis in North Korea: The Failure of De-Stalinization, 1956*

(Honolulu, HI: University of Hawai'i Press, 2005), and in Szalontai, *Kim Il-sung in the Khrushchev Era*. I draw extensively on both volumes below.

44 Szalontai, *Kim Il-sung in the Khrushchev Era*, pp. 70–74.

45 Lankov, *Crisis in North Korea*, p.3.

46 This was Kim's second-longest absence from the North in his lifetime, and very likely reinforced his unease about extended travel outside the DPRK.

47 For some fascinating details on the Mikoyan–Peng visit drawing on newly available Chinese materials, including Mao's personal frustrations with Kim's actions, see Shen, *Alliance of "Tooth and Lips" or Marriage of Convenience?*, pp. 19–20.

48 Memorandum of Conversation between Soviet Ambassador Moskovsky and Romanian Ambassador Bodnaras, 22 August 1963, in Sergey S. Radchenko, *The Soviet Union and the North Korean Seizure of the USS Pueblo: Evidence from Russian Archives* (Washington, DC: Woodrow Wilson International Center for Scholars, Cold War International History Project, Working Paper no. 47, n.d.), pp. 40–41.

49 Szalontai, *Kim Il-sung in the Khrushchev Era*, p. 85.

50 In his 1963 conversation with the Romanian ambassador, Kim claims to have regretted his decision to order the executions, and that 'he now look[ed] at these events with different eyes, and if he had known everything back then, he would not have allowed these events [to take place]'. Memorandum of Conversation, 22 August 1963, in Radchenko, *The Soviet Union and the North Korean Seizure of the USS Pueblo*, p. 41.

51 *Ibid.*, p. 114. On Kim's development of 'on the spot guidance' tours in the late

1940s, see Martin, *Under the Loving Care of the Fatherly Leader*, pp. 57–60.

52 Lankov, *Crisis in North Korea*, p. 205.

53 *Ibid.*, p. 161; Szalontai, *Kim Il-sung in the Khrushchev Era*, p. 118.

54 This paragraph draws extensively on Shen, *Alliance of "Tooth and Lips" or Marriage of Convenience?*, pp. 22–3.

55 Szalontai, *Kim Il-sung in the Khrushchev Era*, p. 130.

56 Quoted in *Ibid.*, p. 118.

57 Dong Wang, *The Quarreling Brothers: New Chinese Archives and a Reappraisal of the Sino-Soviet Split, 1959–1962* (Washington DC: Woodrow Wilson International Center for Scholars, Cold War International History Project, Working Paper no. 49, n.d.), especially pp. 16–30.

58 Szalontai, *Kim Il-sung in the Khrushchev Era*, pp. 137, 143.

59 According to a declassified cable filed by the Hungarian ambassador to the DPRK, Khrushchev was also scheduled to visit North Korea in September 1960, but this visit never took place. 'Report, Embassy of North Korea to the Hungarian Foreign Ministry', 2 July 1960, in James Person (ed.), *Limits of the "Lips and Teeth" Alliance: New Evidence on Sino-DPRK Relations* (Washington DC: Woodrow Wilson International Center for Scholars, Document Reader no. 2, 6 April 2009), p. 6.

60 I am grateful to James Person for this information.

61 Conversation with Albanian party official Myftiu Manush, 10 October 1961, as cited in Weathersby, *Dependence and Mistrust*, p. 13.

62 William Burr and Jeffrey T. Richelson, 'Whether to "Strangle the Baby in the Cradle": The United States and the Chinese Nuclear Programme, 1960–1964', *International Security*, vol. 25, no. 3, Winter 2000/01, pp. 54–99.

Chapter Two

1 Millett, *The War for Korea, 1945–1950*, pp. 48–9. However, declassified US intelligence reports indicate that there was fiercer Japanese resistance to Soviet forces at crucial industrial facilities in remote mountainous locations, including some associated with Japan's clandestine nuclear programme. Robert K. Wilcox, *Japan's Secret War: Japan's Race Against Time to Build Its Own Atomic Bomb* (New York: Marlowe and Company, 1995), p. 195.

2 Seiler, *Kim Il-song*, pp. 45–8. According to Seiler, Stalin personally decided not to permit Korean personnel to accompany the Red Army units entering northeastern Korea, thereby enabling Soviet forces to assert total control over the occupation. *Ibid.*, p. 46.

3 Mao Zedong, 'The Situation and Our Policy After the Victory in the War of Resistance Against Japan', 13 August 1945, in *Selected Works of Mao Tse-tung* [*Zedong*], vol. 4 (Beijing: Foreign Languages Press, 1969), pp. 21–2.

4 Wilcox, *Japan's Secret War*, pp. 36–7, 64, 99. According to Wilcox, US intelligence reports disclosed that there were approximately ten locations where Japan undertook uranium mining operations in Korea, primarily

in mountainous locations in the North. *Ibid.*, pp. 37, 152–3.

5   Lee Choon-geun and Kim Chong-son, 'North Korea's Nuclear and Rocket Technology Development and Its Future Prospects', Seoul Science and Technology Policy Institute [STEPI] Insight No. 22, 15 May 2009; Lee Choon-geun, 'Nuclear Technology and Associated Human Resources in North Korea', Stanford University, unpublished paper, 2008, pp. 1–2; and 'North Korea's Nuclear Program: A History', *Korea Herald*, 15 June 2009. For evidence of early Soviet exploration of North Korean uranium resources, see the top secret protocols of 1946–48 of the Soviet Council of Ministers in Balazs Szalontai and Sergey Radchenko (eds), *North Korea's Efforts to Acquire Nuclear Technology and Nuclear Weapons: Evidence from Russian and Hungarian Archives* (Washington DC: Cold War International History Project, August 2006), pp. 31–3. As Pyongyang's own nuclear efforts accelerated in the 1960s, North Korean specialists informed Soviet counterparts of their plans to undertake intensive exploration efforts of their own. See the remarks of Soviet Ambassador Vasily Moskovsky, 27 September 1963, in *ibid.*, p. 38.

6   Kim is quoted in Shen Zhihua, 'Sino-North Korea Conflict and its Resolution during the Korean War', p. 19.

7   See Roger Dingman, 'Atomic Diplomacy During the Korean War', *International Security*, vol. 13, no. 3, Winter 1988/1989, pp. 50–91; Rosemary Foot, 'Nuclear Weapons and the Ending of the Korean Conflict', *ibid.*, pp. 92–112; Mark A. Ryan, *Chinese Attitudes Toward Nuclear Weapons: China and the United States During the Korean War* (Armonk, NY and London:

M.E. Sharpe, 1989); and *The Unforgotten Korean War*, pp. 697–9.

8   Alexander L. George, *The Chinese Communist Party in Action: The Korean War and Its Aftermath* (New York: Columbia University Press, 1967). The POW interviews (undertaken by Herbert Goldhamer and others at RAND) are also discussed in Peter Hayes, *Pacific Powderkeg: American Nuclear Dilemmas in Korea* (Lexington, MA: D.C. Heath and Company, 1990), pp. 23–6.

9   On US development of tactical nuclear weapons, consult Robert S. Norris, Steven M. Kosiak and Stephen I. Schwartz, 'Deploying the Bomb', in Schwartz et al., *Atomic Audit: The Costs and Consequences of US Nuclear Weapons Since 1940* (Washington, DC: Brookings Institution Press, 1998), pp. 151–61.

10   Hayes, *Pacific Powderkeg*, pp. 35, 49–50, 94. The disclosure on the maximal number of US nuclear deployments is based on Freedom of Information Act data provided to William Arkin, as cited in Oberdorfer, *The Two Koreas*, p. 257; the subsequent reductions are noted in *ibid.*, p. 258.

11   Mansourov bases this judgement on a 1990 interview with a former senior Soviet official responsible for relations with North Korea who 'had known Kim Il-sung personally for decades'. See Alexandre Y. Mansourov, 'The Origins, Evolution, and Current Politics of the North Korean Nuclear Program', in *The Nonproliferation Review*, vol. 2, no. 3, Spring–Summer 1995. pp. 28, 37n. There are few if any statements from Kim Il-sung on his early views of the US nuclear threat, but scattered statements in various Cold War archival materials suggest a keen awareness of how US nuclear

weapons constrained North Korea's options.

12 Hayes, *Pacific Powderkeg*, p. 123.

13 *Ibid.*

14 For one such report, see 'A Physicist Defector's Account of North Korea's Nuke Labs', 20 October 2002, http://www.korean–war.com/Archives/2002/10/msg000166.html.

15 This discussion draws on Mansourov, 'The Origins, Evolution, and Current Politics of the North Korean Nuclear Program'; Lee, 'Nuclear Technology and Associated Human Resources in North Korea'; and Cho Min et al., *Chronicle of the North Korean Nuclear Issue 1955–2009* (Seoul: Korea Institute for National Unification, Online Series 09–51,10 January 2010), http://www.kinu.or.kr.

16 Lee and Kun, 'North Korea's Nuclear and Rocket Technology and Future Prospects'.

17 Song Ui–ho, 'Manpower in North Korea's Nuclear Development Programmes: Its Personal Relationships, Training and Taboos', in *Wolgan Chungang*, March 1994, trans. in FBIS–EAS, 13 May 1994, p. 27.

18 For a detailed depiction of the lead physicists in the DPRK, see Yi Chae-sung, *Pukhanul Umjiginum Tek'unok'uratu* [Technocrats Who Move North Korea] (Seoul: Ilbit, 1998), pp. 98–122. My discussion draws heavily on Yi's account.

19 For still valuable essays on the Soviet Union's early nuclear collaboration with North Korea on which I have drawn, see the chapters by Georgiy Kaurov, Valery Denisov and Alexander Zhebin in Moltz and Mansourov, (eds), *The North Korean Nuclear Program*, pp. 15–20, 21–6, and 27–37, respectively.

20 Zhebin, 'A Political History of Soviet–North Korean Nuclear Cooperation', p. 29; Kaurov, 'A Technical History of Soviet–North Korean Nuclear Relations', p. 17.

21 Ma Linwei, 'Two Experts Behind Nuclear Explosions', *Huanqiu Renwu*, 16 June 2009, pp. 25–6.

22 Group Paektusan, 'Kim Jong-il's Nuclear Missile Scientist: There Is a Genius Scientist Who Supports North Korea's Missile Technology', *Bungei Shunju*, 1–30 September 2006, pp. 166–73; 'Scientists Who Guided DPRK's Nuclear Development', *AERA*, 16 December 2006, p. 35; and Michel Temman, 'The Mysterious Father of North Korea's Bomb', *Liberation*, 23–24 December 2006.

23 I am grateful to James Person for calling this reference to my attention.

24 Kaurov, 'A Technical History of Soviet–North Korean Nuclear Relations', p. 16. Kaurov, a leading technical specialist in Minatom (the Ministry of Atomic Energy), had been directly involved in nuclear technology transfer to the DPRK.

25 Joseph S. Bermudez, Jr, 'North Korea's Nuclear Infrastructure', *Jane's Intelligence Review*, February 1994, p. 77.

26 http://www.naweb.iaea.org/napc/physics/research_reactors/database.

27 Kaurov, 'A Technical History of Soviet–North Korea Nuclear Relations', pp. 16–17. The cost sharing arrangements between Moscow and Pyongyang on Yongbyon's early development (if any) remain obscure. See also Kaurov's comments in the Interior Ministry Press Briefing Regarding Illegal Trafficking in Nuclear Materials, Kremlin International News Broadcast, 10 October 1995. As Kaurov notes, the

provision of nuclear technology and radioactive materials to the DPRK were conducted under the bilateral agreement on peaceful nuclear cooperation and adhered to extant legal procedures.

28 Kaurov, 'A Technical History of Soviet-North Korean Nuclear Relations', p. 17.

29 David Fischer, *History of the International Atomic Energy Agency: The First Forty Years* (Vienna: IAEA, 1997), p. 288; Mansourov, 'The Origins, Evolution, and Current Politics of the North Korean Nuclear Program', p. 26; Albright and O'Neill (eds), *Solving the North Korean Nuclear Puzzle*.

30 On Soviet nuclear assistance to China and its abrogation in the summer of 1959, see John Wilson Lewis and Xue Litai, *China Builds the Bomb* (Stanford, CA: Stanford University Press, 1988), especially pp. 41n, 71–2.

31 Alexandre Mansourov, interview, February 2010.

32 Zhebin, 'A Political History of Soviet–North Korean Nuclear Cooperation', p. 30.

33 Bermudez, 'North Korea's Nuclear Infrastructure'.

34 See the documents of 15 February 1963, 15 April 1963, 27 May 1963, 26 August 1963, 27 September 1963, and 16 October 1963 in Szalontai and Radchenko, *North Korea's Efforts to Acquire Nuclear Technology and Nuclear Weapons*, pp. 35–9.

35 See, for example, the report on a secret visit to Moscow by Kim Il-sung in late 1966 requesting a nuclear power plant; a comprehensive proposal from North Korean technical experts on a December 1967 visit to the GDR; and a sequence of demands for nuclear reactors tabled by Deputy Premier Kang Chin-tae on three separate occasions in 1976 (one made directly to Prime Minister Alexei Kosygin), as discussed in *ibid.*, pp. 42, 44–6, 56–7, 59. As I note later, the frequency and scale of these requests increased notably in the 1970s and 1980s.

36 Pollack and Reiss, 'South Korea: The Tyranny of Geography and the Vexations of History', p. 258.

37 Sergey Radchenko, 'Nuclear Cooperation Between the Soviet Union and North Korea, 1962–63: Evidence from Russian Archives', in Szalontai and Radchenko, *North Korea's Efforts to Acquire Nuclear Technology and Nuclear Weapons*, p. 27.

38 'Conversation between Soviet Ambassador in North Korea Vasily Moskovsky and North Korean Foreign Minister Pak Song-chol', 24 August 1962, in *ibid.*, p. 33. Emphasis added.

39 This conclusion draws on discussions with Chinese scientists on this issue beginning in 2003.

40 Katsuichi Tsukamoto, *Kitachosen: Guntoseiji* [North Korea: Military and Politics] (Tokyo: Harashobo, 2000), p. 232.

41 Oberdorfer, *The Two Koreas*, pp. 252–3.

42 These citations are drawn from *Report of the Embassy of Hungary in North Korea to the Hungarian Foreign Ministry*, 8 January 1965, provided by the North Korea Documentation Project of the Cold War International History Project.

43 Conversation between Alexei Kosygin and Kim Il-sung, 12 February 1965, as cited in Sergey S. Radchenko, *The Soviet Union and the North Korean Seizure of the USS Pueblo: Evidence from Russian Archives* (Washington DC: Woodrow Wilson International Center for Scholars, Cold War International

History Project, Working Paper no. 47, n.d.), p. 8.

44 Less is known about infrastructural progress in the latter half of the 1960s, and Russians involved at Yongbyon during this period have disclosed minimal information. However, as I review in Chapter Three, various facilities were completed in the 1970s and 1980s, clearly suggesting that development had been ongoing in preceding years.

45 'Treaty of Friendship, Co-operation and Mutual Assistance Between the Union of Soviet Socialist Republics and the Democratic People's Republic of Korea,' 6 July 1961, UN Treaty Series, no. 6045, vol. 420, pp. 154–8.

46 Xinhua, 12 July 1961. Emphasis added.

47 Buzo, *The Guerilla Dynasty*, p. 64.

48 These and subsequent references are drawn from Kim Il-sung's meetings with Soviet Ambassador Vasily Moskovsky of 14 August 1962, 1 November 1962, and 10 November 1962, in Radchenko, *The Soviet Union and the North Korean Seizure of the USS Pueblo*, pp. 22–4, 25–8, 29–31.

49 This may have been a request for missile-defence batteries rather than divisions in the usual sense of the term, but the available text does not elaborate on Kim's meaning.

50 Radchenko, *The Soviet Union and the North Korean Seizure of the USS Pueblo*, pp. 3n, 7.

51 Record of Conversation between Soviet Ambassador Moskovsky and North Korean Foreign Minister Pak Song-chol, 29 December 1962, in *ibid.*, p. 31.

52 For a full discussion and depiction, consult Buzo, *The Guerilla Dynasty*, pp. 67–73. The quote is from p. 68.

53 Hans Maretzki, interview, October 2008.

54 Report, Embassy of Hungary in North Korea to the Hungarian Foreign Ministry, 15 February 1963, in Szalontai and Radchenko, *North Korea's Efforts to Acquire Nuclear Technology and Nuclear Weapons*, p. 36.

55 Minutes of Conversation, Pyongyang, 10 June 1971, Archives of the Central Committee of the Romanian Communist Party, in James Person (ed.), *New Evidence on Inter-Korean Relations, 1971–1972* (Washington DC: Woodrow Wilson International Center for Scholars, North Korea International Documentation Project, Document Reader no. 3, September 2009), n.p.

56 *Ibid.*

57 *Ibid.*, p. 70.

58 A North Korean defector interviewed in November 2001 by Korea political-military analyst Daniel Pinkston dates the decision to pursue development of nuclear weapons to 'a Kim Il-sung directive, probably in the 1960s'. Daniel Pinkston, unpublished paper, n.d. Though claims by defectors are often a problematic source and impossible to verify, the assertion is not inherently implausible, given inquiries and comments about nuclear weapons that North Korean officials began to make in 1962 and 1963, as discussed below. Hans Maretzki subscribes to this view as well, seeing 1963 as a plausible starting point of the nuclear-weapons programme, in view of the broader militarisation then underway within the DPRK. Hans Maretzki, interview, October 2008. Other evidence (to be reviewed in Chapter Three) suggests that the actual decision dates from the early to mid-1970s.

59 Mansourov, 'The Origins, Evolution, and Current Politics of the North Korean Nuclear Programme', p. 29.

60 Buzo, *The Guerilla Dynasty*, pp. 72–3.

61 These issues are carefully reviewed and assessed in Michishita, *North Korea's Military–Diplomatic Campaigns, 1966–2008*, pp. 17–51.

62 Hans Maretzki, interview, October 2008.

63 Radchenko, *The Soviet Union and the North Korean Seizure of the USS Pueblo*, p. 9.

64 *Ibid.*, p. 11.

65 This paragraph draws on GDR Embassy reporting in late 1966, as discussed in ample detail in Bernd Schaefer, *North Korean 'Adventurism' and China's Long Shadow, 1966–1972* (Washington DC: Woodrow Wilson International Center for Scholars, Cold War International History Project, Working Paper no. 44, October 2004), especially pp. 19–28.

66 Report, Embassy of Hungary in North Korea to the Hungarian Foreign Ministry, 8 May 1967, in Szalontai and Radchenko, *North Korea's Efforts to Acquire Nuclear Technology and Nuclear Weapons*, pp. 43–4.

67 Report, Embassy of Hungary in the Soviet Union to the Hungarian Foreign Ministry, 25 November 1967, in *ibid.*, pp. 11–5

68 The discussion here draws directly from excerpts of Brezhnev's speech to the CPSU Central Committee Plenum, 9 April 1968, in Radchenko, *The Soviet Union and the North Korean Seizure of the USS Pueblo*, pp. 61–8.

69 *Ibid.*, pp. 17, 19.

70 Embassy of Hungary in the Soviet Union to the Hungarian Foreign Ministry, 12 November 1969, document provided by the North Korea International Documentation Project, of the Cold War International History Project.

71 'Some New Aspects of Korean–Chinese Relations in the First Half of 1965', 4 June 1965, in James Person (ed.), *Limits of the 'Lips and Teeth' Alliance: New Evidence on Sino-DPRK Relations, 1955–1984* (Washington DC: Woodrow Wilson International Center for Scholars, North Korea International Documentation Project, Document Reader no. 2, March 2009), pp. 8–12.

72 According to Hans Maretzki, North Korean soldiers served in Vietnam 'in large numbers', but there are no available studies on the role of DPRK military personnel. Pyongyang also sent several dozen pilots to Vietnam, but it is not certain that the pilots performed a direct role in combat. Hans Maretzki, October 2008.

73 Embassy of Hungary in North Korea to the Hungarian Foreign Ministry, 13 March 1967, in Szalontai and Radchenko, *North Korea's Efforts to Acquire Nuclear Technology and Nuclear Weapons: Evidence from Russian and Hungarian Archives*, p. 42. Kim requested a nuclear-power reactor on this visit, and the Soviet leadership denied his request.

74 GDR Embassy to the DPRK, 'Note on a Conversation with the 1st Secretary of the Soviet Embassy', 15 March 1967, in Person (ed.), *Limits of the 'Lips and Teeth' Alliance*, pp. 39–40.

75 Soviet Ministry of Foreign Affairs, Far East Department, 'Memorandum about Sino-Korean Relations', 7 March 1967, in *ibid.*, p. 33.

76 These events are traced in Schaefer, *North Korean 'Adventurism' and China's Long Shadow, 1966–1972*, especially pp. 6–10.

77 'Information on the Korean Workers' Party', October 1966, in Radchenko,

The Soviet Union and the North Korean Seizure of the USS Pueblo, pp. 21–2.

[78] Soviet Embassy in the DPRK, 'Memorandum on Sino-Korean Relations in 1966', 2 December 1966, in *ibid.*, pp. 23–7.

[79] Schaefer, *North Korean 'Adventurism' and China's Long Shadow, 1966–1972*, p. 14.

[80] GDR Embassy to the DPRK, 'On a Conversation with the 1st Secretary of the USSR Embassy to the DPRK', 29 July 1968, in Radchenko, *The Soviet Union and the North Korean Seizure of the USS Pueblo*, p. 52.

[81] Kim discussed this episode in a meeting with GDR leader Erich Honecker, 31 May 1984, as cited in Schaefer, *North Korean 'Adventurism' and China's Long Shadow*, p. 4.

[82] *Ibid.*, pp. 28–31.

Chapter Three

[1] Paul Rexton Kan, Bruce E. Bechtol, Jr and Robert M. Collins, *Criminal Sovereignty: Understanding North Korea's Illicit International Activities* (Carlisle, PA: US Army War College, The Letort Papers, March 2010), pp. 2–8.

[2] Chen, *Mao's China and the Cold War*, p. 269.

[3] Kim's comments are cited in Buzo, *The Guerilla Dynasty*, pp. 92–3.

[4] See the discussions between Soviet and GDR diplomats, Pyongyang, 13 March 1972, in James Person (ed.), *New Evidence on Inter-Korean Relations, 1971–1972* (Washington DC: Woodrow Wilson International Center for Scholars, North Korea International Documentation Project, Document Reader no. 3, September 2009), n.p.; and Schaefer, *North Korean 'Adventurism' and China's Long Shadow*, p. 36.

[5] Various policy memoranda documenting detailed US Government planning as well as meetings with senior ROK officials (including contentious meetings with a deeply vexed President Park Chung-hee) are compiled in Daniel J. Lawler and Erin R. Mahan (eds), *Foreign Relations of the United States, 1969–1976, Vol. XIX, Part 1 – Korea, 1969–1972* (Washington DC: United States Government Printing Office, 2010), pp. 117–228. As of early 1970, total US military strength on the peninsula was approximately 64,000. 'Draft Minutes of a National Security Council Meeting', 4 March 1970, in *ibid.*, p. 144.

[6] 'Telegram from the Department of State to the Embassy in Korea', 26 October 1970, in *ibid.*, pp. 187–8.

[7] The earliest evidence of ROK pursuit of a nuclear weapons option dates from the early 1970s. Kang Choi and Joon-Sung Park, 'South Korea: Fears of Abandonment and Entrapment', pp. 376–7, 399n.

[8] This discussion draws on declassified records from the Nixon visit. All references are to Memoranda of Conversation, 23 and 24 February 1972, available through the National Security Archives at George Washington University, http://www.seas.gwu/nsarchives/nsa/publications/DOC_readers/kissinger/nixzhou/13–01.htm, and 14-01.htm..

9   Minutes of Conversation between Kim Il-sung and Nicolae Ceausescu, Pyongyang, 10 June 1971, in Person (ed.), *New Evidence on Inter-Korean Relations, 1971–1972*, n.p.

10 Kim Yong-ju spoke at a meeting held in Pyongyang, 28 March 1972, in *ibid.*, n.p.

11 Meeting between Lee Hurak, Kim Il-sung and other senior officials, Pyongyang, 4 May 1972, in *ibid.*, n.p. Emphasis added. Lee was previously Seoul's ambassador to Tokyo and then director of the Korea Central Intelligence Agency; he was generally regarded as the second most powerful leader in the ROK. At this meeting, held after midnight in Kim Il-sung's residence, Kim apologised to Lee for the Blue House raid of 1968 and the attempted assassination of Park Chung-hee, which Kim asserted 'was entirely plotted by the extreme leftists and did not reflect my intent or that of the Party. Back then, we knew nothing about it. I demoted the head of the Security Department, Chief of Staff and the Director of Reconnaissance. Now they work somewhere else.' In light of overwhelming evidence of Kim's open advocacy of the militarisation of North Korean policy over much of the prior decade, his explanation of the Blue House raid and his blaming it on subordinates is highly suspect, though under the circumstances his rationalisation was not unexpected.

12 'On the Three Principles of National Unification', 3 May 1972, in *ibid.*, n.p.

13 Pollack and Reiss, 'South Korea: The Tyranny of Geography and the Vexations of History', p. 262.

14 Interview in *Washington Post*, 26 June 1975, as cited in Kang and Park, 'South Korea', p. 377.

15 Szalontai and Radchenko, *North Korea's Efforts to Acquire Nuclear Technology and Nuclear Weapons*, pp. 42, 45–6.

16 *Ibid.*, pp. 53–4, 56–7, 59–62.

17 Embassy of Hungary in North Korea to the Hungarian Foreign Ministry, 17 February 1979, in *ibid.*, p. 67. This diplomat's observation paralleled the report of a Czech official to a Hungarian counterpart in early 1977, when he characterised a North Korean statement as 'a veiled reference to the fact that the DPRK is equipping itself with nuclear weapons'. Memorandum, Hungarian Foreign Ministry, 16 February 1977. Documentation provided by the North Korean Documentation Project, Cold War International History Project.

18 See, for example, Kim Il-sung, *Answers to Questions Raised by a Journalist Delegation from America's CNN – April 17, 1994* (Pyongyang: Foreign Languages Publishing House, 1994). According to Kim, 'The United States is now clamouring about a nuclear issue ... but their clamour is totally unfounded. As everyone knows, our Republic is a non-nuclear, peace-loving country. We have no nuclear weapons, and do not have any desire or ability to make them. We have no nuclear weapons now, and will not have any in [the] future, either.' *Ibid.*, p. 1. For a more extensive compilation drawn from Kim's conversations with foreign visitors between 1991 and 1994, see the reference materials prepared by the Korea International Institute (Tokyo), 5 February 2008, http://www.koreaii.com/index.html.

19 Mansourov, 'The Origins, Evolution, and Current Politics of the North Korean Nuclear Program', p. 29.

20 I am indebted to Alexandre Mansourov, Visiting Fellow at the US–Korea Institute at SAIS, for his insights into these questions. Though Mansourov's above-cited article dates the onset of the programme from the late 1970s, based on subsequent research he concludes that the actual onset of the programme occurred years earlier. *Ibid*, pp. 26, 29.

21 On the technological and engineering challenges in nuclear weapons development, consult Robert F. Mozley, *The Politics and Technology of Nuclear Proliferation* (Seattle and London: University of Washington Press, 1998), Chapters 2–5; and Richard L. Garwin and Georges Charpak, *Megawatts and Megatons: A Turning Point in the Nuclear Age?* (New York: Alfred A. Knopf, 2001), Chapters 2–3.

22 'On the Six-Year Plan for the Development of the People's Economy of the DPRK', November 1970, as cited in Zhebin, 'A Political History of Soviet–North Korean Nuclear Cooperation', p. 31.

23 *Ibid,*, pp. 31–2. In this context, visitors to the Yongbyon 5 MWe reactor have observed Cyrillic lettering on various knobs and dials on the reactor control panels. This does not represent definitive proof of Soviet involvement in the building of the reactor, but it does illustrate the North's continued reliance on Soviet equipment.

24 A 1976 document in Hungarian Foreign Ministry archives reports claims by a junior North Korean diplomat and deputy military attaché posted to Budapest. They asserted to Hungarian counterparts that North Korea already possessed 'nuclear warheads and carrier missiles', which these officials claimed 'had [been] developed...

unaided through experimentation, and they had manufactured them by themselves'. The report is unsubstantiated by any other evidence. Memorandum, Hungarian Foreign Ministry, 16 February 1976, in Szalontai and Radchenko, *North Korean Efforts to Acquire Nuclear Technology and Nuclear Weapons*, p. 55.

25 http://www.fas.org/nuke/guide/dprk/nuke/index.html.

26 See the report of Hungarian chargé d'affaires in Pyongyang to the Hungarian Foreign Ministry on Kim Il-sung's April–June 1975 tour to China and Eastern Europe, 30 July 1975, in *ibid.*, pp. 52–3. As observed in his report (drawing on conversations with the Chinese ambassador to the DPRK), 'Kim Il-sung considered the possibility of a military solution ... the DPRK wants to create the kind of military situation in South Korea that came into being in South Vietnam before the victory...[but] it is well known that ... China holds back and opposes any kind of armed struggle ... [and] strongly emphasized the importance of the peaceful reunification of Korea ... for his part, Kim Il-sung said nothing, or hardly anything, about his own proposals to find a peaceful solution.'

27 Bernard Gwertzman, 'China Appears to Caution North Korea Not to Attack', *New York Times*, 29 May 1975.

28 Report of the Embassy of Hungary to North Korea to the Hungarian Foreign Ministry, 15 April 1976, in *ibid.*, p. 56.

29 Buzo, *The Guerilla Dynasty*, p. 89.

30 Stephen Linton, interview, January 2010.

31 Satoru Miyamoto, 'DPRK Troop Dispatches and Military Support in the Middle East: Change from Military Support to Arms Trade in the 1970s',

East Asia – An International Quarterly, vol. 27, no. 4, December 2010, pp. 345–59.

[32] Kan, Bechtol and Collins, *Criminal Sovereignty: Understanding North Korea's Illicit International Activities*, p. 2. The correlation of the establishment of the bureau and Kim Jong-il's ascent to party leadership warrants notice.

[33] It is not certain when Kim may have learned about Seoul's covert nuclear programme. It did not become widespread public knowledge until 1978, but it is virtually certain that North Korea was aware of the programme well before then. For an early public disclosure, see Robert Gillette, 'US Squelched Apparent S. Korea A-bomb Drive', *Los Angeles Times*, 1 November 1978.

[34] Archives of the Central Committee of the Romanian Communist Party, Minutes of Conversation (Pyongyang), 10 June 1971, in Person (ed.), *New Evidence on Inter-Korean Relations, 1971–1972*, n.p.

[35] In the view of Hans Maretzki, this was the defining difference between Stalinist Russia, Maoist China and Kimist Korea: neither Stalin nor Mao had a son who could have plausibly served as successor. Maretzki, interview, October 2009.

[36] For a superb reconstruction of this media campaign, see Morgan E. Clippinger, 'Kim Chong-il in the North Korean Mass Media: A Study of Semi-Esoteric Communication', *Asian Survey*, vol. XXI, no. 3, March 1981, pp. 289–309.

[37] You Ji, 'China and North Korea: A Fragile Relationship of Strategic Convenience', *Journal of Contemporary China*, vol. 10, no. 28, August 2001, p. 389.

[38] Interview with former East European diplomat, October 2008. A Chinese interviewee with deep knowledge and experience in the DPRK characterised Kim's attributes in very similar fashion, describing Kim Jong-il as someone of clear intelligence but devoid of practical experience in governance or political imagination. Interview in Beijing, March 2010.

[39] Buzo, *The Guerilla Dynasty*, p. 50.

[40] This episode is based on an interview conducted with a Chinese official in 2000. You Ji, 'China and North Korea', p. 389. You Ji dates this meeting from 1974, but has since acknowledged that the date was a year later, on Kim's extended tour following Hanoi's victory in the Vietnam war. Deng Xiaoping was also present at the meeting with Mao. Correspondence with You Ji, April 2010.

[41] 'An Important Principle for Handling Relations Between Fraternal Parties', 31 May 1980, in *Selected Works of Deng Xiaoping,1975–1982* (Beijing: Foreign Languages Press, 1984), pp. 300–01. This is an excerpt of a longer speech. When it was first published in Chinese media, a photograph of Deng and Kim Il-sung accompanied the article. *Beijing Review*, 22 August 1983, p. 15.

[42] For one such account, see Zhang Fan, 'Kim Il-sung and the Succession of Power from Father to Son', *Zhengming*, no. 37, 1 November 1980, in *FBIS–China Daily Report*, 21 November 1980, p. U1.

[43] You, 'China and North Korea', p. 389. Sino-DPRK relations were generally conducted through party channels, so the purported role of the Ministry of Foreign Affairs in overseeing this process seems somewhat unusual. Although one Chinese source reports that Kim Jong-il travelled with his

father in 1982, this appears implausible. You Ji, personal communication, June 2010. Both China and North Korea describe Kim Jong-il's June 1983 visit to China as his first in a leadership capacity; he did not return to China for another 17 years.

44 William Chapman, 'China Says It is Open to Talks with US About Korean Peninsula', *Washington Post*, 21 October 1983, p. 23.

45 Michael Weisskopf, 'China–US Peace Feelers on Korea Canceled by Rangoon Bombing', *Washington Post*, 17 November 1983; and Clyde Haberman, 'Seoul Rejects North's Offer of Korean Unity Talk', *New York Times*, 12 January 1984.

46 Interview, Beijing, March 2010. See also the recollections of Chas Freeman, Jr, who was serving as the US deputy chief of mission in Beijing in the early 1980s, as reported in Nancy Bernkopf Tucker (ed.), *China Confidential: American Diplomats and Sino-American Relations, 1945–1996* (New York: Columbia University Press, 2001), p. 431. In his late 2000 discussion with Secretary of State Albright, Kim Jong-il asserted that the collapse of the Soviet Union and China's opening to the outside world marked 'the disappearance of our military alliance with either country'. Madeleine Albright with Bill Woodward, *Madam Secretary* (New York: Hyperion, Miramax Books, 2003), p. 589.

47 Kim reportedly undertook a total of 39 trips to China between 1949 and 1994. You Ji, personal correspondence, June 2010.

48 'Deng Warns of Eruption in US–China Ties Over Taiwan', *New York Times*, 12 October 1984.

49 Xinhua, 24 November 1983, in *FBIS–China*, 25 November 1983, p. D8.

50 Zhang's remarks are quoted in a report on the meeting with the JSP delegation, as recounted in *Yomiuri Shimbun*, 25 June 1984, p. 2.

51 Buzo, *The Guerilla Dynasty*, p. 128.

52 These appearances and absences are based on documentation from the Open Source Center.

53 This section is based on discussions with Alexandre Mansourov, who served in the Soviet Embassy in Pyongyang between 1987 and 1989. A North Korean official he describes as a highly trusted source with many years experience with the KWP bureaucracy provided much of this information. Alexandre Mansourov, interview, February 2010.

54 Materials from the 5th and 6th KWP Congresses, as cited in Denisov, 'Nuclear Institutions and Organizations in North Korea', p. 22.

55 Lee, 'Nuclear Technology and Associated Human Resources in North Korea', n.p.

56 ROK Ministry of Unification, *Pukhan Kaeyo 2000* (Seoul: Ministry of Unification, December 1999), p. 414.

57 The fullest accounts remain those in Moltz and Mansourov (eds), *The North Korean Nuclear Program*.

58 For relevant documentation, see Szalontai and Radchenko, *North Korea's Efforts to Acquire Nuclear Technology and Nuclear Weapons*, pp. 67–70.

59 For additional details on this agreement, consult Kaurov, 'A Technical History of Soviet-North Korean Nuclear Relations',, pp. 18–19.

60 Harrison, *Korean Endgame*, pp. 223, 334.

61 See, in particular, Wampler, *North Korea and Nuclear Weapons: The Declassified US Record*.

62 For a full assessment of various choices in reactor development, consult

Garwin and Charpak, *Megawatts and Megatons*, especially Chapters 2,3,5.

63 Yi Chae-sung, *Pukhanul Umjiginum Tekunok Uratu*, Chapter 3.

64 Albright and O'Neill (eds), *Solving the North Korean Nuclear Puzzle*, pp. 146, 160.

65 For relevant data and photographic evidence, see Joshua Pollack, 'Why Does North Korea Have a Gas Graphite Reactor?', *ArmsControlWonk. com*, 16 October 2009.

66 The history of illicit technology transfer from ethnic Korean scientists in Japan to the DPRK is far more extensive than common realised, dating from the earliest years of the DPRK and continuing into the 2000s, possibly including a Japanese specialist on plutonium separation who travelled to North Korea on four separate occasions between 2002 and 2005. For a detailed compilation of much of the available information, consult Katsuhisa Furukawa, 'Japanese Authorities Target Illicit North Korean Technology Procurement', *WMD Insights*, November 2007, http://www.wmdinsights.com/I20/120_EA4.

67 Kiyoshi Sakurai, 'Is There a Nuclear Bomb in North Korea?' *Sekai Shuho*, 25 March 2003, pp. 20–22.

68 Albright and O'Neill (eds), *Solving the North Korean Nuclear Puzzle*, pp. 161–2.

69 Mozley, *The Politics and Technology of Nuclear Proliferation*, p. 53.

70 Mansourov, 'The Origins, Evolution, and Current Politics of the North Korean Nuclear Program', p. 27.

71 http://www.nti.org/e_research/profiles/NK/Nuclear/46.html.

72 Buzo, *The Guerilla Dynasty*, p. 144.

73 Hans Maretzki, interview, October 2009.

Chapter Four

1 For a careful reconstruction of Soviet and Chinese policymaking towards North Korea in the late 1980s and early 1990s, consult Oberdorfer, *The Two Koreas*, pp. 197–228 and pp. 229–48, respectively.

2 Kaurov, 'A Technical History of Soviet–North Korean Nuclear Relations', p. 19.

3 Samuel S. Kim, *The Two Koreas and the Great Powers* (Cambridge: Cambridge University Press, 2006), pp. 117–21.

4 *Ibid.*, pp. 176–80; Buzo, *The Guerilla Dynasty*, pp. 191–3.

5 According to Don Oberdorfer, Gorbachev informed Anatoly Dobrynin, Moscow's long-serving ambassador to the United States, of the underlying reason to pursue relations with South Korea: 'We need some money'. Oberdorfer, *The Two Koreas*, p. 209.

6 *Ibid.*, pp. 206–07.

7 *Ibid.*, pp. 215–16. Kim's remarks are quoted in Georgi D. Bulychev, 'Moscow and North Korea: The 1961 Treaty and After', in Il–Yung Chung and Eunsook Chung (eds), *Russia in the Far East and Pacific Region* (Seoul: The Sejong Institute, 1994), p. 101.

8 Kim's trip to China is discussed in Oberdorfer, *The Two Koreas*, p. 219, based on interviews between Oberdorfer and a former Chinese

diplomat. There are no references in North Korean media to any trips by Kim Il-sung to China between May 1987 and October 1991.

9 My thanks to Ezra Vogel for calling Deng's 1978 visit to the DPRK to my attention.

10 Qian Qichen, *Waijiao Shiji* (Beijing: Shijie Zhishi Chubanshe, 2003), translated as *Ten Episodes in Chinese Diplomacy* (New York: HarperCollins, 2005), pp. 105–26.

11 *Ibid.*, p. 116.

12 Yang Bojiang, 'China and Its Northeast Asian Neighbors', *Contemporary International Relations*, vol. 17, no. 1, January–February 2007, p. 59. Yang further notes that relations were not 'finally restored' until 2000, when Kim Jong-il visited China for the first time in 17 years.

13 Qian Qichen, *Ten Episodes in Chinese Diplomacy*, p. 122.

14 *Ibid.*, p. 123.

15 Sigal, *Disarming Strangers*, pp. 27–30.

16 Han, 'North Korean Behavior in Nuclear Negotiations', p. 42.

17 As cited in Sigal, *Disarming Strangers*, p. 32.

18 The text is available at http://www. nautilus.org.

19 As cited in Sigal, *Disarming Strangers*, p. 30.

20 The text is available at http://www.fas. org/news/dprk/1992/920219–D4129. htm.

21 As cited in Sigal, *Disarming Strangers*, p. 32.

22 Lee Ann Pingel, 'Forcible Repentance: Hostile Nuclear Proliferants and the Nonproliferation Regime – An Interview with Leonard M. Spector', *The Nonproliferation Review*, vol. 1, no. 1, Fall 1993, p. 21.

23 *Ibid*, pp. 18–19.

24 *Ibid.*, p. 39.

25 On North Korea's violations of its NPT commitments, see Fischer, *History of the International Atomic Energy Agency: The First Forty Years*, pp. 287–93.

26 Albright and O'Neill (eds), *Solving the North Korean Nuclear Puzzle*, pp. 7–8; Sigal, *Disarming Strangers*, pp. 22, 26.

27 See in particular Albright and O'Neill (eds), *Solving the North Korean Nuclear Puzzle*.

28 *Ibid.*, pp. 20–21.

29 *Ibid.*, p. 12.

30 According to the official history of the IAEA, the DPRK anticipated completion of the 50 MWe reactor in 1995. Fischer, *History of the International Atomic Energy Agency – The First Forty Years*, p. 288.

31 Discussions at the DPRK Ministry of Foreign Affairs, February 2009.

32 For a contrary interpretation, consult Robert Carlin and John W. Lewis, *Policy in Context: Negotiating with North Korea: 1992–2007* (Stanford University: Center for International Security and Cooperation, January 2008).

33 Bulychev, 'Moscow and North Korea: The 1961 Treaty and After', p. 101

34 Alexandre Y. Mansourov, 'Inside North Korea's Black Box: Reversing the Optics', unpublished paper, available at http://brookings.edu/ views/papers/fellows/oh2004060/ ch4.pdf. Mansourov's account draws on an interview conducted with an unidentified Russian official with direct knowledge of these events.

35 Ryo Hagiwara, *Kim Jong-il's Hidden War* (Washington DC: n.p., 2004), p. 49. Hagiwara was a reporter specialising on Korean affairs for *Akahata* (the newspaper of the Japan Communist Party) for nearly 20 years, including two years in Pyongyang in the early

1970s before being expelled by the DPRK. This volume, first published privately in the United States, was subsequently published in Japanese as *Kin Seinichi: Kakusareta Senso* [Kim Jong-il: Hidden War] (Tokyo: Bungei Shunju, 2006). The volume contains a wealth of information, much of it drawn from official North Korean sources and from novels on North Korean elite politics.

36 *Ibid.*, pp. 49–50.

37 *Ibid.*, p. 50; see also Kim Il-sung's remarks to the Plenary Session of the 6th KWP Central Committee, 8 December 1993, in *Collected Works of Kim Il-sung*, vol. 44 (Pyongyang: Korean Worker's Party Publishing, 1996, p. 281), as cited in *ibid*, p. 50.

38 *The People's Korea*, http://www.korea-np.co.jp.

39 For a careful examination of the origins and functioning of the military first policy, consult O Kyong-sop, 'Military-First Politics and the Changes of the Crisis Management System', *National Strategy*, Vol. 15, no. 4, December 2009, pp. 139–66, http://www.sejong.org.

40 Byung Chul Koh, *Military First Politics and Building A Powerful and Prosperous Nation in North Korea* (Nautilus Institute: Policy Forum Online, No. 05–32A, 14 April 2005) pp. 2–3.; Mansourov, 'Inside North Korea's Black Box', pp. 7–8.

41 Hagiwara, *Kim Jong-il's Hidden War*, pp. 19–21.

42 Wit, Poneman and Gallucci, *Going Critical*, pp. 71–4.

43 On the Carter visit, see Sigal, *Disarming Strangers*, pp. 150–62.

44 The above paragraph draws on and quotes from Fischer, *History of the International Atomic Energy Agency: The First Forty Years*, pp. 290–2.

45 For a detailed if at times sensationalised account of this period, see Hagiwara, *Kim Jong-il's Hidden War*. Hagiwara and others have called attention (albeit speculatively) to the puzzling circumstances of Kim Il-sung's death, noting that Kim's usual complement of medical personnel did not accompany him on this trip. Kim purportedly suffered a massive heart attack in the early morning hours of 8 July 1994, but inclement weather prevented emergency medical help from arriving in a timely manner. One highly knowledgeable Chinese interviewee has also called attention to the odd circumstances of Kim's death, though Kim was 82 years old and under great stress at the time of his death. But Kim's advanced years and uncertain health would have argued for increased emergency medical assistance, not less. Interview with Chinese expert on North Korea, Beijing, March 2010.

46 Wit, Poneman and Gallucci, *Going Critical*, p. 135.

47 Stephen Linton, Interview, January 2010.

48 Sigal, *Disarming Strangers*, p. 156.

49 See, for example, the June 1994 comments of Senior Vice Foreign Minister Kang Sok Ju and of Kim Il-sung, as reported in Harrison, *Korean Endgame*, pp. 222–4.

50 According to South Korean officials who participated in Kim Dae-jung's meetings with Kim Jong-il in June 2000, the North Korean leader acknowledged that Kim Il-sung had been in declining health for years, and had worn a pacemaker since 1991. The release of the results of an autopsy suggests acute sensitivity to the circumstances and causes of Kim's death, though the reference to

51 Kim alluded to the supposed behest in a meeting with PRC State Councilor Tang Jiaxuan. Pyongyang, Korean Central Broadcasting Station, 14 July 2005. I have not located any reference to Kim Il-sung's statement prior to Kim Jong-il's claim in this meeting.

52 According to Siegfried Hecker of Stanford University (who has had extensive direct access both to North Korean nuclear facilities and to DPRK scientific personnel), by 1992 North Korea had made 'significant progress on the construction of the 50MW(e) reactor', but had only 'broken ground on the 200MW(e) reactor'. Siegfried S. Hecker, Sean C. Lee, and Chaim Braun, 'North Korea's Choice: Bombs over Electricity', The Bridge, Summer 2010, p. 7, http://www.nae.edu/Publications/TheBridge.

53 For a careful reflection of the legacy of the Agreed Framework written by the authors of the authoritative history of the negotiations, consult Wit, Poneman and Gallucci, Going Critical, pp. 371–408.

54 For a detailed assessment of the daunting, multiple obstacles confronting the LWR project, see Michael May et al., Verifying the Agreed Framework (Livermore, CA: Center for Global Security Research, Lawrence Livermore National Laboratory, UCRL-ID-142036, CSGR-2001-001, April 2001).

55 For a year-by-year breakdown of US assistance, disaggregated according to food aid, energy assistance, nuclear disablement and medical supplies, see Mark E. Manyin and Mary Beth Nikitin, Assistance to North Korea (Washington DC: Congressional Research Service, 7–5700, 24 December 2008), p. 2. The peak year of US food assistance was 1999; the peak year of US energy assistance was 2002. Cumulative US assistance to North Korea from its inception in 1995 through 2009 amounted to slightly over $1.28 billion.

56 The above quotation is drawn from Kim Il-sung, 'On Making the New Revolutionary Change in Socialist Economic Construction', 6 July 1994, in Collected Works of Kim Il-sung, vol. 44 (Pyongyang: Korean Workers Party Publishing House , 1996), pp. 474–81, as cited in Hagiwara, Kim Jong-il's Hidden War, p. 55. Emphasis added.

57 Kim Il-sung, Speech to 21st Plenary Session of the KWP Sixth Central Committee, 8 December 1993, in Collected Works of Kim Il-sung, vol. 44, p. 283, as cited in ibid., p. 63. The estimated date for completion of the LWRs specified in the Agreed Framework was 2009.

58 This discussion is based on an interview with a Chinese researcher in Beijing, March 2010, and a second interview in April 2010. Kim's final visit to China has not been previously disclosed. There is no record of such a visit in the official coverage of Kim's activities in 1994, though unannounced visits by the North Korean leader to China and of Chinese officials to North Korea were not uncommon. The visit most likely took place shortly after Carter's visit of June 1994, but I have not been able to determine the precise date.

59 Then and now, North Korea has remained an inconsequential trading partner for China. Two-way trade, for example, did not exceed $1bn for

the first time until 2003. For data on bilateral China–North Korea trade between 1981 and 2005, see Scott Snyder, *China's Rise and the Two Koreas: Politics, Economics, Security* (Boulder, CO and London: Lynne Rienner Publishers, 2009), p. 41.

60 *Ibid.*, p. 87.

61 See the especially gripping account of this period in North Korea's rustbelt in Barbara Demick, *Nothing to Envy: Ordinary Lives in North Korea* (New York: Spiegel and Grau, 2009).

62 For a detailed reconstruction of the developments of this period based substantially on the author's personal involvement, consult Smith, *Hungry for Peace*. According to Smith, the most systematic estimates suggest 'about two-thirds of a million people dead through starvation or disease and sickness caused by lack of food'. *Ibid.*, p. 73.

63 Manyin and Nikitin, *Assistance to North Korea*, p. 14. Though WFP contributions have been much more limited since the peak years of food assistance, non-WFP food aid still amounted to more than 700,000 tonnes in 2007.

64 See Kim Jong-il's dialogue with senior party and economic functionaries, 3 October 2001, published as a report by Pyongyang and subsequently acquired and disseminated by a South Korean blog on 24 February 2005, http://blog.naver.com/subbu/120010558967.

65 This composite portrait of Kim draws on discussions and interviews with individuals who have met Kim Jong-il or who have personal knowledge of him, and on conversations between Kim and others where there are credible reports of these conversations, or actual transcripts of these talks. Though there are various purported

insider accounts of Kim Jong-il and his family, some seem of dubious reliability and none can be definitively confirmed, so I do not cite them.

66 Madeleine Albright, *Madam Secretary*.

67 Interview with Chinese expert on North Korea, March 2010.

68 See, in particular, Pulikovsky, *Vostochnyi Ekspress: Po Rossii s Kim Chen Irom*.

69 Kim Hyunga, 'Kim Jong-il revealed in taped conversations', *The Pacific Review*, vol. 9, no. 3, 1996, pp. 455–6.

70 Mansourov describes these changes as a 'revolution from above.' Mansourov, 'Inside North Korea's Black Box', pp. 10–12.

71 For example, in his discussions with Secretary of State Albright, Kim (as paraphrased by Albright) claimed 'there was a 50-50 split within his military on whether or not to improve relations with the United States and that there were people in the foreign ministry who had opposed even his decision to talk to us'. Though it is impossible to determine the veracity of Kim's claims, North Korean officials at times employ these rationales to inhibit negotiated agreements. Albright, *Madam Secretary*, p. 591.

72 As Kim Jong-il acknowledged in an interview with visiting South Korean media representatives in August 2000, 'Among the top officials of the Workers Party, there are several who have worked with President Kim Il-sung so I find it's difficult to revise the [Party] platform. If the platform is changed, a lot of officials present [at this meeting] will have to quit their posts. Some may claim that if I initiate the revision of the platform, I am trying to purge my opponents.' 'Kim Jong-il's Dialogue with South Korean Media Heads',

Chosun Ilbo, English Edition, 13 August 2000.

73 For biographical information on members of the Political Bureau, see KCNA, 29 September 2010.

74 Pak Yong-taek, *Enhanced Position of the North Korean Military and Its Influence on Policy Making* (Seoul: Korea Institute for Defence Analyses, Research Paper, 8 January 2008). Though Pak's paper focuses primarily on the role of the KPA, substantial portions of his analysis are also devoted to decision making and information flows beyond the KPA.

75 Kim Jong-il, 'Let Us Thoroughly Realise the Great Leader Kim Il-sung's Behest for the Reunification of the Fatherland', 4 August 2007, in *Kim Jong-il Sonjip* [Selected Works of Kim Jong Il], Volume 14 (Pyongyang: Korean Workers Party Publishing House, 2000), p. 358. The full text also appeared in *Rodong Sinmun*, 20 August 1997, p. 1.

76 Pyongyang, Korean Central Broadcasting Network, 22 November 1998.

77 This paragraph draws extensively on Koh, 'Military-First Politics and Building a Powerful and Prosperous Nation', p. 5.

78 As quoted in Pulikovsky, *Vostochnyi Ekspress: Po Rossii s Kim Chen Irom*, p. 87.

79 New Year's Day Editorial, 1 January 1999, as cited in Koh, 'Military-First Politics and Building a Powerful and Prosperous Nation'.

80 For a review of US–DPRK interactions, see Carlin and Lewis, *Policy in Context*.

81 For a careful analysis, see Lee Chol-gi, 'The North Korea–US Geneva Agreement: Implications and Violations', *Vantage Point*, December 2002, pp. 45–54. On the Agreed Framework timelines and results, consult Ralph A. Cossa, *The US–DPRK Agreed Framework: Is It Still Viable? Is It Enough?* (Honolulu, HI: Pacific Forum/Center for Strategic and International Studies, April 1999), especially pp. 9–13 and Appendix F. Operational definitions and relevant criteria and milestones are specified in annexes 3 and 4 of the KEDO–DPRK Reactor Supply Agreement, 15 December 1995, as reprinted in James M. Minnich, *The Denuclearisation of North Korea* (Bloomington, IN: First Books Library, 2002), pp. 123–5.

82 *Report of United States Policy towards North Korea: Findings and Recommendations*, Unclassified Report by Dr William J. Perry, US North Korea Policy Coordinator and Special Advisor to the President and the Secretary of State (Washington DC, 12 October 1999).

83 US–DPRK joint communiqué, 12 October 2000.

84 Albright, *Madam Secretary*, pp. 589, 591, 596.

85 This is Leon Sigal's characterisation of the views put forward by opponents of nuclear negotiations with the North. Sigal, *Disarming Strangers*, p. 6.

Chapter Five

1   Funabashi, *The Peninsular Question: A Chronicle of the Second Korean Nuclear Crisis*; Pritchard, *Failed Diplomacy: The Tragic Story of How North Korea Got the Bomb*; and Chinoy, *Meltdown: The Inside Story of the North Korean Nuclear Crisis.*

2   Spokesman of the Ministry of Foreign Affairs, 23 February 2001.

3   Sharon A. Squassoni, *Weapons of Mass Destruction: Trade Between North Korea and Pakistan* (Washington DC: Congressional Research Service, 11 October 2006), pp. 4–5.

4   Lee Chun-geun and Kim Chong-son, 'North Korea's Nuclear and Rocket Technology Development and Its Future Prospects', Seoul, Science and Technology Policy Institute, 15 May 2009. However, Lee and Kim also note that these enrichment plans specified laser and chemical-exchange techniques rather than centrifuge development

5   Doug Struck and Glenn Kessler, 'Hints on N. Korea Surfaced in 2000', *Washington Post*, 19 October 2002.

6   Several prominent scientists (notably, Siegfried Hecker and David Albright) have expressed open skepticism about many of Khan's claims. R. Jeffrey Smith and Joby Warrick, 'Pakistani Scientist Depicts More Advanced Nuclear Program in North Korea', *Washington Post*, 28 December 2009.

7   There has been excellent research on the Khan network. See Christopher O. Clary, *The A.Q. Khan Network: Causes and Implications* (Monterey, CA: Naval Postgraduate School Thesis, December 2005); Mark Fitzpatrick (ed.), *Nuclear Black Markets: Pakistan, A.Q. Khan and the rise of proliferation networks – A net*

assessment (London: The International Institute for Strategic Studies, May 2007); and David Albright, *Peddling Peril: How the Secret Nuclear Trade Arms America's Enemies* (New York and London: The Free Press, 2010). Immediately prior to completion of this manuscript, the Institute of Science and International Security published the most comprehensive assessment to date of North Korean dealings with the A.Q. Khan network and the DPRK's pursuit of uranium enrichment. I have drawn on some of the ISIS findings, but this topic warrants much fuller examination than I have provided. David Albright and Paul Brannan, *Taking Stock: North Korea's Enrichment Program* (Washington DC: The Institute for Science and International Security, 8 October 2010).

8   Albright and Brannan, *Taking Stock*, pp. 6–7.

9   Central Intelligence Agency, Unclassified Report to Congress on the Acquisition of Technology Related to Weapons of Mass Destruction and Advanced Conventional Munitions, July–December 2002.

10 Fitzpatrick (ed.), *Nuclear Black Markets*, p. 78. For a sceptical report of US claims, see Dafna Linzer, 'US Misled Allies About Nuclear Export', *Washington Post*, 20 March 2005.

11 Office of the Director of National Intelligence, 'Background Briefing with Senior US Officials on Syria's Covert Nuclear Reactor and North Korea's Involvement', 24 April 2008; Albright, *Peddling Peril*, p. 167.

12 Mitchell B. Reiss and Robert L. Gallucci, 'Dead to Rights', *Foreign Affairs*, vol. 84, no. 2, March/April 2005, p. 143.

13 Glenn Kessler, 'Uranium Traces Found on N. Korean Aluminum Tubes', *Washington Post*, 21 December 2007.

14 Kessler, 'New Data Found on North Korea's Nuclear Capacity; Intelligence on Enriched Uranium Revives Questions About Weapons', *ibid.*, 21 June 2008.

15 For additional details, consult Mary Beth Nikitin, *North Korea's Nuclear Weapons: Technical Issues* (Washington DC: Congressional Research Service, 16 December 2009), especially pp. 7–9.

16 Siegfried S. Hecker, 'A Return Trip to North Korea's Yongbyon Nuclear Complex', Presentation held at the Center for International Security and Cooperation, Stanford University, 20 November 2010, p. 1.

17 Mark McDonald, '2 Experts Say North Korea Is Building A Reactor', *New York Times*, 20 November 2010.

18 KEDO–DPRK Reactor Supply Agreement, Articles VI and VIII, in Minnich, *The Denuclearisation of North Korea*, pp. 112–13.

19 Mark Hibbs, 'DPRK Enrichment Not Far Along, Some Intelligence Data Suggest', *Nucleonics Week*, 24 October 2002, p. 1.

20 For fuller reconstruction of the Kelly visit, consult Funabashi, *The Peninsular Question*, pp. 93–108; Pritchard, *Failed Diplomacy*, pp. 32–40; and Chinoy, *Meltdown*, pp. 115–26.

21 The US has never released a transcript of Kelly's exchanges with North Korean officials. The above citation is drawn from the statement of the MFA spokesman on the nuclear issue, 25 October 2002, which appears based on Kang Sok-ju's response to Kelly.

22 Howard W. French, 'North Korea Says It Will Bar Atom Inspections', *New York Times*, 23 November 2002.

23 Pyongyang, Korean Central Television, 4 December 2002.

24 Korea Central News Agency, 12 December 2002.

25 'Where is the United States Trying to Lead the Situation?', *Rodong Sinmun* Commentary, Pyongyang Broadcasting Station, 19 December 2002.

26 The above quotes are all drawn from the MFA NPT withdrawal announcement, Pyongyang Central Broadcasting Station, 10 January 2003.

27 *The National Security Strategy of the United States of America* (Washington DC: The White House, 17 September 2002), pp. 13–16. See also *National Strategy to Combat Weapons of Mass Destruction* (Washington DC: The White House, December 2002).

28 Senior Vice Foreign Minister Kang Sok-ju used this evocative phrase during January 2003 discussions with Russian Vice Foreign Minister Alexander Losyukov, as reported in *Chungang Ilbo*, 21 January 2003.

29 Chinoy, *Meltdown*, pp. 150–51.

30 Kang's remarks are quoted in Pritchard, *Failed Diplomacy*, p. 38.

31 This episode is recounted in Chinoy, *Meltdown*, pp. 166–67.

32 The above data are drawn from Open Source Center reporting.

33 Interview, October 2008. The interviewee travelled to North Korea at least twice annually. He was able to undertake extensive travel outside major cities.

34 KWP Central Military Commission, 'On Bringing Forth Wartime Work Guidelines', Directive no. 002, 7 April 2004. The document was serialised in full in *Kyonghyang Sinmun* during January 2005.

35 Statement of the Spokesman of the Ministry of Foreign Affairs, 6 April 2003.

36 Statement of Spokesman of the Ministry of Foreign Affairs, 18 April 2003.

37 Glenn Kessler, 'N. Korea Says It Has Nuclear Arms', *Washington Post*, 25 April 2003.

38 Spokesman of the DPRK Ministry of Foreign Affairs, 8 June 2003. Emphasis added.

39 I am grateful to Frank Jannuzi for his recollection of this meeting and of Vice Foreign Minister Kim's remarks.

40 The phrase employed by Jiang (*buzancheng*) is generally translated as 'disapprove', or 'does not approve', but it has a strongly chastising quality in Chinese. Beijing, Xinhua She, 16 January 2003. On the brief cessation of oil exports, see Jonathan Watts, 'China Cuts Oil Supply to North Korea', *The Guardian*, 1 April 2003.

41 For early evidence of this debate, see the essays by a group of Chinese experts appearing in *Shijie Zhishi* no. 6, 16 March 2003, pp. 11–19.

42 The official is quoted in John Pomfret, 'China Urges N. Korea Dialogue', *Washington Post*, 4 April 2003. According to this official, China transmitted more than 50 messages to Washington and Pyongyang during this period.

43 For a detailed account prepared by a pseudonymous Chinese expert with access to information on Chinese leadership deliberations, see Zong Hairen, 'Hu Jintao Writes to Kim Jong-il to Open Door to Six-Party Talks', *Hong Kong Economic Journal*, 28 August 2003, in Northeast Asia Peace and Security Network Special Report, 5 September 2003.

44 For Chinese export data between 2002 and 2007, see Julia Joo-A Lee, 'To Fuel or Not to Fuel: China's Energy Assistance to North Korea', *Asian Security*, vol. 5, no.1, 2009, p. 54.

45 See the testimony of Siegfried Hecker of the Los Alamos National Laboratory to the Senate Foreign Relations Committee, 21 January 2004. For the North Korean characterisation of the Hecker visit, see the remarks of the Ministry of Foreign Affairs Spokesman, 10 January 2004.

46 Statement of the DPRK Ministry of Foreign Affairs, 10 February 2005.

47 Press Statement of the DPRK Ministry of Foreign Affairs, 31 March 2005.

48 Joel Brinkley, 'China Balks at Pressing the North Koreans', *New York Times*, 22 March 2005; and Joseph Kahn, 'China Says US Impeded North Korea Talks', *ibid.*, 13 May 2005. The latter article contains on the record comments from Yang Xiyu, a Chinese Foreign Ministry official participating in the Six-Party Talks, including the quoted warning to North Korea not to undertake a nuclear test.

49 Zhang Liangui, 'The Korean Nuclear Issue is Already at a Crucial Moment', *Xuexi Shibao*, 28 March 2005. Zhang, a research professor at the Central Party School has been among China's most prolific commentators on the nuclear issue since the breakdown of the Agreed Framework.

50 Pritchard, *Failed Diplomacy*, p. 128.

51 Chinoy, *Meltdown*, pp. 225–51.

52 For a summary of China's drafting efforts, consult Pritchard, *Failed Diplomacy*, p. 120.

53 Joint Statement of the Fourth Round of the Six-Party Talks, Beijing, 19 September 2005.

54 Tong Kim, 'You Say Okjeryok, I Say Deterrent', *Washington Post*, 25 September 2005.

55 Chinoy, *Meltdown*, pp. 252–73.

56 The above account is drawn largely from the translated Japanese version of a confidential Chinese report prepared by group of Chinese analysts and officials following the nuclear test. See Satoshi Tomisaka, *Taikitachosen Chugoku Kimitsu Fairu* [China's Secret File on Relations with North Korea], (Tokyo: Bungei Shunju, 2007), especially pp. 24–34. A well–informed Chinese interviewee characterised the document as 'accurate but not complete'.

57 David E. Sanger, 'US Warns North Korea Against Nuclear Test', *New York Times*, 7 May 2006.

58 In an on the record interview with *Chosun Ilbo*, Chinese Foreign Ministry Spokesman Liu Jianchao remarked: 'Both China and North Korea are sovereign and independent countries ... However, we are not well informed of the internal situation of the North Korean military. The DPRK ... does not listen to what China has to say. It seems that that not only does the DPRK not listen to China, but it also does not listen to itself.' *Chosun Ilbo*, 7 August 2006.

59 Resolution 1695 (2006), Adopted by the Security Council, 15 July 2006.

60 DPRK Foreign Ministry Statement, Korean Central Broadcasting System, 16 July 2006. The statement was made 'with authorisaton', a phrase employed to denote decisions taken at the highest levels of leadership. Foreign Ministry statements are rarely issued, and are therefore deemed highly authoritative.

61 Evan Ramstad, 'Signs in North Korea Point to Nuclear Test', *Wall Street Journal*, 18 August 2006.

62 DPRK Foreign Ministry Statement, Korean Central Broadcasting System, 3 October 2006.

63 Statement by the Office of the Director of National Intelligence on the North Korea Nuclear Test, 16 October 2006; Siegfried Hecker, Report on the North Korean Nuclear Program, Center for International Security and Cooperation, Stanford University, 15 November 2006, p. 3.

64 *Asahi Shimbun*, 11 September 2007.

65 Statement of the Ministry of Foreign Affairs of the People's Republic of China, 9 October 2006.

66 Xinhua Domestic Service in Chinese, 15 October 2006.

67 This paragraph draws on the report of the CCP International Department, 'What Kind of PRC–US Relations and PRC–DPRK Relations Benefit Current Chinese National Interest?', March 2007, in Tomisaka, *Taikitachosen Chugoku Kimitsu Fairu*, pp. 281–6.

68 For official texts of the 2007 agreements, see 'North Korea: Denuclearisation Action Plan', 13 February 2007, http://www.state.gov/r/pa/prs/2007/february/80479.htm; and 'Six-Party Talks – Second Phase Actions for the Implementation of the September 2005 Joint Statement', 3 October 2007, http://www.state.gov/r/pa/prs/ps/2007/oct/93217.htm.

69 Chinoy, *Meltdown*, pp. 330–31.

70 For a detailed accounting of disablement measures undertaken as of February 2008, see Siegfried S. Hecker, 'Denuclearizing North Korea', *Bulletin of the Atomic Scientists*, vol. 64, no. 2, May/June 2008, pp. 44–9, 61–2.

71 Fact Sheet, Office of the Spokesman, US Department of State, Washington DC, 10 May 2008.

72 The author was a member of this non-governmental delegation. The above

quotation is drawn from notes on the conversations with North Korean officials.

73 Siegfried S. Hecker, 'Report of Visit to the Democratic People's Republic of North [sic] Korea, Pyongyang, and the Nuclear Center at Yongbyon', Center for International Security and Cooperation, Stanford University, 12–16 February 2008.

74 See, in particular, Hecker, 'Denuclear-izing North Korea', p. 48.

75 Akiko Horiyama, 'DPRK Nuclear Issue: DPRK Excludes Two Facilities from Declaration, Hiding Their Operation Before 1992', *Mainichi Shimbun*, 6 October 2008.

76 The quote is from State Department spokesman Robert Wood. Choe Sang-Hun, 'North Korea Limits Test of Nuclear Site', *New York Times*, 13 November 2008.

77 Statement of the DPRK Press Spokesman, 26 August 2008.

Chapter Six

1 David Wright and Theodore A. Postol, 'A Post-launch Examination of the Unha–2', *Bulletin of the Atomic Scientists* Web Edition, 29 June 2009, http://www.the bulletin.org/node/7320.

2 Statement of the DPRK Ministry of Foreign Affairs, 14 April 2009, http://www.kcna.co.jp.

3 'DPRK Foreign Ministry Spokesman's Press Statement on Denuclearisation of the Korean Peninsula', 13 January 2009, http://www.kcna.co.jp. Emphasis added.

4 'DPRK Foreign Ministry Spokesman Claims Normalization with U.S., Nuclear Issue "Separate" Issues', 17 January 2009, http://www.kcna.co.jp. Emphasis added.

5 The author served on an expert group visiting the DPRK from 3–7 February 2009, at the invitation of the Ministry of Foreign Affairs. Other meetings held between North Korean officials and non-official American interlocutors during late 2008 and early 2009 reported comparable conclusions.

6 For a fuller elaboration of this issue deriving from the history of the Clinton administration, consult Jeff Goldstein, 'How Light Water Reactors Figure into Negotiations with North Korea', *Bulletin of the Atomic Scientists*, vol. 65, no. 4, July–August 2009, pp. 64–71.

7 The first published reports of Kim Chong-un's designation as the successor appeared in mid-January 2009, with Kim Jong-il purportedly issuing an internal directive on 8 January, Kim Chong-un's birthday. For the initial report, see Kim Hyun, 'N. Korean Leader Names Third Son as Successor: Sources', Yonhap News Agency, 15 January 2009. There are no indications that Kim disclosed the succession plan to Wang Jiarui, but it is not implausible.

8 The photograph of Kim inspecting the rotors did not appear in the North Korean press, but was issued separately by DPRK media. A photograph of the rotor assemblies did, however, appear in *Rodong Sinmun*, 10 May 2009, p. 1. Some technical specialists remain uncertain that the four objects were rotors. However, the unmistakable

resemblance of the objects to rotors in size and configuration and the appearance of the photograph within weeks of North Korea's announced intentions to enrich uranium (and in the presence of the two senior officials most closely associated with the DPRK's advanced weapons development) argues for an affirmative judgement.

[9] A US intelligence assessment, released three weeks after the reported test, disclosed minimal information: 'The US Intelligence Community assesses that North Korea probably conducted an underground nuclear explosion in the vicinity of P'unggye on 25 May 2009. The explosion yield was approximately a few kilotons. Analysis of the event continues.' Office of the Director of National Intelligence News Release No. 23–09, 15 June 2009. ODNI estimated that the yield of the October 2006 nuclear test was 'less than a kiloton', various non-governmental estimates are as low as 200 tons of TNT equivalent. See also Vitaly Fedchenko, 'North Korea's Test Explosion, 2009', *SIPRI Fact Sheet*, December 2009, pp. 1–8. Fedchenko concludes: 'Based on the seismic data, most estimates of the yield of the May 2009 explosion vary between 2 and 7 kilotons', or approximately 'five times stronger than the 2006 test'. Fedchenko, p. 3.

[10] Li Bin, 'An Alternative View to North Korea's Bomb Acquisition', *Bulletin of the Atomic Scientists*, May/June 2010, http://www.thebulletin.org, pp. 38–43.

[11] Siegfried S. Hecker, 'Lessons Learned from the North Korean Nuclear Crises', *Daedalus*, vol. 139, no. 1, Winter 2010, pp. 44–56. The DPRK is theoretically able to reprocess sufficient plutonium for an additional device each year, but reprocessing has been intermittent since the resumption of reactor operations. This suggests technical and material limitations at the facility or a shift towards uranium enrichment in the weapons programme.

[12] For a particularly pointed commentary issued a week prior to the second nuclear test, see Paek Mun-kyu, 'A Strong Countermeasure Will Follow Threat and Blackmail', *Rodong Sinmun*, 19 May 2009, http://www.kcna.co.jp. See also 'Reprocessing of Spent Fuel Rods Completed in DPRK', Pyongyang, KCNA in English, 3 November 2009, http://www.kcna.co.jp. KCNA claims that the reprocessing was completed between April and August.

[13] *North Korea's Nuclear and Missile Programmes* (Seoul and Brussels: International Crisis Group, Asia Report No. 168, 18 June 2009).

[14] Commentator, 'Disgusting Kiss Between Master and Minion at White House Rose Garden – Commenting on Traitor Lee Myung-bak's Junket to the United States', *Rodong Sinmun*, Korean Central Broadcasting System, 25 June 2009.

[15] 'Let Us More Highly Sound the Drums of Economic Agitation at All Sites of 150 Day Battle', *Rodong Sinmun*, 10 August 2009, http://dprkmedia.com.

[16] Song Mi-ran, 'My Country is Big and Powerful', *Rodong Sinmun*, 27 May 2009, http://dprkmedia.com. Song's political essays appear regularly in *Rodong Sinmun*. Her writings were once praised in a handwritten note from Kim Jong-il. She is evidently entrusted with essays on extremely sensitive political topics, including leadership succession. Song wrote an equally lengthy and comparably effusive encomium to the attempted

satellite launch, also appearing in the paper two days following the event. Song, 'Knocked on the Gate to a Powerful State', *ibid.*, 7 April 2009, http://dprkmedia.com.

[17] http://www.un.org/News/Press/docs//2009/sc9679.doc.htm.

[18] Analysts continue to disagree about the economic toll of the heightened sanctions regime on the DPRK. For an assessment emphasising the narrowing of the DPRK's economic options in the aftermath of the second nuclear test, see *North Korea under Tightening Economic Sanctions*, (Seoul and Brussels: International Crisis Group, Asia Briefing No. 101, 15 March 2010). For a more cautionary view emphasising the North's growing trade with the Middle East and its far greater trade dependence on China, see Stephan Haggard and Marcus Noland, 'Sanctioning North Korea: The Political Economy of Denuclearisation and Proliferation', Peterson Institute for International Economics, Washington DC, Working Paper Series, WP 09–4, July 2009.

[19] 'DPRK Foreign Ministry Spokesman on Unreasonable Call for Resumption of Six-Party Talks', 27 July 2009, at http://www.kcna.jp.

[20] Korean Central Broadcasting Station in Korean, 4 August 2009.

[21] 'N. Korea Steps Up Threats over Kaesong Complex', *Chosun Ilbo*, 10 November 2008, http://english.chosun.com.

[22] The Committee on the Peaceful Reunification of Korea in late January declared: 'All agreements adopted between the North and South in the past have already become dead letters and blank sheets of paper, ' thereby 'nullify[ing] all agreed upon matters related to resolving the state of political and military confrontation between the North and the South'. Pyongyang, Korea Central Broadcasting Station, 29 January 2009.

[23] For a detailed overview of Chinese leadership deliberations during 2009 on which this paragraph draws, see *Shades of Red: China's Debate Over North Korea* (Seoul, Beijing and Brussels: International Crisis Group, Asia Report No. 179, 2 November 2009).

[24] This section draws on discussions with Chinese analysts and officials during visits to Beijing in 2009 and 2010 and additional interactions with Chinese scholars and diplomats.

[25] Zhang Liangui, 'Reality Starts to Teach Everyone a Lesson', *Shijie Zhishi*, no. 12, 16 June 2009, pp. 14–20.

[26] Wang Zaibang and Li Jun, 'Searching for the Root of the DPRK's Second Nuclear Experiment, and Diplomatic Thoughts', *Xiandai Guoji Guanxi* [Contemporary International Relations], no. 7, 20 July 2009, pp. 38–44. Wang is a vice president of the China Institutes of International Relations; Li is an associate researcher.

[27] Zhu Feng, 'The DPRK Nuclear Crisis After the Second Nuclear Test: The Six-Party Talks and "Coercive Diplomacy"', in *Xiandai Guoji Guanxi*, no. 7, 20 July 2009, pp. 44–50. Zhu is a Professor in the School of International Studies at Peking University, and a frequent commentator on strategic and security issues, especially US–China relations.

[28] For more details, see Jonathan D. Pollack, 'China's North Korea Conundrum: How to Balance a Three Legged Stool', *YaleGlobal Online*, 23 October 2009, http://yaleglobal.yale.edu.

29 John S. Park, 'North Korea, Inc.: Gaining Insights into North Korean Regime Stability from Recent Commercial Activities', United States Institute of Peace, Washington DC, Working Paper, 22 April 2009; Haggard and Noland, 'Sanctioning North Korea'.

30 Col. Wang Yisheng of the China Academy of Military Science, as quoted in 'Military Diplomacy Creates a Peaceful Periphery', *Liaowang*, No. 48, 30 November 2009, p. 34.

31 Security Council Resolution 1874.

32 Beijing, CCTV–4 in Mandarin, 10 October 2009. Emphasis added.

33 'DPRK's Will to Strive for Building Nuclear–free World Reiterated', 30 September 2009, http://www.kcna.co.jp.

34 'China Upping Investment in North Korea but Success of Development Projects Uncertain', *Kyodo Clue III Online*, 1 April 2010, http://clue3.kyodonews.jp.

35 See Jiro Ishimaru, 'What Should be Read from Kim Jong-il's Trip to China?', *Sande Mainichi*, 23 May and 30 May 2010.

36 Choe Sang-hun, 'North Korea is Said to be Seeking China's Aid', *New York Times*, 3 April 2010.

37 Xinhua, 7 May 2010.

38 Yoshihiro Makino, 'North Korea Demands U.S. Lifting of UN Sanctions as Condition to Return to Six-Party Talks', *Asahi Shimbun*, 2 January 2010, http://www.asahi.com.

39 Secretary of State Hillary Rodham Clinton, Remarks at the United States Institute of Peace, Washington, DC, 21 October 2009.

40 Joint Editorial of *Rodong Sinmun* and other lead North Korean newspapers, Korean Central Broadcasting Station, 1 January 2010.

41 The characterisations are found in Siegfried S. Hecker, 'A Return Trip to North Korea's Yongbyon Nuclear Complex', Centre for International Security and Cooperation, Stanford University, 20 November 2010.

42 Joint New Year's Day editorial of *Rodong Sinmun* and other lead North Korean publications, Korean Central Broadcasting Station, 1 January 2009.

43 Kim's remarks at the Songjin Steel Complex are cited in Korea Central News Agency in English, 19 December 2009, http://www.kcna.co.jp; see also the comments of Kim Yong-nam (Political Bureau Member, president of the Supreme People's Assembly Presidium, and nominal chief of state): 'The great success of our-style iron and steel-making methods ... is a great immortal victory of the *juche* idea and is a more stunning demonstration of national power than that of [a] third nuclear test.' Korean Central Television, 25 December 2009.

44 Joint Editorial, 1 January 2010.

45 *Rodong Sinmun*, 9 January 2010, as cited in *Chosun Ilbo Online*, 11 January 2010, http://english.chosun.com.

46 Ri Tong-ch'an, Pang So'ng-hwa and Kim Sun-yo'ng, 'Let Us Drink a Toast on the Frontline of Victory', *Rodong Sinmun*, 30 December 2009, http://dprkmedia.com.

47 *Nuclear Posture Review Report* (Washington DC: Department of Defense, April 2010), pp. vi–vii.

48 Spokesperson of the DPRK Ministry of Foreign Affairs, Pyongyang, Korean Central Television Station, 9 April 2010.

49 Kim Chi-yong, in *Choson Sinbo* (Electronic Edition), 8 April 2010, http://www.dprkmedia.com.

50 All citations are drawn from 'Memorandum of the DPRK Ministry of

Foreign Affairs – The Korean Peninsula and Nuclear Weapons', Pyongyang, Korean Central Broadcasting System, 21 April 2010. My emphasis.

Conclusions

1 Jonathan D. Pollack, 'North Korea's Nuclear Weapons Programme to 2015: Three Scenarios', *Asia Policy*, no. 3, January 2007, pp. 105–23; Hecker, 'Lessons Learned from the North Korea Nuclear Crisis.'

2 Hecker, Lee and Braun, 'North Korea's Choice: Bombs over Electricity', p. 9.

3 Kim Chi-yong, 'Increasing Electric Power Production: "Self Reliance" for Light Water Reactors as Well', *Choson Sinbo*, 13 November 2009, http://dprkmedia.com; Hecker, 'A Return Trip to North Korea's Yongbyon Nuclear Complex'. Other claims have extended to nuclear fusion. See Ryo Myong Hui, 'Nuclear Fusion Technology for Development of New Energy of the Future', *Rodong Sinmun*, 15 May 2010, http://dprkmedia.com.

4 Reiss, *Bridled Ambition*, pp. 19–24.

5 See, in particular, Daniel Pinkston, 'WMD Deals between Pyongyang and Islamabad: When Did It all Begin?' unpublished paper, n.d.; *Officials Involved in DPRK–Iran Relations, 1992–Present* (Washington DC: Foreign Broadcast Information Service, FEA 20020304001702191919, 7 March 2005); Siegfried S. Hecker and William Liou, 'Dangerous Dealings: North Korea's Nuclear Capabilities and the Threat of Export to Iran', *Arms Control Today*, March 2007, http://www.armscontrol.org/print/2290; and 'Report to the Security Council from the Panel of Experts established Pursuant to Resolution 1874 (2009)'.

6 Pyongyang, Korean Central Broadcasting Station, 27 September 2010.

7 Mansourov, 'Inside North Korea's Black Box', pp. 12–13.

8 See, for example, Bradley O. Babson, 'Transformation and Modernisation of North Korea: Implications for Future Engagement Policy', Washington DC, SAIS US–Korea Institute, Paper for Project on 'Improving Regional Security and Denuclearising the Korean Peninsula: US Policy Interests and Options', n.d.

9 On North Korean economic deliberations in the early 2000s, see Robert L. Carlin and Joel S. Wit, *North Korean Reform: Politics, Economics and Security* (London: The International Institute for Strategic Studies, Adelphi Paper 382, July 2006). On the DPRK's policy reversion, see Andrei Lankov, 'Pyongyang Strikes Back: North Korean Policies of 2002–08 and Attempts to Reverse 'De-Stalinization from Below'', *Asia Policy*, Number 8 July 2009, pp. 47–71.

10 Such sentiments were conveyed very explicitly by Kim Jong–il's sister in a 2009 article published in an important economic journal. Kim Kyong-hui, 'Strengthening Centralised and

51 Spokesman of the DPRK Ministry of Foreign Affairs, 24 May 2010, http://www.kcna.co.jp.

Unified State Guidance Over Economy Is a Basic Requirement for Improving Socialist Economic Management', *Kyongje Yonggu*, 20 August 2009, pp. 4–5, http://dprkmedia.com. Madame Kim serves as director of the KWP Light Industry Department, but this title understates her power and influence in decision-making.

11 On these possibilities, see Andrei Lankov, 'Changing North Korea', *Foreign Affairs*, vol. 88, no. 6, November/ December 2009, pp. 95–105.

12 Stephan Haggard and Marcus Noland, 'Reform from Below: Behavioural and Institutional Change in North Korea', Peterson Institute for International Economics, Washington DC, Working Paper Series, WP 09–8, September 2009.

13 Albert O. Hirschman, *Exit, Voice, and Loyalty–Responses to Decline in Firms, Organisations, and States* (Cambridge, MA: Harvard University Press, 1970).

14 Interview, Washington DC, March 2010. For details drawn from semi-structured interviews with a cross section of defectors, consult Cho Chong-a et al., *Everyday Life of the DPRK Residents* (Seoul: Korea Institute for National Unification, 31 December 2008), at http://www.kinu.or.kr.

15 Joint Editorial of *Rodong Sinmun* and other leading North Korean newspapers, 1 January 2010.

16 For some representative examples of these two approaches, Phillip Wonhyuk Lim, 'North Korea's Economic Futures – Internal and External Dimensions', in Pollack (ed.), *Korea: The East Asian Pivot*, pp. 171–95; and Nicholas Eberstadt, *The End of North Korea* (Washington DC: American Enterprise Institute Press, 1999).

17 See, for example, Bonnie S. Glaser and Scott Snyder, with See-won Byun and David Szerlip, *US–China–South Korea Coordination: Addressing Conflicting Interests and Approaches to North Korea* (Washington DC: Center for Strategic and International Studies, May 2010).

18 Lankov, 'Pyongyang Strikes Back'.

19 This section draws on several extended conversations with Stephen Linton, who has negotiated extensively with North Korean officials during approximately 70 trips to the DPRK over a 30- year period.

20 See, in particular, Shin, *Ethnic Nationalism in Korea*.

21 I am indebted to Morton Halperin for this insight. For a decidedly contrary view placing much greater emphasis on the risks posed by nuclear-armed regional states (including the possible risks of small-scale nuclear use by such an adversary), see David Ochmanek and Lowell H. Schwartz, *The Challenge of Nuclear-Armed Nuclear Adversaries* (Santa Monica, CA: RAND Corporation, 2008).

22 Byung–Kook Kim, 'The Politics of National Identity: The Rebirth of Ideology and Drifting Foreign Policy in South Korea', in Pollack (ed.), *Korea: The East Asian Pivot*, pp. 79–120; Sung-Yoon Lee, 'Engaging North Korea: The Clouded Legacy of South Korea's Sunshine Policy', *Asian Outlook* (Washington, DC: American Enterprise Institute, April 2010).

23 For a particularly harsh reconstruction, see Donald Kirk, *Korea Betrayed – Kim Dae-jung and Sunshine* (New York: Palgrave Macmillan, 2009), especially pp. 155–216. Scott Snyder notes that the start date of Kim Dae-jung's visit to the North was delayed by a day, until Kim Jong–il was certain that the

entire promised sum was deposited in North Korean-controlled accounts in the Banco Delta Asia in Macao. Snyder, *China's Rise and the Two Koreas*, p. 122. As another long-time observer of Korean politics and someone highly sympathetic to the sunshine policy observes, 'Kim Dae-jung gambled and lost. There is a Korean supposition that you can change people through generosity. This applies in the South. Kim's miscalculation is that he thought it would also apply in the North.' Interview, January 2010.

24 This estimate, derived primarily from Ministry of Unification data, does not include the $500 million paid to North Korea immediately prior to the June 2000 summit. Additional international assistance totaling $2.4 billion is also excluded from this estimate. 'Aid to N. Korea Increased Under Roh', *Dong-A Ilbo*, 8 September 2006.

25 See the text of President Lee Myung-bak's national address, 24 May 2010, http://english.yonhapnews.co.kr; Statement of the Spokesman for the Committee for the Peaceful Reunification of the Fatherland, Pyongyang, Korean Central Broadcasting Station, 25 May 2010; and Statement of the General Staff of the Korean People's Army, Pyongyang, KCNA, 27 May 2010.

26 Yi So'k, 'The Effectiveness of Economic Sanctions on North Korea: Can DPRK–China Trade Substitute North–South Trade?', Korea Development Institute, Seoul, Issue Analysis, 24 May 2010, http://www.kdi.re.kr.

27 For estimates on the balance of trade over the past decade, see 'Report to the Security Council from the Panel of Experts established Pursuant to Resolution 1874 (2009)', Table 1, p. 16.

28 *North Korea under Tightening Sanctions* (Seoul/Brussels: International Crisis Group, Asia Briefing no. 101, 15 March 2010), pp. 4–5, 13.

29 This section draws on exchanges with Chinese experts and Chinese officials undertaken since the early 2000s, especially meetings and interviews conducted since the North's first nuclear test in October 2006.

30 For a discerning overview of Chinese assessments of the war and its consequences, see Steven M. Goldstein, 'Chinese Perspectives on the Origins of the Korean War: An Assessment at Sixty', *International Journal of Korean Studies*, vol. XIV, no. 2, Fall–Winter 2010, pp. 45–70.

31 He Di, 'The Last Campaign to Unify China: The CCP's Unrealised Plan to Liberate Taiwan, 1949–1950', in Mark A. Ryan, David M. Finkelstein and Michael A. McDevitt (eds), *Chinese Warfighting – The PLA Experience Since 1949* (Armonk, NY and London: M.E. Sharpe, 2003), especially pp. 83–8.

32 For a particularly harsh Chinese assessment, consult the speech of China's vice president and presumptive future leader Xi Jinping to a forum marking the 60th anniversary of the intervention of Chinese forces in the Korean War, Xinhua Domestic Service, 25 October 2010.

33 The data on Chinese expenditure and combat losses are derived from Xu Yan, 'Korean War: In the View of Cost Effectiveness'. US estimates of Chinese combat deaths and casualties are far higher and subject to ample variation, with some estimates approaching one million. By comparison, Chinese estimates are far more precise.

34 Zhou Zhiren, 'Sino-DPRK Friendship Continued by Future Generations',

Renmin Ribao Online, 6 April 2010, p. 3.

35 Yang Xiyu, 'Several Legal Issues Concerning the Establishment of a Korean Peninsula Peace System', *Guoji Wenti Yanjiu*, no. 4, 13 July 2009, pp. 30–31, 33–4. The journal is a publication of the China Institute of International Studies, which is subordinate to the Ministry of Foreign Affairs.

36 *Ibid.*, p. 35.

37 Interview, Chinese Ministry of Foreign Affairs, October 2006.

38 See Snyder, *China's Rise and the Two Koreas: Politics, Economics, Security*, pp. 23–108. See also Piao Jianyi et al., *Zhongguo Dui Chaoxian Bandao De Yanjiu* [Chine's Research on the Korean Peninsula] (Beijing: Minzu Chubanshe, 2006).

39 Carla Freeman and Drew Thompson, 'The Real Bridge to Nowhere – China's Foiled North Korea Strategy', United States Institute of Peace, Washington DC, Working Paper, 22 April 2009, http://www.usip.org; Wu Delie, '3+3: A New "Six Party Talks Cooperation Mechanism"?' *Shijie Zhishi*, no. 8, 16 April 2010, especially pp. 28–9.

40 For a discerning analysis, see Heungkyu Kim, 'From a Buffer Zone to a Strategic Burden: Evolving Sino–North Korea Relations during the Hu Jintao Era', *The Korean Journal of Defence Analysis*, vol. 22, no. 1, March 2010, pp. 57–74.

41 Unidentified Chinese diplomat, as quoted in the preface to International Crisis Group, *Shades of Red*.

42 Wit et al., *US Strategy Towards North Korea*, p. 5.

43 Memorandum of the DPRK Ministry of Foreign Affairs, 'The Korean Peninsula and Nuclear Weapons', Pyongyang, Korean Central Broadcasting Station, 21 April 2010, available at http://www.kcna.jp.

44 Pyongyang, Korean Central Broadcasting Station, 25 June 2010. The reference to '100 year sworn enemy' has appeared very rarely in North Korean media coverage; Kim Jong-il in 1997 even asserted that 'we do not intend to view the United States as our 100–year sworn enemy'. It seems certain this reference would not have been employed in the 2010 speech without Kim Jong-il's concurrence.

45 Spokesman of the DPRK Foreign Ministry, Pyongyang, Korean Central Broadcasting System, 24 May 2010.

Adelphi books are published eight times a year by Routledge Journals, an imprint of Taylor & Francis, 4 Park Square, Milton Park, Abingdon, Oxfordshire OX14 4RN, UK.

A subscription to the institution print edition, ISSN 1944-5571, includes free access for any number of concurrent users across a local area network to the online edition, ISSN 1944-558X

2011 Annual Adelphi Subscription Rates			
Institution	£491	$864 USD	€726
Individual	£230	$391 USD	€312
Online only	£442	$778 USD	€653

Dollar rates apply to subscribers outside Europe. Euro rates apply to all subscribers in Europe except the UK and the Republic of Ireland where the pound sterling price applies. All subscriptions are payable in advance and all rates include postage. Journals are sent by air to the USA, Canada, Mexico, India, Japan and Australasia. Subscriptions are entered on an annual basis, i.e. January to December. Payment may be made by sterling cheque, dollar cheque, international money order, National Giro, or credit card (Amex, Visa, Mastercard).

For more information, visit our website: **http://www.informaworld.com/ adelphipapers.**

For a complete and up-to-date guide to Taylor & Francis journals and books publishing programmes, and details of advertising in our journals, visit our website: **http://www.informaworld.com.**

Ordering information:
USA/Canada: Taylor & Francis Inc., Journals Department, 325 Chestnut Street, 8th Floor, Philadelphia, PA 19106, USA. **UK/Europe/Rest of World:** Routledge Journals, T&F Customer Services, T&F Informa UK Ltd., Sheepen Place, Colchester, Essex, CO3 3LP, UK.

Advertising enquiries to:
USA/Canada: The Advertising Manager, Taylor & Francis Inc., 325 Chestnut Street, 8th Floor, Philadelphia, PA 19106, USA. Tel: +1 (800) 354 1420. Fax: +1 (215) 625 2940.

UK/Europe/Rest of World: The Advertising Manager, Routledge Journals, Taylor & Francis, 4 Park Square, Milton Park, Abingdon, Oxfordshire OX14 4RN, UK. Tel: +44 (0) 20 7017 6000. Fax: +44 (0) 20 7017 6336.

The print edition of this journal is printed on ANSI conforming acid-free paper by Bell & Bain, Glasgow, UK.